Paroling Authorities

Recent History

and Current Practice

Edward E. Rhine, William R. Smith, Ronald W. Jackson

With
Peggy B. Burke and Roger Labelle

This publication may be ordered from:
American Correctional Association
8025 Laurel Lakes Court
Laurel, Maryland 20707
(301) 206-5059

Publications Director: Patricia L. Poupore
Managing Editor: Elizabeth Watts
Editor: Linda J. Walter
Editorial Assistant: Becky Hagenston
Inside Design: Ann Tontodonato
Cover Design: Kristen Mosbaek

ISBN 0-929310-51-9

Contents

Contents

Tables and Figures

Tables

Tables and Figures

Figures

Foreword

Even before it came under fire during the 1988 Presidential campaign, parole was a controversial issue. As the authors put it at the beginning of Chapter 3, "No other |parole| decision is more scrutinized or invokes the public's ire more than the decision to release potentially dangerous criminals into society." How that decision is made, who makes it, which offenders will be released, and under what conditions are concerns of both the public and corrections practitioners.

All of these issues are addressed in this book—the only comprehensive volume on the parole process. After years of hard work, the American Correctional Association's Task Force on Parole has put together a valuable reference that fills a gap in the literature on this important topic. The authors—all experienced parole practitioners or academics—discuss major issues and controversial areas that every parole board may have to address. The inclusive data assembled from all fifty states and the District of Columbia will provide valuable assistance to paroling authorities responding to legislative inquiries or developing programs and budgets.

The American Correctional Association is proud to have cosponsored (with the Association of Paroling Authorities International) this important work. We encourage other groups to work with ACA to help us attain our goal of providing current, practical information to the corrections profession.

Anthony P. Travisono
Executive Director

Acknowledgements

From 1986 to 1988, an American Correctional Association Task Force on Parole met to review the status of parole and to make recommendations concerning its future. The monograph that follows draws significantly from the discussions of the task force and from a comprehensive survey that it developed and distributed to paroling authorities in the United States and Canada. Task force members to whom we are indebted for both inspiration and guidance include Benjamin Baer, James L. Byrd, Jackie Crawford, John J. Curran, Jr., Gail Hughes, Bert Koon, Anabel Mitchell, Richard Mulcrone, Lloyd Rupp, and B. Norris Vassar, as well as two of the authors.

A very special acknowledgement is owed to T. Don Hutto, former President of the American Correctional Association, under whom the Task Force on Parole was originally formed, and former President Su Cunningham, under whose leadership the task force prospered. A grateful acknowledgement must also be extended to ACA Executive Director Anthony P. Travisono for his steadfast support of the task force and the publication of this monograph.

Deep appreciation must also be extended to the National Institute of Corrections. The chief of the community corrections division, George Keiser, provided generous technical assistance to ensure the successful completion of the Task Force on Parole survey. Kermit Humphries, also of the National Institute of Corrections, served as a member ex-officio on the task force and offered thoughtful suggestions throughout the preparation of the monograph.

Sincere gratitude is clearly due to the Association of Paroling Authorities International for its active support of this undertaking and its commitment to a more sensible, effective, and professional system of parole. We owe a special thanks to former APAI Presidents Christopher Dietz, B. Norris Vassar, Ronald W. Jackson, "Jack" Curran, Wayne Snow, and current President Gladys Mack for their tireless commitment to serving their parole colleagues across the country. Sincere gratitude must also be expressed to the parole board chairs and executive staff who gave so generously of their time to complete the Parole Task Force survey.

We are also grateful to our parole colleagues in Canada. Fred Gibson, chair of the National Parole Board, was supportive at all times and participated in the completion of the task force survey. Doyne Ahern, Manager of Publications, and Linda Goldberg, Research Officer, both of the National Parole Board, provided expertise and assistance in preparing the material on the Canadian parole process. A warm acknowledgement must be extended as well to William R. Outerbridge, former parole board chair, who offered valuable guidance during the initial stages of this project.

A publication such as this requires skilled and dedicated editors. We are indebted to Elizabeth Watts at the American Correctional Association for her extraordinary assistance on our behalf and Linda J. Walter for her meticulous attention to detail and thoughtful review of the monograph. We also wish to thank the Director of Communications and Publications, Patricia Poupore, for her longstanding support and patient willingness to see this project through to completion.

Finally, as this monograph was written between the interstices of the authors' full-time jobs, it goes without saying that it was completed occasionally at the expense of spending time with those we love. It was through the continuous support and reassuring presence of our families that we were able to finish our work.

EER
WRS
RWJ
PBB
RL

December 1990

Introduction

For well over half of the twentieth century, parole was considered an integral part of a criminal justice system that was based on indeterminate sentencing and the rehabilitative ideal. Though parole was subjected to frequent criticism, especially during its most formative years in the 1920s and 1930s, it was the practice rather than the concept that was challenged. As recently as the formation of the President's Commission on Law Enforcement and Administration of Justice (1965-67), the legitimacy of parole, as well as the sentencing structure on which it rested, remained unquestioned.

Beginning in the early 1970s, parole boards were exposed to a growing series of criticisms challenging the fairness of their decision-making procedures and the unbridled exercise of discretion in the absence of accountability. The most emphatic of the critics called for the outright abolition of parole. These concerns, however, were rooted within a larger challenge to the fairness and legitimacy of indeterminate sentencing.

For a variety of reasons, most notably the politicization of crime control policy and the loss of faith in the ability of rehabilitative programs to effect offender change, jurisdictions across the country began to emphasize greater determinacy in sentencing. This drive was coupled with the passage of mandatory sentencing provisions, sentencing enhancements, and other measures designed to stiffen criminal penalties. As a result, prison populations began to rise with the decade of the eighties witnessing a historically unprecedented increase in the number of inmates confined in state and federal prisons.

The movement from indeterminate to determinate sentencing codes exposed paroling authorities to crosscutting pressures. On the one hand, discretionary parole release was abolished or sharply curtailed in a number of states. On the other hand, in many jurisdictions the parole board was called upon to manage escalating prison populations through emergency release mechanisms and other measures. In some states, the paroling authority actually became the de facto regulator of prison population levels.

These contradictory pressures on parole continue. Despite its diminishing role, discretionary parole release remains the primary method of release from confinement. As a consequence of the incessant pressures associated with prison crowding, the rate of growth currently associated with parole supervision is comparable to or exceeds that of the other correctional components, including probation and confinement in prisons and jails. While parole has been abolished in some determinate sentencing jurisdictions, it coexists within a determinate sentencing framework in others.

How parole will evolve in the decade ahead, and what role paroling authorities will play within the context of future sentencing reforms, remains unclear and to a large extent unexplored. Recent works on sentencing reform choose not to consider what contributions parole might make within a comprehensive system of sanctioning (see, for example, Morris and Tonry's (1990) otherwise excellent monograph, *Between Prison and Probation*).

The goal of this book is to offer a systemic and sympathetic appraisal of the parole process, including release, supervision, and revocation. Information is drawn from existing (though all too often dated) literature on parole, and from the work of an American Correctional Association Task Force on Parole. The Task Force, which met from 1986 to 1988, was established to consider the issues then having an impact on the philosophy, administration, and practice of parole. Its membership was composed of parole board chairs and executive staff, parole field service administrators, and practitioners representing other facets of parole.

During its tenure, and with support from the National Institute of Corrections, the Task Force distributed a forty-six page survey to paroling authorities in the United States and Canada. The purpose of the survey was to gather information on the organization and administration of parole boards, release and revocation practices, and parole supervision. A final section of the survey focused on the issues confronting paroling authorities, and on parole board chairs' views of those issues.

The survey was sent to parole boards by the American Correctional Association in February 1988. A follow-up request was sent two months later to boards that had not responded. With further assistance from the ACA and the Association of Paroling Authorities International, a 100-percent response rate was obtained in December 1988. Some of the more salient findings drawn from responses from the fifty states and the District of Columbia are highlighted throughout the book.

Chapter 1 provides a review of the history and changing philosophical context of parole. It emphasizes the importance of the Progressive Era in shaping the future direction of parole, the subsequent impact of sentencing reform and prison crowding on parole, and recent efforts by some boards to adopt a structured approach to parole decision making.

Chapter 2 describes the jurisdiction, political environment, administration, and organizational variation of paroling authorities. It also discusses parole boards as policy-making bodies. The chapter concludes with a description of background characteristics of parole board chairs.

Chapter 3 addresses what is arguably the most controversial component of parole: discretionary parole release. It considers the trend toward greater rationalization in parole decision making, mainly through parole guidelines. It also discusses various initiatives to open the parole hearing process through victim input and other means.

The fourth chapter discusses the uneasy relationship between prison crowding and parole. It reviews the use of emergency powers acts by parole boards. It also looks at the experiences of three states that rely on expedited parole release to relieve or manage limited correctional resources. The chapter concludes with a discussion of the policy quandaries facing parole boards as they are called on or expected to assume an active role in prison population control.

Chapter 5 explores the other half of the parole system: parole or postrelease supervision. The organization of parole field services is discussed, as are conditions of supervision and the use of classification and case management. A special section is devoted to what is often overlooked in discussions of a similar topic in probation: the presence of an intensive supervision movement in parole.

The sixth chapter examines parole revocation. It discusses parole board compliance with the requirements of the Supreme Court's well-known decision *Morrissey v. Brewer* (1972). It also highlights developments in several jurisdictions that have begun to rely as a matter of policy on intermediate sanctions in response to parolee violations. A final section addresses the meaning and implications of parole revocation and parolee recidivism.

Chapter 7 leaves the United States for a discussion of the parole system in Canada. This chapter provides a comparative context for the book as a whole. As this chapter shows, the Canadian parole system is mainly a federal system. Although it has experienced serious criticism and reform, the status of parole north of the border is reasonably secure.

The eighth chapter offers a series of prescriptions for reforming parole in the United States. It argues for a much closer interdependence between parole boards and departments of corrections, as well as between the boards and parole field services. It also suggests that paroling authorities must assist departments of corrections in managing limited prison resources, although parole boards alone cannot be responsible for resolving the correctional crowding crisis.

The chapter concludes with some thoughts on the need for a rational system of parole within the context of future sentencing reform. Parole, properly designed, contributes to a sensible balance between a system of just sanctioning, public protection, and meaningful offender change.

Chapter 1

The Development and Philosophical Context of Parole

The concept of parole, though not the term, may be traced to revolutionary innovations in prison management during the mid-nineteenth century in Australia and Ireland. These innovations are credited to Alexander Maconochie, superintendent of the Norfolk Island Prison Colony from 1840-44, and Sir Walter Crofton, who became chairman of the board of directors of the Irish prison system in 1854 (Cavendar 1982). Though Crofton borrowed (and subsequently expanded) many of the principles first developed by Maconochie, both men accepted that the primary purpose of imprisonment was the reformation of the offender. The principles and methods they developed were influential in shaping the reformatory movement and eventually the birth of parole in the United States in the 1870s.

Maconochie's principles of reform were developed in response to the debasing brutalities he associated with the English system of transportation to and prison administration in the Australian penal settlements.[1] Norfolk Island was considered the dumping ground of the penal colonies. Located several hundred miles off the coast of Australia, it housed individuals who had been convicted of additional crimes after transportation to the penal colonies (Cavendar 1982, 13). Before Maconochie's arrival, it was a place ruled by terror, cruelty, and brute force.

Maconochie immediately set about to change the philosophy and methods of prison management on the island. He argued that a prisoner should be taught self-discipline and personal responsibility through hard labor and frugal living. He introduced a system of graded classification based on the concept of "marks" (Barry 1972). Prisoners on Norfolk Island were expected to earn back their freedom by successfully moving from highly regimented to less restrictive stages.

The final stage, resulting in release, came to be known as the "ticket-of-leave." Although this concept did not originate with Maconochie, and there is some controversy over whether it is actually the forerunner of parole (White 1976), it became the mechanism of release from Norfolk Island. For Maconochie it was the final stage from which offenders would be discharged as free men without supervision or constraint. In fact, most of those granted a ticket-of-leave remained on Norfolk Island.

The system that Maconochie developed was never fully implemented. Not surprisingly, his principles and methods as superintendent were subjected to criticism, resulting in his dismissal in 1844. Nonetheless, his experiment was considered by many to have been a success, and along with continuing opposition to transportation, played a role in the passage of the English Penal Servitude Act of 1853. This act formalized several of Maconochie's reforms, extending some of its key features to Ireland, where they were incorporated by the director of the prison system, Sir Walter Crofton (Cavendar 1982, 14).

As a disciple of Maconochie, Crofton borrowed Maconochie's concept of graded classification (i.e., movement through stages) and the acquisition of marks leading to greater levels of personal freedom. A prison reformer in his own right, Crofton developed two additional features: graduation to an intermediate prison, and strict supervision while on a ticket-of-leave.

Relative freedom was granted to prisoners who, after progressing successfully through several classification stages involving more independence and less control, were transferred to intermediate prisons. These prisons held approximately 100 men, who were employed in manufacturing and farming. Placement in these institutions was designed to test each prisoner's self-control and ability to function under conditions approximating those in the free community.

Those offenders who performed well were granted a ticket-of-leave. Certain conditions, however, were attached. Offenders were expected to send monthly reports and were to avoid association with known criminals. The work ethic was reinforced with a provision against idleness. Surveillance of the releasee was occasionally provided by the police or by prisoners' aid societies. Violations of these conditions could lead to reimprisonment.

The principles and methods devised by Maconochie and Crofton provided the foundation for developments that led eventually to the birth of parole in the United States. These reformers emphasized offender reformation over retribution, preparation for release during confinement through a system of graded classification, and successful performance while on a ticket-of-leave (or supervision). Yet, as Lindsey (1925, 13) points out:

> the ticket-of-leave or conditional liberation, which was the forerunner of our modern parole systems, arose out of experience in the care and handling of convicts and was developed by men in charge of prisoners as a practical method of dealing with them. Its origin was in practical experience rather than in theoretical reasoning and it became established because it produced results in the matter of prison discipline more favorable than had ever been secured without it.

The works of Maconochie and Crofton were widely discussed by Dr. Enoch Wines, Gaylord Hubbell, and Theodore Dwight before the New York Prison Association. In 1866, Hubbell, who at the time was warden of Sing Sing Prison, visited Ireland and reported favorably on Crofton's model. Wines and Dwight surveyed prison and reformatory practices in the United States and Canada and urged the adoption of offender reformation as the primary object of imprisonment.

Widespread concern over an apparent "increase in social disorder and crime," coupled with disillusionment with the effectiveness of congregate prisons (Pisciotta 1983, 614) provided the impetus in 1869 for New York's legislature to authorize the construction of an "industrial reformatory" for males aged sixteen to thirty. Though Elmira was eventually selected as the site for the new institution, the legislation was silent on how the reformation of young offenders would be achieved.

The philosophical foundation and a set of governing principles were provided in 1870 when the newly formed American Prison

Association held its first National Congress on Penitentiary and Reformatory Discipline in Cincinnati, Ohio. With Rutherford B. Hayes presiding, the Congress adopted a Declaration of Principles, thirty-seven paragraphs that called for a new and more humanitarian approach to prison reform.

These principles reflected many of the assumptions of the Positive School of criminology. Three of the more salient principles with respect to the "reformatory movement" and the origin of parole in the United States are provided below (Lindsey 1925, 20).

> II. The treatment of criminals by society is for the protection of society. But since such treatment is directed to the criminal rather than to the crime, its great object should be his moral regeneration. Hence the supreme aim of prison discipline is the reformation of criminals, not the infliction of vindictive suffering.
>
> V. The prisoner's destiny should be placed, measurably, in his own hands; he must be put into circumstances where he will be able, through his own exertions, to continually better his own condition. A regulated self-interest must be brought into play and made constantly operative.
>
> VIII. Peremptory sentences ought to be replaced by those of indeterminate length. Sentences limited only by satisfactory proof of reformation should be substituted for those measured by mere lapse in time.

The core features of the reformatory system, that is, the means to accomplish the end of "moral regeneration," included the indeterminate sentence, the progressive classification of prisoners based on a regulated schedule of marks, academic and industrial education, religious instruction, the cultivation of the prisoner's self-respect, and parole.

These ideas came to fruition with the appointment of Zebulon R. Brockway as superintendent of Elmira Reformatory in 1876. One of the authors of the original Declaration of Principles, Brockway was instrumental in drafting legislation providing for an indeterminate sentence and parole. With its passage in 1877, Brockway was authorized to develop a system of prison management that linked performance in school, work, and elsewhere in the institution to the duration of confinement and thus parole. The indeterminate sentence imposed on the inmate was used only to establish the maximum term that he might serve.

Once prisoners earned the requisite number of marks over a twelve-month period, they became eligible to appear before the Board of Managers. This board, in consultation with the superintendent, determined their readiness for parole. Jurisdiction, however, was retained over those who were released. Those who violated the conditions of their parole could be returned to custody.

The conditions of parole required that the parolees have a job upon release and that they submit monthly work reports cosigned by their employers (Pisciotta 1983, 618). Parolees were also expected to conduct themselves with "honesty, sobriety, and decency."

Supervision was provided not by parole officers, but by police chiefs, district attorneys, New York Prison Association members, and citizen volunteers. If, after a six-month probationary period, the Board of Managers determined that there was a "strong or reasonable probability" that the parolee would "live and remain at liberty without violating the law" and that "his release [was] not incompatible with the welfare of society," they recommended an "absolute release from imprisonment" to the governor. The governor retained the discretion to restore the individual to full citizenship.

The year 1877 marks the official birth of parole, the reformatory, and the indeterminate sentence in the United States.[2] It is important to note, however, that while parole and the indeterminate sentence presuppose a reformatory regime, through the end of the nineteenth century Elmira remained a singular exception to prevailing prison practices.

It is ironic that despite the commitment to offender reformation expressed in the Declaration of Principles and the promise of Elmira, the years 1870-1900 may very well have been the most brutal in the history of American corrections (Rothman 1983; Johnson 1987).[3] Throughout this period, most states' criminal codes were characterized by fixed-time sentences. To cope with the growing burdens imposed by fixed sentencing, especially crowding and inmate disciplinary problems, wardens relied upon good-time measures, governors' pardons, and the generous use of corporal punishment.

Within this context, parole was introduced and often served functions unrelated to offender reform. In some states, parole legislation was enacted to relieve governors of the time and trouble associated with the review of petitions for executive clemency.[4] In other states, it was used as a safety valve to reduce prison crowding and thus avoid the expense of new prison construction (Rothman 1983). Finally, it was championed by wardens and superintendents who viewed it as an effective tool for maintaining order and control inside prison walls.

Nonetheless, the concept of parole was seeded during this time. By 1900, twenty states had adopted a system of parole though only eleven of these states also had indeterminate sentencing provisions (Lindsey 1925, 40). If at this point parole was valued more for its contributions to prison management than to offender treatment and change, its role and functions were to be significantly redefined during the Progressive Era.

Parole During the Progressive Era

The Progressive Era began during the first quarter of the twentieth century (Hofstadter 1955; Weibe 1967). Characterized by an ardent commitment to broad-scale societal reform, the Progressives focused on a wide array of social problems they believed were caused by the unregulated demands of an expanding industrial economy: child labor abuses, dangerous occupations, poorly ventilated factories, dilapidated settlement housing, and slums (Rothman 1980). What is striking about the Progressive Era is the optimism and confidence behind the various reforms that were proposed.

When they turned their attention to the problem of crime, the Progressives firmly believed that if their programs and methods were properly implemented, criminal behavior would be reduced, if not eliminated. Their agenda for criminal justice reform consisted of four principles.

The first principle was rooted in positivist criminology and reflects the growing influence of the social sciences. Positivism argues against free will and assumes that behavior is determined or caused by factors over which the offender has no control (Mannheim 1972). These factors may be biological, psychological, or social. However complex the factors may be, the causes of criminal behavior can ultimately be discerned and appropriate treatment provided.

The second principle represents perhaps the essence of the Progressive approach to criminal behavior. Whatever treatment is provided must be individualized to meet each offender's unique needs. A case-by-case study offers the most suitable method for understanding the causes of the individual's criminality and for prescribing appropriate programming. The individualization of treatment—the cornerstone of the Progressive agenda—required that sentencing judges fit the punishment to the criminal, not the crime.

As their third principle of reform, the Progressives urged the adoption of the indeterminate sentence. Critical of the rigidity of fixed or flat-time sentences, they argued that indeterminate sentencing schemes were necessary to provide prison officials and parole authorities with sufficient discretion and flexibility to determine when an offender was ready for release. Such a system also offered offenders an incentive to change through program participation and positive institutional behavior. Just as important, those not amenable to treatment would remain confined for the duration of their maximum sentence.

The fourth Progressive principle was a "fundamental trust in the power of the state to do good" (Rothman 1980, 60). These reformers had a deep and abiding belief that the state would carry out its responsibilities in a manner that balanced the needs of the community against the welfare of the offender. If their proposals increased official discretion and thus the power of the state, the Progressives believed that it would be properly exercised in the interest of promoting law-abiding behavior.

The ideological legacy of the Progressive Era on criminal justice for much of the twentieth century is hard to underestimate. Yet, while the principles of Progressivism have provided an enduring vision for criminal justice reform, actual practices have invariably lagged behind. This is nowhere more apparent than in the area of parole.

The first several decades of the 1900s, which witnessed the ascendancy of Progressive ideology within the criminal justice system, also saw the rapid-fire passage of parole statutes in nearly every state and jurisdiction across the country. Between 1900-1910, thirty-two states and the federal government adopted a system of parole. By 1922, forty-four states had a parole system, along with the territory of Hawaii (Lindsey 1925, 58-69). By 1927 only three states—Florida, Mississippi, and Virginia—were without a parole system (National Commission on Law Observance and Enforcement 1931, 127).

While the rapidity of this change is notable, what is even more striking is that state after state enacted parole legislation with a minimum of debate (Rothman 1980, 44). According to Rothman, this reflected the broad-based nature of the coalition supporting parole:

> Concerned citizens, settlement house workers, criminologists, social workers, psychologists, and psychiatrists stood together with directors of charitable societies, judges, district attorneys, wardens, and superintendents (1980, 44-45).

Parole quickly became the principal means of releasing inmates from confinement. In 1927, a total of 44,208 inmates were released from state prisons and reformatories (National Commission on Law Observance and Enforcement 1931, 127). Of these, 49 percent were paroled, 42 percent were released upon expiration of their maximum sentence, and 9 percent were set free by other means.

Even with the growing reliance on parole in many states, it was from the start the most controversial and most unpopular of the reforms recommended by the Progressives (Rothman 1980).[5] It was viewed by the public as an act of leniency and an indefensible method for turning "hardened criminals" loose before the full service of their term. Public opposition to parole was at times strident and uncompromising.

Although a convenient target for systemic inadequacies that cut across criminal justice as a whole, the shortcomings of parole were clearly identified by a wide array of investigative bodies and crime commissions formed to assess its operation. Two of these—The National Commission on Law Observance and Enforcement and the *Attorney General's Survey of Release Procedures*—are especially notable for their criticisms of parole; notable because their criticisms fully embrace the principles informing the Progressives' vision of criminal justice.

In 1931, the National Commission on Law Observance and Enforcement issued its *Report on Penal Institutions, Probation, and Parole* (hereafter cited as the Wickersham Report). As the commission observed, there were at the time four main avenues of release from imprisonment. First, inmates could be released upon service of their full sentence. Second, they could be released through "an automatic time allowance for good conduct within the institution." Third, they could be granted executive clemency by the governor. Finally, they could be paroled. In the commission's view, parole represented the safest method of release by providing for an extension of the state's period of control over the offender. It did so by adding

> to the period of imprisonment—a further period involving months or even years of supervision during which the offender may be reimprisoned without the formality of [the] judicial process (Wickersham Report 1931, 129).

According to the commission, a properly administered system of parole "enables the state to complete the work of reformation which it has begun within the institution" (Wickersham Report 1931, 132). Anticipating the development of prison classification systems, the commission viewed both parole release *and* supervision as the principal means by which to bring "the process of social reconstruction through to its necessary conclusion" (Wickersham Report 1931, 132). Each component was found to be seriously deficient.

With respect to release practices, the commission reported that in twenty states, parole was authorized by the governor or by a board of pardons. It was viewed as a form of executive clemency. In another twelve states, the authority to grant parole was vested in institutional boards where it was treated as incidental to prison administration. At this time, only fourteen states had separate agencies to make parole release decisions. Of these, however, three used a single official to select offenders for parole, while six states relied on part-time, unpaid or "ex-officio boards." Along with the federal government, only five states—Illinois, Ohio, Massachusetts, New York, and Texas—had salaried, full-time parole boards (Wickersham Report 1931, 133).

If separate and autonomous parole boards were the exception rather than the rule, there was apparently some standardization in the factors used in granting parole. Drawing on a study by Clair Wilcox, the commission's director of research, the Wickersham Report (1931, 133-35) observed that four factors were emphasized in the decision to release.

Prison conduct was the most important factor, though its prominence is not surprising given the presence at the time of prison wardens on parole boards or institutional boards of trustees. The second factor was the nature of the crime for which the offender was incarcerated. The third was the offender's prior criminal history, while the final item was the offender's general demeanor or appearance at the hearing.

In the commission's view, such standardization undermined the Progressives' emphasis upon individualized treatment and a case-by-case evaluation tailored to the offender's progress and reform during confinement. This shortcoming was exacerbated by problems associated with parole supervision.

The most serious deficiencies were found in the quality of supervision provided to parolees after release. In eighteen states, contact was maintained with parolees only through correspondence. Written reports were required, but their accuracy was not verified. In seven states, this system of control was supplemented by the use of employers, "first friends," and sponsors who were willing to guarantee that the parolee would remain law-abiding. However, these persons were not held accountable for the parolee's behavior. Some states also relied on the assistance of religious, charitable, or welfare organizations (Wickersham Report 1931, 135-36).

Only eight states provided parole supervision through a central, administrative agency. Fourteen states were without parole officers altogether, while the number of parole officers in another nineteen states ranged from one to four. Even in those states with more parole officers, the caseloads were often excessive, numbering 300, 600, 800, and in one instance, 2,000 parolees. Formal training was nonexistent.

While the commission argued that parole supervision should be grounded in "careful, conscientious, social casework" (1931, 304-5), it recognized that the application of this principle was nowhere to be found. Less than a decade later, the concerns of the commission would be voiced again.

In 1939, a five-volume study was published entitled the *Attorney General's Survey of Release Procedures* (Wayne Morse, ed.; hereafter cited as the *Attorney General's Survey*). It began by examining the various methods for releasing convicted offenders either by the courts or from prison. In terms of parole, it noted that while its functions and purposes have often been misunderstood, "at no period has the entire institution been the object of so much controversy and attack or viewed with so much suspicion by the general public as it has been during the past four or five years" (*Attorney General's Survey* 1939, vii). Although it strongly endorsed the concept of parole, the *Attorney General's Survey* offered a critical assessment of its operation.

Parole, it observed, is both a procedure for releasing offenders from prison and a method of treatment. It represents an extension of correctional treatment in a manner that permits the parolee to exercise personal responsibility while under supervision. Echoing the Wickersham Report, the purpose of parole "is, or should be, to bridge the gap between the closely ordered life within the prison walls and the freedom of normal community living" (*Attorney General's Survey* 1939, 5).

Like the Wickersham Report, the *Attorney General's Survey* reviewed both parole release and supervision. With respect to release, it found that three different agencies (or offices) were responsible for paroling inmates from reformatories or state prisons: central boards, the governor, and institutional boards (1939, 44). Parole decision-making powers were vested in centralized boards composed of three to five members in twenty-nine jurisdictions (twenty-six states). In another seventeen states the authority to grant parole belonged to the governor. In most of these states, however, the governor received recommendations from advisors or advisory boards, including wardens or other cabinet-level officials. Institutional parole boards were used to varying degrees in seven states.

The *Attorney General's Survey* questioned the wisdom of placing responsibility for granting or denying parole in the governor's office. The absence of special training or qualifications, the myriad duties, and the political nature of the office, it argued, conspired against fair and thorough case-by-case review.

It was also critical of institutional parole agencies claiming that their primary concerns were to maintain prison discipline and reward good behavior. Parole was not viewed as a sound correctional device in its own right.

The *Attorney General's Survey* urged the adoption of centralized parole boards with full-time members. It noted that "[in] many states the granting of parole is looked upon merely as a minor incidental function which can be taken care of by a state official when he can squeeze in a few hours a few times a year" (1939, 55). Full-time paroling authorities were found in only ten states, New York City, and the federal government (Rothman 1980, 162). Maryland, Missouri, and Texas maintained full-time agencies with the power only to recommend pardons and paroles to the governor. In all other states, either state officials with other duties or part-time appointees made parole decisions.

In terms of parole board composition, the *Attorney General's Survey* was highly critical of the absence of any formal qualifications or criteria for appointing the membership (1939, 59). Appointment to the parole board was most often based on party loyalty, rather than any particular experience or training (Rothman 1980, 163). According to the *Attorney General's Survey*, this factor more than any other contributed to the public perception that the parole system had broken down.

The absence of qualifications and training also undermined the quality of parole hearings. The standard practice at the time was to conduct monthly hearings at an institution, giving brief consideration to each case. Because many of the boards were composed of "inexperienced laymen" who had "no conception of their true function," pertinent questions were not asked while "wholly irrelevant considerations predominated" (*Attorney General's Survey* 1939, 166). In marked contrast to the Progressives' emphasis upon a thorough and objective (i.e., scientific) review of the case history of each offender, "[purely] subjective and emotional elements" determined the decision to grant or deny parole (1939, 171).

The concerns with release practices carried over into parole supervision as well. At the time of the survey, the parole granting agency also administered parole supervision in thirty-five jurisdictions. The supervision of parolees was performed by a separate agency in only seven states. Another ten states followed Wisconsin and the federal parole system by combining probation and parole supervision under the same administrative agency (*Attorney General's Survey* 1939, 65).

The principal criticisms were directed at the methods for supervising parolees. Though there was some regional variation, every state relied on written reports, unpaid volunteers, parole officers, or some combination of the three (1939, 200-201). Eleven states merely required written reports from parolees. In twenty-six states (and the District of Columbia), supervision consisted of written reports supplemented by unpaid volunteers. The majority of jurisdictions (N = 30) employed parole officers to perform supervision.

The *Attorney General's Survey* questioned the value of requiring parolees to submit written reports as the sole basis for supervision. It was also skeptical of the effectiveness of using volunteers. It argued that only trained parole officers with appropriately sized caseloads could achieve social casework goals during the course of supervision. Only a few states, however, had a sufficient number of parole officers to perform this task. The number of parolees assigned to parole officers showed significant variation, ranging from 50 to 600 (1939, 227).[6]

Despite the criticisms of parole contained in the Wickersham Report and the *Attorney General's Survey*, both were supportive of the theory and purposes behind the concept. Support for parole was evident at the national level as well. In 1939, the Attorney General of the United States, with the backing of President Roosevelt, sponsored the first National Parole Conference.

President Roosevelt, who spoke at the conference, considered parole "the most promising method of terminating a prison sentence" (National Probation and Parole Association 1957, 7). He went on to comment, however, that parole had become a "serious national concern" because of a combination of neglect (in funding and personnel) and abuse (through the granting of political or personal favors) (National Probation and Parole Association 1957, 7).[7]

The prominence and leadership of the speakers and delegates underscored the commitment at the time to a sound and effective system of parole. At the end of the conference, the delegates adopted a Declaration of the Principles of Parole (National Probation and Parole Association 1957, 182-83). The declaration provided parole with a sense of mission and purpose on a national level that had not existed previously. The principles themselves reflected the core assumptions of Progressivism. As will be seen, they were to inform the philosophy, if not the practice, of parole for the next thirty years.

From Progressive Ideology to the Rehabilitative Ideal

The Progressives recognized that an effective system of parole was dependent upon a reformatory method of prison governance. The 1930s and 1940s, however, reflected the era of the "big house," with an emphasis on firm discipline and hard labor (Clemmer 1958; Irwin 1980; Johnson 1987). Remedial, or treatment-oriented programs, were still an exception to the rule. It was not until after World War II that the "big house" was replaced by the "correctional institution." Although this transition represents more of a change in degree than kind, there was a discernible increase in amenities and services (Johnson 1987, 44). More important, it was accompanied, if not fueled, by the rise of the "rehabilitative ideal" (Allen 1981).

The ascendancy of the rehabilitative ideal occurred during a period of unparalleled confidence in American institutions, the economy, and the political system (Matusow 1984; Zalman 1987; Useem and Kimball 1989). With respect to criminal justice, "the crime rate was low in the 1950s, and declining for some types of crime" (Useem and Kimball 1989, 9). The state and federal prison population totaled 166,000 in 1950, showing an actual decline of 8,000 from 1940. Moreover, there was a growing belief that rehabilitation should be the primary purpose of imprisonment.[8]

The rehabilitative ideal was to exercise an ideological hegemony over the field of corrections through the 1960s. At its core, the term suggests that

> a primary purpose of penal treatment is to effect changes in the characters, attitudes, and behavior of convicted offenders, so as to strengthen the social defense against unwanted behavior, but also to contribute to the welfare and satisfactions of offenders (Allen 1981, 2).

As it developed, the rehabilitative ideal came to incorporate or express four key features: a system of classification, treatment programs, the indeterminate sentence, and discretionary parole release (Wright 1973). Each component was considered essential to the success of the others.

The ACA first published a *Handbook on Classification* in 1947. At the time only two states, New York and California, had a classification system for adult offenders. McKelvey reports that by 1960, "most state penal systems had endorsed the concept of classification" and had hired professional staff to diagnose and evaluate inmates at the time of admission (1977, 30). The goal of classification was to fit the institution and the program to the inmate (Wright 1973, 49).

While the practice of classification spread quickly during this period, a wide array of treatment programs were also introduced. The oldest forms of institutional programs—education, vocational training, and religious services—were expanded under the inspiration of the rehabilitative ideal. Perhaps the most distinctive feature of this period was that behavioral experts were recruited into the prison setting, including counselors, psychologists, and caseworkers. Their coming resulted in individual and group counseling programs, behavior modification, and alcohol and drug treatment (Irwin 1980; Marshall 1981).

Treatment programs were designed to help inmates understand their problems with the assistance and support of experts. If treatment was to be individualized, so also was the offender's parole release date, subject to the maximum term that could be imposed under an indeterminate sentence.

While fixed sentences remained relatively common in the South, most jurisdictions were influenced increasingly by the movement toward indeterminate sentencing (Tonry 1987). In fact, indeterminacy in sentencing in tandem with parole acquired a newfound legitimacy under the rehabilitative ideal. Together they "institutionalized the notion that individuals should be released only when they have been 'cured' of their criminality" (Marshall 1981, 22).

Under indeterminate sentencing codes, parole boards were given broad discretion to set release dates. The fact that parole eligibility ripened long before the maximum sentence expired presupposed that the parole board—composed of "experts" in evaluating behavioral change—was capable of discerning that moment during confinement when the offender was rehabilitated.

As the rehabilitative ideal acquired growing prominence in the vocabulary of American penologists, paroling authorities struggled to achieve its lofty goals in practice. With the passage of a parole statute in Mississippi in 1944, every state had a system of parole. In a majority of jurisdictions, however, its authority was decentralized, its membership part-time or ex-officio, statutory qualifications for appointment largely nonexistent, and the hearing process relatively unstructured and informal (Rubin 1949).

Nonetheless, the concept of parole continued to gain broad support at the national level. This is most clearly evidenced by the caliber of participants who gathered for the Second National Conference on Parole in Washington, D.C., in 1956.

The conference was convened by then Attorney General Herbert Brownell, at the request and in cooperation with the National Probation and Parole Association and the U.S. Board of Parole. The governor of every state and territory was invited to send three delegates to help produce a manual on parole. The document that was issued reaffirmed the 1939 Declaration of Principles and provided for the first time national standards for the practice of parole (National Probation and Parole Association 1957).[9]

Throughout the conference proceedings and workshop reports there is an expressed faith in the importance of parole. Parole was defined by the conferees as

> a method of selectively releasing an offender from an institution prior to the completion of his maximum sentence, subject to the conditions specified by the paroling authority, a method whereby society can be protected and the offender can be

provided with continuing treatment and supervision in the community (National Probation and Parole Association 1957, 65-66).

Reflecting the imprint of Progressive ideology and the rehabilitative ideal, one of the workshop reports strongly endorsed indeterminate sentencing to accord "the parole board the discretion necessary to determine that moment when the optimum response to the correctional-educational program of the institution indicates that the offender is ready to be returned to society" (National Probation and Parole Association 1957, 72).

This argument was coupled with an assumption that board members would be selected based on education, experience, and personal integrity, not political loyalty. Moreover, the paroling authority itself would be independent of prison administration. The delegates recommended that it be a centralized agency with autonomous decision-making power (National Probation and Parole Association 1957, 77).

In his speech before the conferees, James V. Bennett, the director of the Federal Bureau of Prisons, commented that "a parole system cannot rise above the level of institutions from which parolees are released" (National Probation and Parole Association 1957, 56). Furthermore, if prison programs were to be based on a rehabilitative model, as recommended in another workshop report (National Probation and Parole Association 1957, 95), a period of parole supervision was considered essential to parole success.

In 1955, nearly half of the inmates released were discharged at the expiration of their maximum sentence without assistance or control. Acknowledged by the conferees as a continuation of correctional treatment, parole supervision would be based on the application of casework principles and methods (National Probation and Parole Association 1957, 127). Calling for case classification, one of the workshop reports urged that the maximum number of cases assigned to a parole officer not exceed fifty (National Probation and Parole Association 1957, 132-33).

The principles and recommendations endorsed at this conference were based on a philosophy of rehabilitation. Within this framework, parole release and supervision represented a vital component of crime control policy working in concert with the institution. The indeterminate sentence, parole board autonomy, discretion, and expertise would be combined with a social casework approach to supervision to ensure a sound system of parole.

The dominance of rehabilitative ideology was again reaffirmed less than a decade later through the President's Commission on Law

Enforcement and Administration of Justice (1965-67). The commission was created to develop an effective strategy for responding to the problem of crime confronting American society in the mid-1960s. Its reports were "intended to improve criminal justice in America by a variety of means, including a thoroughgoing program of rehabilitation and indeterminacy in corrections and sentencing" (Zalman 1987, 545).

With respect to parole, at the time of the commission's work, more than 60 percent of adult felons were released on parole prior to the expiration of their maximum sentence (President's Commission on Law Enforcement and Administration of Justice—*Task Force Report: Corrections* 1967, 60; hereafter cited as *Corrections*). According to the commission, when used appropriately, parole accomplishes the goals of public protection and offender reintegration (*Corrections* 1967, 62). The commission observed, however, that "there are wide discrepancies between...what parole purports to be and the actual situation in most jurisdictions" (*Corrections* 1967, 62).

The task force report devoted a chapter to parole drawing on a national survey conducted by the National Council on Crime and Delinquency (National Parole Institutes 1963). It examined three major areas of parole: the organization of paroling authorities, release decision-making, and parolee supervision. Though it found practices in each area deficient to varying degrees, the task force report argued that an effective parole system was an essential element in the fight against crime.

Significantly, the problems highlighted in the task force report echoed those also discussed in the Wickersham Report and the *Attorney General's Survey of Release Procedures*. As long as the rehabilitative ideal maintained its dominance within corrections, it was assumed that by reforming deficiencies in practice, societal protection and offender welfare could be achieved.

The President's commission endorsed the legitimacy of parole as well as the sentencing structure with which it was associated. It is ironic that shortly after the commission completed its work, the core ideas of its reform-oriented agenda—the rehabilitative ideal, indeterminacy in sentencing, and parole—would be seriously challenged by both liberals and conservatives.

The Demise of Rehabilitation and the Assault on Parole

The rehabilitative ideal served as the reigning paradigm in corrections for nearly three decades, from the 1940s through the early 1970s. Its assumptions reflected and expanded those of the Positive School of criminology and the legacy of Progressivism. Its dramatic decline was precipitated by changes in the social and political order that caused the public, politicians, academicians, and others to lose faith in these assumptions; a loss that made them, in turn, receptive to a fundamental shift in criminal justice policy (Gendreau and Ross 1987; Cullen and Gendreau 1989).

It is important to recall that the decade preceding the challenge to rehabilitation was characterized by political turmoil and unrest. Civil rights demonstrations, widespread protests against the Vietnam War, the failure to eradicate poverty, a seeming tolerance for drug use, and discouraging trends in the rate of crime combined, along with other factors, to create the perception that America was coming unraveled (Matusow 1984; Zalman 1987).

This perception carried enormous implications for the criminal justice system. For the first time the problem of crime, if not law and order more generally, emerged as a serious concern in public opinion polls (Finckenauer 1978). While conservative politicians began to criticize the system of criminal justice as ineffectual in its response to crime, their liberal colleagues expressed serious misgivings over unfair and discriminatory sanctioning practices (Cullen and Gilbert 1982; Griset 1987).

The politicization of criminal justice policy coalesced around a series of challenges that engineered the demise of rehabilitation. The first focused on the disparities associated with the indeterminate sentence. The second questioned the efficacy of correctional programming and treatment. The final and most significant challenge targeted the very legitimacy of rehabilitation. Parole was implicated throughout each of these concerns.

The opening salvo in the challenge to the indeterminate sentence was the publication in 1971 by the American Friends Service Committee of *Struggle for Justice*. This was followed by The Twentieth Century Fund Task Force on Criminal Sentencing report *Fair and Certain Punishment* (1976), and von Hirsch's *Doing Justice* (1976), two of the most influential tracts of the decade. These works urged the adoption of determinate or fixed sentencing structures that would focus on the nature of the offense, not the offender. According to the proponents, the primary purpose of sentencing should be retribution, not crime control per se. Von Hirsch argued forcefully for a "just deserts" model, which would reduce disparity and ensure equity as like offenders would receive like terms. In essence, the proposals embraced a return to a neoclassical conception of criminology by arguing that the punishment should fit the crime and not the criminal.

The attacks on the indeterminate sentence were also rooted in a concern that by its very nature it granted unlimited and thus unaccountable discretion to criminal justice functionaries, most notably judges, corrections officials, and parole boards. The abuse of discretion that inevitably followed was exacerbated by the ineffectiveness of treatment throughout the correctional process.

A number of existing studies had already raised serious questions concerning the impact of treatment programs on subsequent criminal behavior (e.g., Wooton 1959). An article, however, published by Robert Martinson in 1974 entitled "What Works? Questions and Answers About Prison Reform," provided an apparently irrefutable, research-based critique of the capacity of corrections to correct.

Martinson's article, and the 1,400-page report from which it was drawn (Lipton, Martinson, and Wilks 1975), called into question the entire correctional enterprise with the comment that as far as offender recidivism is concerned, "nothing works." Basing his conclusion on a review of 231 studies of programs designed to rehabilitate criminal offenders, which were conducted between 1945 and 1967, Martinson, in effect, dismissed the whole of correctional treatment:

> With few and isolated exceptions, the rehabilitative efforts that have been reported so far have had no appreciable effect on recidivism. Studies that have been done since our survey was conducted do not present any major grounds for altering that conclusion (1974, 25).

While he was later to recant the stridency of his original remarks with supportive statements concerning the efficacy of some forms of treatment (Martinson 1979), the rehabilitative ideal suffered a dramatic, perhaps irreparable, loss of legitimacy.[10] The reasons for this loss are rooted in the findings of science, as well as ideology (Cullen and Gendreau 1989). Together with the critique of the indeterminate sentence, the very legitimacy of the rehabilitative ideal was undermined seemingly overnight.

As belief in and commitment to rehabilitation justifies and requires the expertise of parole boards to determine that moment when an offender is ready for release, it is not surprising that parole itself was subjected to attack. The assault on parole began with a call for its outright abolition (American Friends Service Committee 1971).

Others, however, quickly joined the chorus, urging that parole be eliminated or drastically reformed (New York State Special Commission on Attica 1972; Morris 1974; Citizen's Inquiry on Parole and Criminal Justice 1975; Fogel 1975; Stanley 1976; Schmidt 1977; McCleary 1978; von Hirsch and Hanrahan 1979). While several surveys undertaken during this period showed that significant changes were taking place in the field as a whole (O'Leary and Nuffield 1972; O'Leary and Hanrahan 1976; Parker 1975; Carlson 1979), they received far less attention and thus did not contribute to the growing debate over the value of parole.

Many of the most scathing criticisms were directed at the parole release hearing. Hearing practices in New York (Citizen's Inquiry on Parole and Criminal Justice 1975), as well as those of the Federal Parole Board, the District of Columbia, California, Colorado, Georgia, and Wisconsin (Wright 1973; Stanley 1976) were found to be seriously deficient. These studies concluded that parole release decision making was arbitrary and unfair, secretive, not subject to review and thus, inherently flawed.

At the time, parole hearings were generally conducted by panels of three to five board members, one of whom usually read the case file while the others interviewed the inmate. Most of the questions asked were stock queries, based on a cursory review of the case file (Citizen's Inquiry 1975, 46). Board members often conducted fifteen to twenty routine interviews each day while at an institution, after which they voted "yes" or "no" to grant parole. Most of the hearings in New York lasted no more than six to twelve minutes (Citizen's Inquiry 1975, 49).

While a parole hearing was conducted presumably to determine whether an inmate was rehabilitated and thus ready for release, board members were criticized for lacking the necessary training or expertise to make this determination. A national survey by Parker (1975, 57-60) revealed that in thirty-six of the fifty-four jurisdictions from which he solicited information, there were no statutory qualifications for parole board members.

Even if board members had the requisite expertise, numerous studies reported that the factors considered at the time of the hearing had little to do with rehabilitation. Rather, board members often focused on the seriousness of the offense, the inmate's prior criminal record, and compliance with institutional rules and regulations (Wright 1973; Carlson 1979; Cavendar 1982).

Though most of the criticisms were leveled at parole release decision making, parole supervision was also challenged. Several commentators noted that while parole supervision was designed to provide surveillance and assistance, the control function tended to predominate (Citizen's Inquiry 1975; Studt 1978; von Hirsch and Hanrahan 1979).[11] Most critics acknowledged, however, that the degree of control maintained over parolee behavior was sporadic to nonexistent. General concern was expressed over the amount of time parole officers devoted to assisting parolees and the arbitrary enforcement of the conditions of parole.

Time studies suggested that individual parolees received very little officer attention or assistance. One study (of federal probation) reported that officers spent an average of seven minutes per week with individuals on their caseloads, while another (in Georgia) found the average time to be eight minutes per week (Megathalin 1973; Stanley 1976, 125-26). Moreover, most of the contacts with parolees were conducted not in the field, but in the office. Office-bound contacts were the norm, according to Stanley, who characterized them as "typically amiable, superficial and brief...an empty formality" (1976, 95-101).

A more serious criticism targeted the enforcement of parole conditions. The conditions of parole at the time tended to be comprehensive in reach and frequently moralistic with respect to parolee behavior (Arluke 1969). More important, the same rules were subject to varying interpretations by different officers (as well as the same officer). In fact, Studt observed that the amount of control experienced by parolees depended in large measure on the officer to whom they were assigned (1978, 140).

The discretionary enforcement of parole conditions was criticized as being unfair, often intrusive, and not subject to any accountability.[12] More generally, these studies called into question the effectiveness of parole supervision by arguing that its crime control and rehabilitative value was negligible.

Nonetheless, these criticisms were not new. From the Progressive Era through the late sixties, numerous commissions and studies found that the practice of parole was seriously flawed. Yet, there was a strong belief that while practices were in need of reform, the concept itself was sound. During the 1970s, many of the same criticisms were made—albeit with a sharper edge. The demise of the rehabilitative ideal gave these criticisms new meaning. In the environment of the time, the problems associated with parole were viewed as symptomatic not of a disparity between theory and practice, which could be overcome, but of an inherently flawed concept that should be abolished.

Sentencing Reform and Parole Abolition

Growing public concern over the problem of crime, the marked loss of faith in the rehabilitative ideal, and the politicization of criminal justice policy sparked the movement toward determinate sentencing reform that began in the 1970s. For more than three decades prior to 1975, every state and the federal system had sentencing codes characterized by indeterminacy (Tonry 1987). These codes reflected a widespread consensus that offender rehabilitation was the primary rationale for imprisonment. If this consensus in sentencing policy is remarkable for its duration, the suddenness of its demise is equally noteworthy.

In the decade that followed, all fifty states, the District of Columbia, and the federal government revised or considered replacing indeterminate with determinate sentencing codes (Shane-DuBow et al. 1985). Sentencing guidelines projects were created or considered in many states. While a majority of jurisdictions ultimately retained their indeterminate sentencing codes, between 1976 and 1982 at least fifteen states passed determinate sentencing legislation and thus adopted a new philosophy to govern the sanctioning of criminal offenders (Shane-DuBow et al. 1985).[13]

As Tonry points out, during this period "the monolith of American indeterminate sentencing dissolved, to be replaced not by another monolith, but by a diverse assortment of sentencing approaches that varied state by state" (1987, 6). Even in states where sentencing changes were not so sweeping, criminal penalties were increased, mandatory sentencing laws were enacted, and habitual or repeat offender laws were either passed or strengthened.

Even though no model came to predominate, the impact on parole, especially discretionary parole release, was dramatic. With Maine leading the way, between 1976 and 1979 six states either eliminated or severely limited parole release (California, Colorado, Illinois, Indiana, Maine, and New Mexico). From 1980 to 1984 another five states followed suit (Connecticut, Florida, Minnesota, North Carolina, and Washington). Only one other state (Delaware) has since abolished parole through legislation that became effective in 1990.[14]

At the federal level, the Comprehensive Crime Control Act of 1984 was enacted, creating the U.S. Sentencing Commission to develop sentencing guidelines. At the same time, this legislation abolished the U.S. Parole Commission, which will be phased out in 1992.[15] Certain offenders will continue to be supervised upon their release.

Nonetheless, the abolition of parole does not necessarily follow the adoption of a determinate sentencing structure (e.g., New Jersey) or sentencing guidelines (Pennsylvania), nor is it irreversible even where it occurs. In 1979, Colorado eliminated discretionary parole release. In 1985, it restored this function. North Carolina, which placed severe limitations on its parole commission in 1981, has since given it more discretion. Florida, which adopted sentencing guidelines in 1983 and abolished parole, recently returned the function under the new name "Controlled Release Authority."

Regardless of the type of sentencing structure, the wave of sentencing reform that began in the 1970s has resulted in a significant diminution of parole boards' discretionary authority to release. Between 1977 and 1988 the proportion of inmates granted parole release relative to mandatory release showed a steady decline (Bureau of Justice Statistics [BJS] 1989b). Approximately 72 percent of those released from prison in 1977 were paroled. The comparable figure in 1988 was 40 percent. During this same period, the percentage of mandatory releasees increased nearly fivefold from 6 percent in 1977 to 31 percent in 1988. Mandatory releasees leave prison upon service of their maximum sentence minus time off for program participation or good behavior during confinement. They are generally subject to a period of supervision equal to the amount of good time deducted. They are not subject to review by a paroling authority.

While the discretionary authority of parole boards has been eliminated in some states and significantly curtailed in others, the movement to abolish parole has slowed considerably. Though parole boards are still subject to challenge, the first wave of sentencing reform has brought in its wake unprecedented prison and jail crowding. Ironically, the very factors that contributed to the assault on parole under the rubric of determinacy and just deserts in sentencing have now provided a reprieve from outright abolition, as parole is being called on increasingly to manage growing prison populations.

Prison Crowding in the 1980s: A Reprieve for Parole

Throughout the twentieth century, the rate of incarceration in the United States has showed remarkable stability ranging from 75-125 offenders per 100,000 population (Austin and McVey 1988). Since 1972, however, the nation's prison population and rate of imprisonment have shown historically unprecedented levels of growth. Fueled in part by the movement toward determinate sentencing reform, as well as mandatory sentencing laws and sentencing enhancements, the philosophy of just deserts in the 1970s gave way to a singular reliance upon a philosophy of incapacitation during the 1980s (Burke 1988).

In 1970, there were 196,429 inmates in state and federal prisons. The rate of incarceration was 96 per 100,000 (Blumstein 1988). Between 1980 and 1989, the rate of incarceration increased from 139 to 274 per 100,000. The prison population grew to a record high of 710,054. As of 30 June 1990, a record-breaking total of 755,425 inmates were confined, and the rate of incarceration stood at 289 per 100,000 (USA Today, 9 September 1990). It is likely that the prison population will continue upwards in the 1990s (Blumstein 1989).

The enormous jump in the rate of imprisonment, combined with escalating costs associated with prison construction, focused the attention of policy makers and legislators on ways to cope with correctional systems that seem out of control (National Conference of State Legislatures 1989). In a number of states that have engaged in massive prison construction programs and have spent hundreds of millions of dollars in an effort to manage the growth, there is now a recognition that it is not possible nor desirable to continue to expand bedspace to match the demand (Strasser 1989).

The heightened concern with managing finite correctional resources under growing fiscal constraints has tempered the rush to abolish discretionary parole release. In fact, the prison crowding crisis of the eighties has been the single most important determinant in derailing the movement to eliminate parole (Burke 1988). Nonetheless, the crisis in correctional crowding, which has provided a reprieve for parole, now threatens to reduce the function of paroling authorities to de facto regulators of unmanageable prison population levels.

Parole boards have always been the historical "back-door keeper" of America's prisons (Garry 1984). At times they have served as a safety valve to relieve crowded institutions (Messinger et al. 1985). The record growth in the number of those imprisoned has, however, placed unprecedented pressure on paroling authorities in many states to release offenders, regardless of their suitability or eligibility for parole.

The responsibility for managing prison population levels has been thrust upon paroling authorities in several ways. The most visible mechanism has been emergency early release. In 1980, not a single state had an emergency powers act (EPA). Since then twenty-one jurisdictions have enacted such acts, although in some states the legislation has expired and in others it was never triggered (Rhine et al. 1989).

EPAs are designed to serve as a short-term, infrequently used option to reduce a state's prison population when it exceeds a specified capacity for a certain period of time. Generally, the legislation directs that an authority, usually the governor, when notified of a crowded condition, declare an emergency and award increments of time credits to inmates to advance either their parole eligibility or mandatory release dates. The first group of inmates, whose parole eligibility is advanced, represents the pool that is reviewed by the parole board for release.

Even where they have been triggered frequently, EPAs have not been a panacea for measurably reducing prison crowding. Under these circumstances, the parole board is subject to immense pressure to release a certain percentage of inmates who would not otherwise have been given such consideration. Moreover, by repeatedly invoking their EPA, several states have found that those inmates directly affected have often been awarded huge time credits. Inmates confined in Texas prisons from

1987-89 had their sentences reduced by twenty-one months through the awarding of EPA time credits (Jackson et al. 1989).

Paroling authorities in states with and without EPAs have also been called upon to manage the prison population in other ways. Some parole boards (e.g., Georgia) have received legislative authority and direction to control the prison population by adjusting their formal guidelines for release. Other boards (e.g., Texas) have been told informally by the governor's office to grant parole through a quota system wherein the number of releases must approximate the number of admissions. In such instances paroling authorities are obligated to adjust, if not completely disregard, their decision-making criteria to increase and expedite the number of inmates who are released.

The staggering increase in prison populations and the attendant pressure to manage the overflow has created a quandary for paroling authorities that is both philosophical and practical. With respect to the latter, there is a tacit acknowledgement that parole boards represent the most viable agency for releasing offenders. Even if this involves only a cursory review of each case, the process provides a more orderly method for screening offender risk than systems characterized by mandatory release (e.g., California). As indicated earlier, this recognition recently prompted the state of Florida to restore parole under an agency renamed the Controlled Release Authority. This newly named authority is composed of the same membership as the former Parole Commission.

If the pressing reality of prison crowding has focused attention away from the abolition of parole, at least for now, it also threatens to undermine developments that were beginning to refocus the philosophy of parole release decision making. The most notable development is found in the area of structured parole decision making.

In response to widespread criticism in the 1970s over the absence of standards to govern release decisions, paroling authorities began to experiment with parole guidelines (Gottfredson et al. 1978). The first and best-known guidelines project was initiated by the U.S. Parole Commission (then the U.S. Board of Parole) in 1972. Gradually, other boards followed suit. By 1986 eighteen jurisdictions reported that they used formal guidelines in making parole decisions (Baird and Lerner 1986). The number has grown since then, although there is no one common definition of parole guidelines. In some states a matrix approach is used, while in others a listing of aggravating and mitigating factors informs the decision to release.

Many states that use parole guidelines also include some form of risk assessment as well. Predicting which inmates may be returned safely to the community has always been a concern of parole boards. The assessment of offender risk through objective decision-making tools represents a relatively new development that has occurred simultaneously with the adoption of parole guidelines.

The trend toward managing both discretion and offender risk through the application of structured decision-making tools has gone relatively unnoticed during the past decade.[16] Nonetheless, this trend reflects a significant philosophical shift with respect to parole decision making in the direction of balancing just deserts concerns with the management of offender risk. Whether it will be or can be firmly integrated within the parole process is unclear, given the incessant pressures produced by prison crowding to expedite the release of offenders.

What is clear is that parole will continue to be subjected to powerful cross-currents in the years ahead. The most serious challenge to parole continues to center around its contribution to, and thus its very legitimacy within, the criminal justice system. The correctional crowding crisis represents an equally profound threat to the integrity of the entire parole process. How paroling authorities are responding to these and other issues will be addressed in the chapters to follow.

Notes

1. In 1837, Maconochie submitted a report that was generally supportive of transportation but highly critical of the treatment experienced by felons during their overseas transit and following their arrival. While residing on Van Dieman's Land (Australia), he published a series of pamphlets on prison administration that, together with his earlier report, secured his eventual appointment as Superintendent of Norfolk Island (Barry 1972, 88-92).
2. Champion (1990, 247) points out that early release, based on an inmate's earning good-time credits, was authorized by New York long before, in 1817. Other states quickly followed suit.
3. Brockway himself was accused of using harsh disciplinary methods and was eventually forced to "quietly resign" following an investigation of Elmira (Pisciotta 1983).
4. Messinger et al. (1985) argue that parole was initially introduced in California in 1893 as a way to reduce the demands on the governor's time caused by the need to review an ever-growing number of petitions from prisoners seeking executive clemency.
5. Though it spread rapidly, there was substantial variation in the extent to which parole was relied upon in different jurisdictions. In 1936, fifteen states paroled 80 percent or more of those released from imprisonment. In fourteen states, parole accounted for less than 25 percent of those released. This variation, reported in the *Attorney General's Survey of Release Procedures* (1939, 122), nonetheless reveals the growing relationship between parole and the indeterminate sentence.

177209

6. Many states had only one parole officer assigned to supervision. Regardless of the number of such staff, the *Attorney General's Survey of Release Procedures* was highly critical of the complete absence of qualifications or training for parole officers.

7. Other prominent speakers at the conference included Earl Warren, the attorney general of California; James V. Bennett, director of the U.S. Bureau of Prisons; the governor of New York; and the president of the University of Chicago.

8. This belief was symbolized on the national level when in 1954 the American Prison Association changed its name to the American Correctional Association to more effectively convey its purpose (McKelvey 1977, 327).

9. In addition to the attorney general, who brought greetings from President Eisenhower, the 475 delegates in attendance heard from Chief Justice Earl Warren, James V. Bennett, and J. Edgar Hoover.

10. Other surveys were to draw similar conclusions (e.g., Sechrest et al. 1979). At the time they were published, they simply reinforced what Allen (1981) refers to as the "new orthodoxy."

11. Cavender (1982) argues that the emphasis given to the rehabilitative value of parole has been much overstated. According to the author, from the very beginning its primary function has been that of social control. See chapter 2 in Cavender for an elaboration of this position.

12. McCleary found that the arbitrary enforcement of parole rules was shaped by bureaucratic culture. Within this culture, "discretion was not unlimited, but governed by organizational norms emphasizing the parolee's potential for making trouble or disrupting the organizational dynamic" (1978, 43). Parole officers learned how to avoid unnecessary problems by correctly typing parolees.

13. There is considerable variation and complexity in the determinate sentencing statutes enacted among the states. According to a major survey of sentencing reform, "it would be a mistake to assume that all states with determinate sentencing have essentially similar sentencing laws" (Shane-DuBow et al. 1985, 279). For this reason, there is no one commonly accepted definition of determinacy. See Chapter 3 for further discussion of this issue.

14. Parole or postrelease supervision was also affected in most of the states adopting determinate sentencing legislation. In three states (Florida, Maine, and Washington), the supervision component was abolished altogether. In a number of the others, the period of postrelease supervision was narrowed to a fixed term ranging from one to three years, as in California, Indiana, and Illinois (Hussey and Lagoy 1983).

15. Although a 1989 U.S. Supreme Court decision affirmed the constitutionality of the U.S. Sentencing Commission in *Mistretta v. U.S.* 109 S.Ct. 102 L. ed. 2d 714, the Congress recently extended the U.S. Parole Commission to 1997.

16. Between 1985 and 1987, the National Institute of Corrections provided technical assistance funding for parole decision makers. Its major goal was to support paroling authorities in their efforts to develop a policy-based, structured approach to decision making. Nine states received technical assistance in this area. The project, which was managed by the COSMOS Corporation in concert with the Center for Effective Public Policy, was extended for two more years to cover additional states.

Chapter 2

Organization and Administration of Paroling Authorities

Paroling authorities or parole boards are located within the executive branch of government.[1] Although they are executive branch agencies, they enjoy quasi-judicial immunity under limited circumstances (del Carmen and Louis 1988). As agencies within the criminal justice system, the scope and consequences of their actions—statutory and administrative—are enormous. Their decisions determine the actual period of time many offenders spend behind bars or under supervision on the streets.

Though they may assist states in managing limited correctional resources by adjusting the criteria for granting parole, they may also contribute to prison and jail crowding through shifts in parole revocation policy. The decisions of paroling authorities also affect public safety and the achievement of a state's sentencing goals. As McGarry states, given their relative size, "[in] no other part of the system is so much power concentrated in so few hands" (1988, 18).

Parole boards play a pivotal, though not exclusive, role within the overall parole process. The parole process refers to three principal components: release, supervision, and revocation. Although these functions or components are interdependent, in most states they are housed in separate agencies: parole boards and parole field services.[2]

Paroling authorities have the statutory responsibility for deciding if and when an inmate may be released from confinement and whether parole should be revoked if rules violations occur during supervision. The decision to grant or deny parole is a quasi-judicial function and is vested solely in the board. There is no constitutional right to parole (Knight and Early 1986). On the other hand, the revocation of parole is bound by the constraints of procedural due process—see *Greenholtz v. Inmates of the Nebraska Penal and Correctional Complex*, 442 U.S. 1 (1979). If the allegations are sustained, the board is authorized to revoke parole and, within what remains of the original sentence, require that the parolee serve additional prison time.

In most states, the actual supervision of parole is carried out by parole field services. These agencies are usually housed under the department of corrections. They are responsible for enforcing the conditions of parole—conditions that are established by, and thus represent, the decision goals of the board (McGarry 1988, 91). If the parolee commits a crime or violates other rules during supervision, the field service agency may initiate revocation proceedings and refer the parolee to the board for a final determination.

The percent of jurisdictions in which paroling authorities have the statutory responsibility for release, revocation, and supervision are shown in Figure 2.1. Of the fifty-one jurisdictions included in the ACA Parole Task Force survey, 98 percent have statutory authority over parole release.[3] Minnesota is the exception.

Forty-nine jurisdictions, or 96.1 percent, have jurisdiction over revocation; Oklahoma and Wisconsin represent the exceptions. In terms of supervision, while parole boards set the conditions that the parolee is expected to abide by in 98 percent of the jurisdictions, they are directly responsible for supervising parolees in only thirteen states. Parole supervision is performed by an independent field service agency in thirty-eight jurisdictions.[4]

Although there is considerable variation state by state, Figure 2.1 illustrates that parole boards are authorized by statute to carry out a significant number of additional functions and responsibilities. Thus, in forty-seven jurisdictions (92 percent) the parole board may rescind a

Figure 2.1

Statutory Jurisdiction of Paroling Authorities

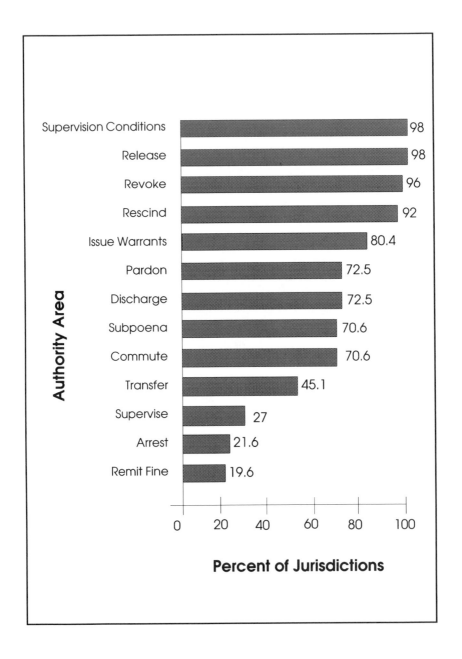

parole date that has already been set. Under such circumstances, an inmate with an established parole date who commits a serious disciplinary violation will be reheard to determine if release is still appropriate. Arrest warrants may be issued by the board in forty-one jurisdictions (80.4 percent), while in thirty-six states (70.6 percent) the board has subpoena power when conducting hearings. In thirty-seven states (72.5 percent) the board may grant final discharge for satisfactory performance while on parole.

Reflecting the historical development of parole in the United States, most paroling authorities still have statutory responsibility to either recommend or grant a pardon (N = 37) or commutation of sentence (N = 36) to the governor. Pardons and sentence commutations are forms of executive clemency. A pardon represents an act of grace and forgiveness that is "usually granted to people who are no longer incarcerated, but who wish to regain certain rights that were lost or suspended on conviction" (National Governors' Association 1988, 4). It may be distinguished from a commutation of sentence, which "substitutes a new, lesser punishment for the original sentence" (National Governors' Association 1988, 5). With respect to commutations, in most states with capital sentencing statutes paroling authorities play a role in determining whether to permit an execution to go forward or to reduce a death sentence to life imprisonment.

The range of matters over which parole boards have statutory jurisdiction is substantial, despite the differences that may be noted state by state. Nevertheless, how they exercise this authority is influenced not just by the provisions of state statutes, but also by the parole board's relationships to other governmental agencies and decision-making elites, most notably the governor's office, the legislative branch of government, and the department of corrections.

Paroling authorities are part of the political process and empowered by it, a distinction they share with all executive branch agencies. In contrast, however, to most agencies within the executive branch in which only the head of the department is appointed by the governor, in a majority of states the governor nominates the entire membership of the parole board. While this serves to increase the accountability of the parole board, it also renders its decision making vulnerable to political pressure.[5]

Although the appointment and confirmation process shows some variation, the key player in most states is the governor. In forty-one jurisdictions, the governor has the authority to make appointments to the parole board, subject to legislative confirmation. In another four states, the governor shares the appointing authority with another body. The

Table 2.1

Statutory Qualifications for Parole Board Membership in Selected Jurisdictions

Jurisdiction	Statutory Qualifications for Membership
Montana	Academic training that qualifies board member for professional practice in a field such as criminology, education, psychiatry, psychology, law, social work, sociology, or guidance and counseling. Related work experience in the areas listed may be substituted for these educational requirements. One board member must have particular knowledge of Indian culture and problems.
New York	Each member of the board shall have graduated from an accredited four-year college or university with a degree in the field of criminology, administration of criminal justice, law enforcement, sociology, law, social work, corrections, psychology, psychiatry, or medicine, and shall have had at least five years of experience in one or more of such fields.
Ohio	No person shall be appointed a member of the board who is not qualified by education or experience in correctional work, including law enforcement, probation, parole, in law, in social work, or in a combination of the three categories.
Pennsylvania	An individual shall have at least six years of professional experience in parole, probation, social work, or related areas, including one year in supervisory or administrative capacity, and a bachelor's degree. Any equivalent combination of experience and training shall be acceptable.
West Virginia	Each member of the board shall have had experience in the field of social science or administration of penal institutions and shall be familiar with the principles, practices, and problems thereof and shall be otherwise competent to perform the duties of his office.

governor does not play a key role in the appointments process in only six states. In five of these states the director or commissioner of corrections makes the appointment (Idaho, Michigan, Minnesota, Ohio, Wisconsin), while the secretary of public safety does so in the other (Maryland).

In most states the governor enjoys wide latitude when nominating someone to the parole board. The qualifications for appointment as a parole board member have not changed appreciably during the past twenty years. A survey conducted in 1972 found that twenty-eight boards had statutory requirements for appointment (O'Leary and Nuffield 1972). The same survey conducted again in 1976 found that the number had increased to thirty-five (O'Leary and Hanrahan 1976). By 1979 this upward trend had reversed itself with only twenty-four parole boards reporting such requirements (Carlson 1979). While these differences may reflect variations in wording across the surveys, the findings are consistent with those of other studies (Parker 1975).

These findings are also mirrored in the 1988 ACA Parole Task Force survey. It found that twenty-nine jurisdictions (56.9 percent) reported that there were no professional qualifications, defined by statute, for parole board membership. In these jurisdictions, the governor may nominate individuals without regard to education, training, or experience.

Even in states with professional qualifications, the statutes may be stated in very general terms and thus afford the governor generous discretion. The results of the ACA Parole Task Force survey indicate that of the twenty-two states (43.1 percent) that have statutory requirements for parole board membership, only six require a bachelor's degree (Indiana, Kentucky, Massachusetts, Michigan, New York, and Pennsylvania). One state requires a master's degree (Iowa). Nine states responded that they require some experience in criminal justice or a related field, although the number of years is not specified. A minimum number of years of experience in criminal justice or a related field is required in another nine states, most often five years.

The qualifications for parole board membership in five of the twenty-two states reporting such requirements are presented in Table 2.1. They are drawn from jurisdictions representing different regions of the country and parole boards of varying sizes and jurisdiction. They illustrate how general, if not permissive, the statutory language is with respect to parole board appointments.

The political nature of the appointments process, as well as the absence of statutory qualifications for parole board membership, has long been subjected to criticism (National Commission on Law Observance and Enforcement 1931; Morse 1939; National Probation and Parole Association 1957; Parker 1975). As with executive branch agencies generally, if the

Table 2.2

Active Groups on Parole Issues

Person/Group	Activity Level (Percent)			
	Plays No Role	Rarely Active	Sometimes Active	Always Active
Governor	11.8	11.8	51	25.5
Citizens' Crime Comm.	19.6	21.6	33.3	25.5
Democratic Leader (State Senate)	16	18	50	16
Republican Leader (State Senate)	22	16	50	12
Democratic Leader (State House)	18	18	44	20
Republican Leader (State House)	24	18	50	8
State Senate Corrections Committee	15.7	5.9	27.5	51
State House Corrections Committee	12	8	28	52
Head of State Corrections Dept.	9.8	2	45.1	43.1
State Attorney General	13.7	27.5	45.1	13.7
State Bar Association	31.4	41.2	27.5	0
Police Chiefs of Large Departments	21.6	31.4	47.1	0
American Civil Liberties Union	27.5	29.4	31.4	11.8
Ex-Offenders Org.	58.8	15.7	17.6	7.8
Assoc. of Corrections Personnel	35.3	25.5	35.3	3.9

environment in which paroling authorities operates is highly political, this same environment provides them with access to policy makers and other state elites who may affect parole legislation, board operations, and ultimately, the very survival of the agency.

The Political Environment of Parole

To address the importance of those individuals and groups who may be active in shaping legislation that affects parole, the ACA Parole Task Force survey asked parole board chairs to rate the activity levels and influence of different elites and groups within their state.[6] The methodology employed drew on an earlier study by Berk and Rossi (1977). In that study (of state correctional elites and prison reform), as well as in the survey, it was assumed that states vary in the ways in which legislation affecting corrections (and by implication parole) is brought before the legislature and enacted. In some states a large number of groups and individuals may participate actively, while in others only a few key groups and persons may actually be involved.

It is important to emphasize that these findings express the perceptions or views of parole board chairs on who they regarded as influential in enacting parole legislation in their particular state. Nonetheless, the results illustrate the complicated mix of individuals and groups who potentially wield power within the political environment in which parole boards carry out their myriad and often controversial responsibilities.

Table 2.2 highlights how parole board chairs rated the activity levels of those groups and persons usually participating in legislative initiatives that affect parole. The levels were categorized as "always active," "sometimes active," "rarely active," and "plays no role." As Berk and Rossi (1977, 87) found, the level of activity is perceived to vary quite significantly across the different groups.

Ten of the groups or individuals were viewed as "sometimes active" to "always active" 50 percent or more of the time. Within these groups, however, four were rated as showing such activity 75 percent of the time or more. These include the head of the state department of corrections (88.2 percent), followed by the state House corrections committee (80 percent), the governor (76.5 percent), and the state Senate corrections committee (76.5 percent). Five groups were assessed as playing "no role" or "rarely active" more than 50 percent of the time, including ex-offenders organizations (74.5 percent), the state bar association (72.6 percent), associations of corrections personnel (60.8 percent), the American Civil Liberties Union (56.9 percent), and the police chiefs of large police departments (53 percent).[7]

The survey also asked the respondents to assess which groups actually had the power or "clout" to secure or block passage of parole legislation. Thus, one question was, "[if] you wanted to get a piece of parole legislation through the state legislature, which of these groups or individuals would it be very important to get on your side?" Another question asked for a response to the statement, "Opposition from these groups or individuals could make it impossible or very difficult to get parole legislation passed." Table 2.3 summarizes those groups considered essential for passage and those viewed as capable of stopping legislation on parole.

According to at least 60 percent of the chairs, three individuals/groups were viewed as being very important to—as well as capable of stopping—parole legislation: the governor, and the corrections committees of both the House and the Senate. At least 40 percent of the chairs rated the Democratic leaders in the House in the same way. The Republican leadership was not considered as essential to passing a bill, but it was viewed by nearly 40 percent as able to stop passage. Although the heads of the department of corrections were considered the most active in Table 2.2, they were not viewed as very powerful in passing or blocking bills concerning parole.

Following Berk and Rossi (1977), a correlation matrix was constructed using each of the variables to measure how essential a given person/agency is to parole issues in a state. In looking at three states (Florida, Illinois, and Washington), Berk and Rossi found two very broad but influential categories, an "administrative coalition" and an "executive coalition." The responses of the parole board chairs point to a similar result. Although most parole chairs recognize that the governor is essential, there are only three statistically significant correlations (see Table 2.4) between "governor is essential" and any of the other persons/groups: Democratic leader of the Senate, of the House, and the head of the department of corrections. The Democratic and Republican leadership of the House and Senate constitute a similar group of "essential" individuals for parole issues—thus, the relatively high correlations among those four variables.[8]

Another set essential to parole issues consists of the corrections committees of both the House and Senate. Neither of these variables correlate highly with any of the others in Table 2.4, suggesting that these committees are perceived to be essential independent of the other individuals/groups, including the party leadership of the Senate and the House

The head of the department of corrections tends to be perceived as essential where the following are also perceived as such: the governor,

Table 2.3

Reputation for Power on Parole Issues

Person/Group	Percent Claiming Group Essential for Passage of Bill	Percent Claiming Group Can Stop Passage of Bill
Governor	72.5	68.6
Citizens' Crime Committee	11.8	21.6
Democratic Leader (State Senate)	48	64
Republican Leader (State Senate)	26	42
Democratic Leader (State House)	42	64
Republican Leader (State House)	26	38
State Senate Corrections Committee	60.8	62.7
State House Corrections Committee	66	62
Head of State Corrections Department	27.5	37.3
State Attorney General	11.8	39.2
State Bar Association	5.9	13.7
Police Chiefs of Large Police Departments	7.8	21.6
American Civil Liberties Union	2	7.8
Ex-Offenders Organization	2	3.9
Association of Corrections Personnel	5.9	7.8

Table 2.4

Correlation Matrix of Persons/Groups Considered Essential for Passage of a Bill on Parole Legislation

	1	2	3	4	5	6	7	8	9	10	11	12	13	14
Governor	1.00													
Citizen's Crime Committee	.22	1.00												
Democratic Leader Senate	.42**	.14	1.00											
Republican Leader Senate	.17	.20	.62**	1.00										
Democratic Leader House	.35*	.06	.80**	.51**	1.00									
Republican Leader House	.17	.06	.53**	.79**	.51**	1.00								
Senate Corrections Committee	.23	.08	.13	.11	.12	.11	1.00							
House Corrections Committee	.21	.01	.18	.14	.18	.04	.88**	1.00						
Head of Dept. of Corrections	.38**	.32*	.47**	.34*	.46**	.24	.22	.17	1.00					
Attorney General	.25	.24	.26	.34*	.19	.48**	.17	.14	.18	1.00				
State Bar Association	.15	.17	.26	.23	.30*	.23	.03	.18	.03	.43**	1.00			
Police Departments	.18	.35*	.16	.33*	.05	.16	.23	.21	.47**	.35*	.24	1.00		
American Civil Liberties Union	.09	.39**	.15	.24	.17	.24	.11	.10	.23	.39**	.57**	.48**	1.00	
Ex-Offender Organizations	.09	.39**	.15	.24	.17	.24	.11	.10	.23	.39**	.57**	.48**	1.00	1.00
Association of Correctional Personnel	.15	.17	.26	.23	.30*	.23	.20	.18	.41**	.17	.29*	.24	.57**	.57**

* Signif. LE .05
** Signif. LE .01 (2-tailed)

citizens' crime committee, leaders of both houses and both parties, police departments, and associations of correctional personnel. Thus, the importance of the head of a department of corrections is generally shared with several others.

Citizens' groups, as well as civil liberties associations, ex-offender associations, and police departments also seem to cluster in terms of importance: few parole chiefs see them as essential.

In summary, Table 2.4 suggests the following groups as being important—and relatively autonomous—for legislation relevant to parole: the governor, the party leadership of the House and Senate, corrections committees of the legislatures, the head of the department of corrections, and least of all, more broadly based citizens, civil liberties, ex-offender, and correctional personnel groups.

Perceptions of who are the powerful players help form a general framework for understanding the political process of parole. The actual involvement of parole board chairs represents another aspect of that process. Table 2.5 presents information on the extent of personal knowledge and contact between the respondents and the groups and individuals discussed thus far. The first question asked, "[are] there any of these groups in which you know the key members well enough to call them about something concerning parole issues?" A second item asked, "[have] you ever contacted any of these individuals or group members about parole issues?"

On the whole, the extent to which the parole board chairs claim to know the various persons and groups is rather high and well distributed. With but three exceptions (the state bar association, the American Civil Liberties Union, and ex-offender associations), the chairs reported knowing everyone well enough to call 40 percent or more of the time. The head of the department of corrections is the best known, closely followed by the governor and the Senate and House corrections committees.

This pattern is for the most part repeated with respect to those chairs stating that they have actually contacted the various individuals and groups on parole-related matters. Again, the head of the department of corrections was contacted most often, followed by the governor and the corrections committees of the Senate and the House. The groups least often contacted (by less than 40 percent of the chairs) included those already mentioned above and the citizens' crime committee, police chiefs of large police departments, and the association of corrections personnel.

Tables 2.2 through 2.5 suggest that from the parole board chairs' perspective, there are a limited number of persons and groups who are influential with respect to parole-related legislative initiatives. The Senate and the House corrections committees appear to be the most important

Table 2.5

Extent of Personal Contact on Parole Issues

Person/Group	Percent Knowing Person/Group Well Enough To Call	Percent Who Have Contacted Person/Group
Governor	66.7	74.5
Citizens' Crime Committee	41.2	37.3
Democratic Leader (State Senate)	52	54
Republican Leader (State Senate)	48	48
Democratic Leader (State House)	58	54
Republican Leader (State House)	48	48
State Senate Corrections Committee	62.7	66.7
State House Corrections Committee	64	66
Head of State Corrections Department	70.6	78.4
State Attorney General	54.9	52.9
State Bar Association	35.3	23.5
Police Chiefs of Large Police Departments	51	37.3
American Civil Liberties Union	23.5	13.7
Ex-Offenders Organization	17.6	13.7
Association of Corrections Personnel	41.2	23.5

overall. They are regarded as quite active in dealing with parole bills, essential to passage, and able to block the enactment of parole legislation. The governor and the head of the department of corrections are also viewed as key players and are well integrated into the interpersonal network and "legislative coalition" that forms the political environment of parole.

Corrections and Parole

Not only is the relationship of parole to the political process important, but so too are interagency relations. The department of corrections is especially critical to the parole board. Regardless of where the parole board is located, its functions and responsibilities bring it into daily contact and interaction with the corrections department.

Paroling practices also exert a tangible influence on correctional administration. While each group has substantial autonomy in most states, the work of each has a dramatic impact on the other. Although it varies by state, there are three main areas where their interdependence is most apparent: institutional support during the preparole process, prison management and inmate control, and the management of correctional resources.

With respect to the first area, in most, if not all states, the department of corrections provides logistical and other assistance to the paroling authority during the preparole process. This assistance includes the provision of office space for institutional parole staff, the sharing of and ongoing access to classification files and other information (e.g., psychological reports) on inmates eligible for parole, and the coordination and scheduling of preparole and parole hearings within the daily routine of the facility. The extent of cooperation and communication that exists between prison officials and paroling authority staff who are housed within the institution is critical—although often unrecognized—to the smooth flow of the parole process.

The impact of parole on prison management has long been acknowledged. Before the 1920s and 1930s, when parole boards began to centralize and acquire some independence from departments of corrections, the most enthusiastic advocates of parole release were wardens and superintendents (Rothman 1980). Their enthusiasm changed to concern, however, in the 1970s as parole release discretion was curtailed sharply in several states in response to the move toward determinate sentencing reform (Carlson 1979).

According to prison administrators and others, the prospect of parole release contributes to order and stability within the walls. It does so by providing inmates with an incentive to comply with institutional rules and participate in work, treatment, and other programs (e.g., education) that enhance their chances for release when they appear before the parole board. Even for those inmates who are serving long prison terms, the possibility that they may eventually be paroled provides a measure of hope and thus may encourage positive behavior over time.[9]

Parole board practices also strongly affect the management of a state's correctional resources. As is well recognized, parole boards have at different times served as a "safety valve" at the back end of the correctional system (Garry 1984). Paroling authorities have traditionally enjoyed both the flexibility and discretion to adjust their release policies to maintain a certain equilibrium with respect to prison population levels. Doing so has on occasion reduced the pressure to build new prisons or expand existing prison capacity.

Clearly, an expansive parole release policy assists a state in managing its finite correctional capacity. Conversely, a restrictive policy on parole release may strain correctional resources and exacerbate prison crowding. Whether responding to public concerns or legislative criticism, if a parole board tightens its policies on release, the cumulative effect of its more conservative decisions will be felt directly by those with responsibility for managing the state's prison population.

If the impact of parole release policy on correctional resources is generally understood, the implications of shifts in revocation policy are not. Whether gradual or sudden, changes in a parole board's policy on parolee revocation may produce a discernible change in the size of a state's prison population. If a significant percentage of parolees who violate the conditions of their supervision have their parole revoked and are returned to custody, especially in a state experiencing serious prison crowding, the consequences may be staggering.

Austin (1989) reports that in 1987 prison admissions in California totaled 62,729. Of this number, 31,581 (50.3 percent) were parole violators. Roughly 80 percent of those were returned to prison as technical violators without a new prison sentence. According to the research, confining the 25,000 offenders who were returned for technical parole violations (for an average of 125 days) was estimated to cost $242 million. How parole boards choose to respond to parole violators, especially those who commit technical violations, clearly implicates how limited correctional resources are allocated.

It is evident that the policies and operations of the parole board are functionally interdependent with the department of corrections. Nonetheless, in the vast majority of states the parole board is organizationally a separate and independent agency. To assess the extent of this autonomy, one of the questions on the ACA Parole Task Force survey asked if "the parole board was autonomous and not subject to the control and supervision of another agency, such as the department of corrections." As Figure 2.2 shows, in 1988 forty (78.4 percent) parole boards reported that they were autonomous, while eleven (21.6 percent) boards indicated they were part of another state agency.

Most paroling authorities have operated in an autonomous and independent fashion for over a decade. As Figure 2.2 illustrates, however, since 1966 there has been a discernible movement from autonomy to consolidation and back again to autonomy.

Of fifty jurisdictions reporting (Carlson 1979), in 1966 forty were autonomous, while ten were part of a larger state agency or department of corrections. During the ensuing six years, there was a dramatic movement away from independence toward consolidation. Thus, in 1972, thirty jurisdictions indicated they were consolidated under another agency, while twenty stated they were autonomous. By 1976 this trend had begun to reverse itself with an even number of parole boards reporting that they were consolidated or autonomous. During the next three years, however, autonomous parole boards began once again to predominate. According to Carlson, in 1979 "thirty-nine states reported that their parole boards were independent state agencies or departments while only thirteen reported that their parole boards were consolidated into other state units" (1979, 8).[10]

These shifts were housed within the more general attempts to reorganize state governments that occurred from the mid-sixties through the mid-seventies. At the same time, they also reflect the imprint of a series of national commissions that called for states to reorganize their correctional systems (Marcelli 1977). The most notable commissions included the President's Commission on Law Enforcement and Administration of Justice in 1967 and the National Advisory Commission on Criminal Justice Standards and Goals in 1973. The objectives were to increase the political accountability of correctional agencies, improve managerial control, and enhance programmatic services. While states varied in the extent to which the objectives were accomplished, the commitment to reorganization was extraordinary: between 1965 and 1975, forty-two states reorganized their correctional systems; twenty-nine did so twice (Marcelli 1977, ix).

With respect to corrections and parole, one of the organizational models proposed (and adopted in some jurisdictions) served to consolidate all correctional agencies under a human services or public safety umbrella. As Figure 2.2 shows, this model is still present in eleven states. Another model called for the creation of independent departments of corrections. The return to paroling authorities that were autonomous

Figure 2.2

Organizational Setting of Parole Boards

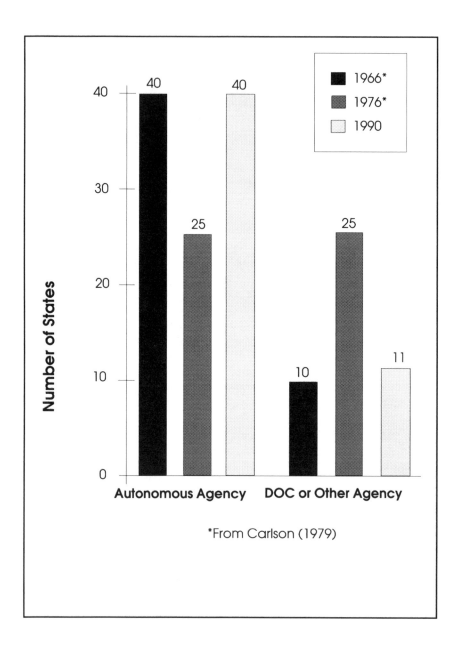

*From Carlson (1979)

and separate from the department of corrections reflects, in part, the movement toward independent departments of corrections.[11]

Although paroling authorities and departments of corrections are autonomous agencies within the executive branch, they are functionally interdependent by virtue of their jurisdiction and scope of responsibilities. Together their operations form the core of a state's correctional system. Nonetheless, while the work of each has a significant impact on the other, they carry out their respective duties in separate organizational and administrative contexts under the direction of different chief executive officers. With respect to parole boards, who they are headed by, how they are organized, and the staff responsible for administering their affairs varies widely.

Parole Board Chairs, Paroling Authorities, and Organizational Variation

The administration of paroling authorities and the organizational variation they display is shaped, in part, by the statutory and administrative responsibilities assigned to the parole board chair as chief executive officer of the agency. There are a number of studies—though none of them recent—that address the organization of parole boards (National Parole Institute 1963; O'Leary and Nuffield 1972; Parker 1975; O'Leary and Hanrahan 1976; Carlson 1979). Very little is known, however, about the heads of paroling authorities either with respect to who they are, what they do, or even what they believe is their role as manager of the parole process. Yet, it is reasonable to assume that their stewardship of the agency is critical to its stability and success.

The ACA Parole Task Force survey devoted an entire section to the background and views of parole board chairs. Parole board chairs from all fifty-one jurisdictions completed this section. In addition, other questions in the survey asked for information on the chairs' executive and organizational relationship to the paroling authority. The results suggest that to understand organizational variation among paroling authorities, it is appropriate to begin with parole board chairs.

With respect to their backgrounds, forty-three of the chairs (84.3 percent) were male, while eight (15.7 percent) were female. In terms of age, twenty of the chairs were thirty-three to forty-five years of age, while twenty-four ranged in age from forty-six to sixty. The remainder were sixty-one years of age or older. With respect to race and ethnicity, thirty-seven (72.5 percent) of the chairs were white, ten were black (19.6 percent), and four (7.8 percent) were Hispanic. All of the chairs stated they had some college education. While eleven (21.6 percent) reported that they graduated from college, the majority (N = 34, or 66.7 percent) indicated that they had an advanced degree (frequently in law).

As with corrections commissioners, despite some notable exceptions, it is often the case that parole board chairs enjoy an uneven and often abbreviated tenure.[12] Although a number of the chairs had already served as a board member prior to their being elevated to head of the agency, more than one-third of them had been chair for only one year. On the other hand, thirteen of the respondents (25.6 percent) had been chair for five years or more. More generally, while twenty-five (49 percent) of the respondents noted they had been chair for two years or less, the remaining twenty-six (51 percent) had been chair for three years or more.

Nonetheless, being chair of the paroling authority is not synonymous with being the agency's chief executive officer. The ACA Parole Task Force survey asked if the chair of the agency was the chief executive officer (that is, the person who directed agency operations and management). Thirty-seven jurisdictions (72.5 percent) reported that the chair was the chief executive officer, while fourteen jurisdictions (27.5 percent) answered no to this question. The fourteen states were Alabama, Alaska, Arkansas, Idaho, Iowa, New Hampshire, North Dakota, Ohio, Oklahoma, South Carolina, South Dakota, Texas, Utah, and Wyoming. With the exception of five of these states, the parole board operates on a part-time basis.

An issue of obvious importance to parole board chairs pertains to the method by which they are selected. The governor alone selects the chair when exercising the authority to appoint in twenty-nine states (56.9 percent). In another six states (11.8 percent), the governor shares this authority with others (e.g., attorney general, chief justice). In three states (Michigan, Minnesota, and Ohio), the director or commissioner of corrections selects the chair. In another thirteen states (25.5 percent), the parole board chair is selected by fellow board members. In one of these states (Georgia), the parole board chair is chosen on a rotating basis every two years.

Even though board members in one-quarter of the states select the chairs, it is not always the case in these or other states that the former share responsibility with the latter for setting policy or assisting in administration. One question on the ACA Parole Task Force survey asked, "Do board members share responsibility with the chair for the administration (management and operations) of the agency?" Of the forty-eight jurisdictions responding to this question, twenty-five (52.1 percent) said no, while twenty-three (47.9 percent) stated that such responsibility was shared. In most of the states answering yes to this question, how this responsibility is shared is determined by statute or by administrative regulations.

Regardless of whether the authority to manage the agency is shared, the continuity of paroling authority operations is affected by board members' terms of appointment. Unlike commissioners of corrections, whose terms are often coterminous with those of the governor, appointment to the parole board is usually for a fixed term. In twenty jurisdictions (39.2 percent), board members are appointed to four-year terms, while six-year appointments are reported in thirteen states (25.5 percent). Though less common, board members are appointed to three-year terms in three states (5.9 percent), and five-year terms in nine states (17.6 percent). No specific term of appointment is served by board members in six states (11.8 percent): Georgia, Michigan, Minnesota, Ohio, West Virginia, and Wisconsin.

The continuity of parole board operations is also affected by whether board members' terms are staggered or run concurrently. Staggered terms ensure that there are always some board members who can share their experiences, provide training, and as a group serve as an institutional memory for new board members to draw on. Forty-one (80.4 percent) of the jurisdictions in the ACA Parole Task Force survey indicated that board members serve staggered terms. In ten jurisdictions (19.6 percent) they do not. With respect to the latter, in five of these states board members do not serve fixed terms (Michigan, Minnesota, Ohio, West Virginia, and Wisconsin). In several of the remaining states, when changes occur, the entire membership of the board is replaced literally overnight (e.g., North Carolina).

Another organizational variable affecting the administration of paroling authorities is their status as full- or part-time agencies. Since 1966 there has been a gradual trend toward increasing parole boards to full-time status (Carlson 1979). In 1966, there were twenty-four full-time parole boards, while in 1976 this number had increased to thirty. It remained at thirty in 1979 as well. According to the ACA Parole Task Force survey, there are now thirty-one (60.7 percent) full-time boards, thirteen (25.4 percent) part-time boards, and seven boards (13.7 percent) with a mixture of full-time and part-time membership. In the latter states, the chair is usually full-time. Thus, Connecticut, Delaware, Hawaii, Minnesota, and Mississippi have full-time chairs while the board members serve part-time. In Iowa and Utah the chair and at least one other member are full-time while at least two board members serve part-time.

The size of paroling authorities has shown steady but incremental growth since 1966, when there were 221 board members (Carlson 1979). By 1972 this figure had increased to 240; in 1976, to 259. By 1979 there were

Table 2.6

Selected Organizational Features of Paroling Authorities

Jurisdiction	Chair CEO	Chair/Board Members Share Administration	Length of Term	Full/ Part-time	Number of Members
Alabama	No	Yes	6	Full	3
Alaska	No	No	5	Part	5
Arizona	Yes	Yes	5	Full	7
Arkansas	No	No	5	Part	5
California	Yes	No	4	Full	9
Colorado	Yes	No	3	Full	5
Connecticut	Yes	Yes	4	F/P	11
Delaware	Yes	Yes	4	F/P	5
D.C.	Yes	Yes	5	Full	5
Florida	Yes	No	4	Full	6
Georgia	Yes	Yes	7	Full	5
Hawaii	Yes	No	4	F/P	3
Idaho	No	No	5	Part	5
Illinois	Yes	No	6	Full	12
Indiana	Yes	No	4	Full	5
Iowa	No	Yes	4	F/P	5
Kansas	Yes	Yes	4	Full	3
Kentucky	Yes	No	4	Full	7
Louisiana	Yes	Yes	4	Full	5
Maine	Yes	No	4	Part	5
Maryland	Yes	Yes	6	Full	7
Massachusetts	Yes	Yes	5	Full	7
Michigan	Yes	No	7	Full	7
Minnesota	Yes	No	7	F/P	2

Jurisdiction	Chair CEO	Chair/Board Members Share Administration	Length of Term	Full/ Part-time	Number of Members
Mississippi	Yes	No	4	F/P	5
Missouri	Yes	No	6	Full	5
Montana	Yes	Yes	4	Part	4
Nebraska	Yes	Yes	6	Full	5
Nevada	Yes	No	4	Full	5
New Hampshire	No	Yes	5	Part	5
New Jersey	Yes	Yes	6	Full	7
New Mexico	Yes	No	4	Full	3
New York	Yes	No	6	Full	19
North Carolina	Yes	No	4	Full	5
North Dakota	No	Yes	3	Part	3
Ohio	No	No	7	Full	7
Oklahoma	No	No	4	Part	5
Oregon	Yes	Yes	4	Full	5
Pennsylvania	Yes	No	6	Full	5
Rhode Island	Yes	No	3	Part	5
South Carolina	No	No	6	Part	7
South Dakota	No	No	4	Part	3
Tennessee	Yes	Yes	6	Full	5
Texas	No	Yes	6	Full	6
Utah	No	Yes	6	F/P	6
Vermont	Yes	Yes	5	Part	5
Virginia	Yes	Yes	4	Full	5
Washington	Yes	No	5	Full	7
West Virginia	Yes	Yes	7	Full	3
Wisconsin	Yes	Yes	7	Full	7
Wyoming	No	No	6	Part	5

278 board members. The ACA Parole Task Force survey shows that nearly a decade later the number of board members had increased to 291. (This figure excludes the U.S. Parole Commission, which would make the total more than 300.) The modal number of board members is five, although the size of parole boards ranges from two (Minnesota) to nineteen (New York).

Table 2.6 summarizes several of the organizational features by jurisdiction. It highlights whether the chair is the agency's chief executive officer, whether responsibility for administering the agency is shared with board members, the length of board members' terms, whether the board is full- or part-time, and the total number of board members.

In most jurisdictions, the work of board members is supported by a variety of executive and professional staff. Depending on the parole board's jurisdiction and range of responsibilities, these staff may be assigned to correctional institutions to monitor inmates' parole eligibility, conduct preparole interviews or hearings, prepare case summaries for board member review, conduct victim input hearings, review executive clemency applications, perform training, supervise parolees, conduct revocation interviews or hearings, engage in research or data collection, or act as legal counsel to the board.

The actual size of parole board staff displays significant variation, ranging from one person in Vermont to 2,000 in New York. (The latter has jurisdiction over and thus includes parole field service staff.) Thirteen boards (25.5 percent) employed four or fewer staff, while the size of the boards' professional staff in another fourteen jurisdictions ranged from 103 to several thousand.

In thirty-nine jurisdictions (76.5 percent), the paroling authority is administered by an executive director who is not a member of the parole board. In most states the executive director shares to a varying extent administrative responsibility for policy, planning, media relations, and legislative issues with the chair and board members. In nearly every jurisdiction, the executive director was involved in personnel matters and the development of the agency's budget.

In an effort to discern the extent of parole board specialization, the ACA Parole Task Force survey asked respondents if they had a full-time training officer, public information officer, legislative liaison, and legal counsel.

Only nine boards (17.6 percent) reported that they had a full-time training officer, although five stated that they were planning to create or were considering creation of such a position. Twelve paroling authorities (23.5 percent) indicated that they had a full-time public information officer, fourteen (27.5 percent) had a legislative liaison, and fifteen (29.4 percent) had in-house legal counsel. Most parole boards without legal counsel (N = 36) obtained legal advice through the attorney general's office.

Since 1979 correctional agencies, including paroling authorities, have been able to seek accreditation through the American Correctional Association. The accreditation process involves an independent evaluation by outside auditors using nationally recognized standards against which an agency is compared.[13] Two separate manuals cover the administration of parole. The first is *Standards for Adult Paroling Authorities* (1981) and the second, *Standards for Adult Probation and Parole Field Services* (1981).

Although the ACA Parole Task Force survey asked if the respondent had ever participated in accreditation activities under either of the manuals, the results reflect only the extent of participation among adult paroling authorities. Twelve parole boards (23.5 percent) have at some point sought accreditation; thirty-nine (76.5 percent) have not. Of the twelve, eight were accredited, one withdrew, and three are currently participating in the process.

Once an agency is accredited, it may seek reaccreditation after a certain period of time. Five of the eight agencies mentioned above have been reaccredited, while one is currently seeking reaccreditation. Two of the parole boards that were already accredited withdrew from the reaccreditation process. Of those parole boards that have not at any point participated in accreditation, twenty-seven stated that they were not planning to seek accreditation, while eleven said they were either going to or were considering entering the process. (One state was missing.)

Accreditation is designed to give an agency an opportunity to review its policies and procedures and to improve its overall performance. Although a sizable number of paroling authorities indicated that they were considering the issue, the last year a parole board was granted an initial accreditation award was 1986. An earlier study of paroling practices found that thirty-six parole boards were at that time working to achieve compliance with the accreditation standards (Carlson 1979, 30-34). The apparent decline in interest reflects to some extent uncertainty over the value of going through the accreditation process.

One of the ACA Parole Task Force survey questions asked parole board chairs to respond to the following: "[accreditation] offers parole boards a sound management tool for increasing the effectiveness of their operations." While very few chairs disagreed with this statement, nineteen (37.3 percent) were uncertain how to respond. Twenty-four chairs (47.1 percent), or just under half of the total respondents, expressed agreement.

The uncertainty over the value of accreditation is symptomatic of a more general issue that many paroling authorities have yet to address. Parole board members in many states still view their primary role as that of individual case decision makers with responsibility for conducting parole release hearings. Setting policies, reviewing agency operations and procedures, and engaging in strategic planning that includes but is not limited to release decision making are not considered core functions. Yet, by virtue of their responsibilities and the reach of their jurisdiction, paroling authorities' decisions implicate, if not express, the sanctioning policy of the state.

Paroling Authorities as Policy-making Bodies

When making individual case decisions, parole board members are expected to achieve competing, if not contradictory, goals. These goals, which go to the heart of any state's sanctioning policy, include deterrence, incapacitation, retribution, and rehabilitation. Additional, albeit more pragmatic concerns, also enter into the parole decision. These concerns revolve around reducing sentencing disparities and thus ensuring that inmates serve comparable time for comparable offenses, maintaining institutional order, and assessing the risk or likelihood that the parolee will commit another offense subsequent to release (Carlson 1979; McGarry 1988).

The cumulative impact of the decisions parole board members make as individuals establish de facto policy for the agency. Thus, individual board members may emphasize risk considerations over rehabilitation in deciding to grant or deny parole. Or, their aggregate decisions may reflect a concern for serving sufficient time (incapacitation) given the seriousness of the offense. The impact and implications of balancing these concerns for agency policy as a whole is often unrecognized by the very persons who are responsible for parole decision making.

If parole board members perceive themselves as individual case decision makers, it is because in many states most of their time is, in fact, spent conducting parole release hearings. The hearing schedules of many parole boards require that board members travel to institutions throughout the state to consider inmates for parole release. The overwhelming demands placed on board members reduce the time they have to devote as a group to agency policies and goals. Moreover, as stated earlier, in just over half of the jurisdictions surveyed parole board members do not share responsibility with the chair for agency administration and thus for setting or reviewing policy.

One of the more salient trends with respect to paroling authorities is a growing recognition that the decisions they make should be informed by a policy-driven consensus over goals and objectives that link release decision making with supervision and revocation. The movement to incorporate, if not structure, parole decision making is reflected in the results of two technical assistance projects sponsored by the National Institute of Corrections working in concert with the COSMOS Corporation and the Center for Effective Public Policy.[14]

The first project ran from November 1985 to August 1987 and involved the provision of technical assistance to nine paroling authorities: Alaska, Massachusetts, Mississippi, Nebraska, Ohio, South Carolina, Tennessee, Texas, and Virginia. The primary focus of this undertaking was structuring release decision making. As defined by the project managers, a structured approach to parole decision making incorporates the following features:

1. Explicitly stated goals for decision-making practices (e.g., just deserts, rehabilitation, risk management);
2. Explicit, written policy covering topics such as release, offender eligibility for parole, setting terms, conditions of parole release, supervision levels;
3. Explicit decision-making tools (e.g., rating sheets, risk prediction devices);
4. Revocation policy;
5. Explicit rules for overriding policy;
6. Tracking systems to document decision makers' compliance with policy; and
7. Systems for periodic review and revision of policy. (Burke et al. 1987, 3).

The second project extended from January 1988 through 1989. Again, nine jurisdictions received technical assistance, four of which were recipients during the first undertaking. The nine jurisdictions were the District of Columbia, Florida, Kansas, Massachusetts, New York, South Carolina, Tennessee, Utah, and Virginia (Burke et al. 1990a).

Although attention focused on structuring release decision making, several paroling authorities also addressed the need to develop a comprehensive policy on revocation to handle offenders who violate the conditions of parole while under supervision. These boards considered the issue of parole revocation not in terms of how long offenders should be confined for violating parole conditions, but in relation to options that might be developed as a matter of policy to assist parole field services and the agency itself in responding to parolee violations. The revocation of parole is in this context only one of a number of possible responses (Burke et al. 1990a).

The results of these efforts show that developing structured decision-making policy involves far more than simply stating goals. It also covers more than parole release. Incorporating structure, and thus developing policy goals to be achieved through parole decision making, places the parole board in a new role, a role that carries enormous implications for the administration and organization of the agency.

Within this context, policy-driven parole decision making links parole release with supervision and revocation. This linkage has significant implications for the relationship of paroling authorities with departments of corrections, an issue that will be discussed in the final chapter. For now it is sufficient to note that structured decision making necessarily involves first and foremost the most controversial component of the parole process—the parole release decision.

Notes

1. The fact that the paroling authorities are in the executive branch and that the sentencing of the offender is within the judiciary presents possible organizational conflict, which has not been systematically explored. For example, the punishment of an offender is not determined by the judiciary alone—the parole board decides when a "parolable" offender is released. Although this is well known, we do not know of research that has tried to link the branches of government to different goals or to different ways of achieving goals.

2. In terms of professional self-image, these agencies generally view themselves as independent of each other. This is reflected in their affiliation with different professional associations. Parole board members and staff belong to the Association of Paroling Authorities International, while parole supervision officers participate in the American Probation and Parole Association.

3. Throughout this chapter and those that follow, the terms *state* and *jurisdiction* will be used interchangeably. The jurisdictions referred to in the ACA Parole Task Force survey include all fifty states and the District of Columbia.

4. Since the completion of the survey, the number of parole boards with jurisdiction over field services has dropped to twelve. As part of a general reorganization of criminal justice in Texas, parole supervision was transferred from the Board of Pardons and Paroles (now the Parole Board) to the Department of Corrections (now the Institutional Division). These functions are housed under an umbrella agency known as the Texas Department of Criminal Justice.

5. This is most evident in those states where paroling authorities have been called upon to release offenders under emergency powers acts or by relaxing their criteria for granting parole. See Chapters 1 and 4 for a more detailed discussion of this issue.

6. Every parole board chair responded to this section of the survey, which was designed for them alone. For more information on the

chairs, see the next section in this chapter, entitled "Parole Board Chairs, Paroling Authorities, and Organizational Variation."

7. The average activity levels were calculated in a fashion comparable to Berk and Rossi. Each group's level of activity was converted to a four-point scale ("no role" = 1, "rarely active" = 2, "sometimes active" = 3, and "always active" = 4). In general, the groups with the highest mean ratings are the same groups that were rated as active by the chairs. The head of the department of corrections had a mean of 3.216, the House corrections committee a mean of 3.2, the Senate corrections committee a mean of 3.137, and the governor a mean of 2.902. The least active groups were the state bar association at 1.961 and the organization of ex-offenders at 1.745.

8. The Republican leadership of the Senate and House does not correlate significantly with the governor in terms of sharing importance, while the Democratic leadership does. This may reflect the predominance of the Democratic party in these bodies across the states.

9. The social control function that parole serves within an institution can backfire if parole board practices are viewed as unfair by the inmate population. One of the grievances expressed by inmates after the riot at Attica in 1971 focused on arbitrary and capricious parole release practices (New York State Special Commission on Attica 1972).

10. The number of jurisdictions varies in each of the surveys. Although the ACA Parole Task Force survey solicited information from the U.S. Parole Commission, it is not included here.

11. Historically, three distinct models have been proposed for locating parole organizationally: an institutional model (generally associated with juvenile corrections); an autonomous model; and a consolidation model. For a discussion of the comparative advantages and disadvantages of the different models, see O'Leary and Hanrahan (1976, 6-9).

12. A recent study of corrections commissioners found that they serve on average three years before they are fired (DiIulio 1990b). This research indicates that "[between] 1973 and 1987, in less than one-third of all adult corrections agencies did commissioners enjoy an average tenure of five years or more; in over one-third they held office for an average of three years or less" (1990b, 5).

13. Until recently, the audit process was carried out under the auspices of the Commission on Accreditation for Corrections. The commission worked closely with, but was independent of, the American Correctional Association. In 1986, it merged with the latter and is now part of the Standards and Accreditation Division within the ACA.

14. The movement toward structured parole decision making reflects a more general trend toward formal classification systems and the adoption of objective decision-making tools in criminal justice. For an in-depth discussion of this more general development, see Gottfredson and Tonry (1987).

Chapter 3

Parole Release and the Management of Discretion

No other parole decision is more scrutinized or invokes the public's ire more than the decision to release potentially dangerous criminals into society. Release on parole involves an implicit decision that the goals associated with the incarceration of the offender have been achieved and that the offender may return to life in the community.

It is a decision made within the broader context of the many goals of imprisonment discussed in Chapter 2, such as rehabilitation, deterrence, retribution (or just deserts), incapacitation, and maintaining tolerable population levels in prisons (Clear and Cole 1990; Burke 1988). The legitimacy of parole boards' unbridled authority to decide how to balance these goals has been challenged in the past two decades—leading, on the one hand, to a movement to abolish it and, on the other hand, toward reforms to better legitimate the authority parole boards exercise.

Through the 1960s, parole release decisions were usually made with few outside constraints. When offenders were deemed suitable for release, it was presumably because there was no reason to hold them. Decisions to release were generally unchallenged—unless a mistake was made that drew media attention. The mode by which these decisions were made·is often referred to as *clinical*—that is, based on professional or expert judgment, drawing on the experience of the decision maker(s) in relation to the normative parameters established in past cases (Monahan 1981). Clinical decision making is based on an interview and/or a reading of the offender's personal file and draws on the past experience of the decision maker. In some states (e.g., Illinois), the decision was guided by actuarial evidence that certain characteristics associated with the risk of recidivism might be used to help decide a case, but generally, it was a judgment call by parole boards that determined release (probably even where risk instruments were used—see Glaser 1987).

By the early 1970s, parole release decision making began to change. Of primary concern was the *philosophical basis* for the decision to release (which goals should have priority? or how should they be mutually considered?), as well as the *process* by which such decisions should be made. The first concern was triggered by the growing ideological hegemony of retributionist or just deserts goals. The second and related concern led to attempts to limit the discretion of the individual decision maker: legislatively imposed statutory restrictions, and the parole guidelines movement. The historical and political context for the growth of retributionist goals has been discussed briefly. The nature and impact of the statutory changes and the guidelines movement on parole release are now considered in detail.

The Shifting Statutory Context of Parole Release: From Indeterminacy to Determinacy

The challenge to parole at the state and federal level brought to the fore the conflict between retribution and crime control goals. The proposed reforms urging greater determinacy in sentencing called into question when, and for whom, parole eligibility applied. As the emphasis shifted toward the philosophical goals of retribution and away from crime control goals, the parole board's release decision-making authority was sharply limited and in some states abolished by legislatively established determinate sentencing laws or through presumptive sentencing guidelines promulgated by a sentencing commission (Tonry 1987, 1988; Morris and Tonry 1990).

Within the context of statutory determinate sentencing, a mandatory period or minimum number of months must be served before an offender may be considered for parole. The primary factor driving the severity of the sentence, according to this philosophy, is the seriousness of the presenting offense, although offense history is generally considered as well.

Regarding parole release, it is sometimes difficult to discern what constitutes a pure determinate sentencing state, in contrast to a state that may be labeled indeterminate. Distinctions of many types may be drawn:

1. "presumptive sentencing," in which the offender essentially is guaranteed at sentencing a set period of time to be served, assuming good behavior
2. "mandatory minimum terms," or set times to be served, varying by offense type before parole eligibility
3. "mandatory proportions" (e.g., offender must serve time ranging usually from one-fourth to two-thirds of a minimum sentence before parole eligibility, varying across as well as within states, depending on the offense or offender chronicity), with further time subtracted for good-time credits
4. "mandatory proportions," as in "3" above, with good-time reductions subtracted from the maximum time, not the minimum proportions
5. "indeterminate" states, where an offender is eligible for parole any time before the maximum time to be served

These classifications only scratch the surface of the complexity of eligibility for parole and mandatory release. Usually the term *determinate* is used to characterize states for some variation of 1 through 4. Yet, this is often a somewhat inaccurate, if not misleading, usage of determinate, since in some states the mandatory minimum terms may be so short that the state may be better characterized as indeterminate.[1] Other complexities exist as well.[2]

Strict comparability across jurisdictions is lacking because offense classifications themselves, as well as the prescribed sentences for these crimes, vary from state to state.[3] Even within crime types (e.g., robbery, burglary), there is considerable variation across states as to the crime's "degree structure." Thus, the same act of robbery committed in different states may result in a different classification by degree structure and result in different (or the same) punishment. Furthermore, prosecutors have considerable discretion to define an act relative to the criminal code of a state.[4]

An adequate comparison requires individual-level data on a state-by-state basis to determine what happens to offenders between offense and punishment, in addition to qualitative information as to the legal and regulatory variations in codes. In the absence of such data, it is necessary to rely on more qualitative assessments of how states handle offenders (e.g., Shane-DuBow et al. 1985; Vassar 1987) and crude aggregate statistical evidence.

Such assessments are nonetheless difficult to evaluate since some states may appear more determinate than they really are. Some jurisdictions' legislatures have passed so-called determinate sentencing legislation to suit political purposes—giving the appearance of "getting tough" on crime—while in fact the system may be best described as indeterminate. Determinate sentencing laws may be passed that pertain to only a small percentage of offenders. Alternatively, states may have determinate laws for a broad range of sentences, but with very short mandatory terms and/or the option of a probation sentence.

This variation suggests that a straightforward classification of states into discrete categories as determinate or indeterminate is unlikely to be completely accurate. Although such a classification is of general value, many states may not be clearly classified into these discrete categories. Nonetheless, what follows examines the actual use of parole across the states to better understand the extent to which discretionary parole release has been affected by the movement toward greater determinacy in sentencing.[5]

One relatively recent and thorough classification of states, which is used in the analysis below, is that of Shane-DuBow et al. (1985). It is the result of a qualitative analysis of each of the fifty states (and Washington, D.C.). The validity of these classifications of determinacy versus indeterminacy may be ascertained by establishing their relative use of parole release compared to other types of release from prison. Statistics are reported yearly (BJS 1988b) on each of the states in relation to the type of release from prison: parole release, probation release (usually called *split sentences*), other supervised release, mandatory release (offender has served the maximum sentence, less good-time credits) with supervision, expiration of sentence, and commutation of sentence. One indication of the extent to which a state uses determinate sentencing is the proportion of releases that can be accounted for by alternatives to parole: mandatory release, and expiration of sentence.

Table 3.1 presents data from the years 1974 and 1987. These years were chosen because 1974 immediately precedes the beginning of the movement from indeterminate toward determinate sentencing practices, while 1987 is the most recent year for which data are available.[6] Probation

63

Table 3.1

Releases on Parole (ROP) in 1974 and 1987

State Name	%ROP '74	#ROP '74	%ROP '87	#ROP '87	% Decrease	Determinate
HAWAII	100.0	106	93.0	385	-7.0	0
WASHINGTON	97.7	1288	62.7	1847	-35.0	1
NEW MEXICO	95.1	371	82.7	1078	-12.4	1
NEW HAMPSHIRE	94.5	225	71.9	192	-22.6	0
VERMONT	94.3	116	42.4	70	-51.9	0
RHODE ISLAND	94.3	132	93.9	291	-.4	0
NEW JERSEY	93.9	3447	80.2	4281	-13.7	1
OHIO	93.2	3655	41.5	3684	-51.7	1
KANSAS	93.2	682	87.0	1255	-6.2	0
MONTANA	92.7	227	76.6	298	-16.0	0
PENNSYLVANIA	92.5	3390	89.4	4144	-3.1	0
MINNESOTA	92.3	863	3.7	62	-88.6	1
CALIFORNIA	92.2	5058	0.0	0	-92.2	1
IDAHO	92.1	211	68.1	318	-24.0	0
COLORADO	92.0	1083	92.2	1793	.2	1
MICHIGAN	91.9	3668	92.0	4471	.1	0
UTAH	90.6	212	95.5	660	4.9	0
ARKANSAS	86.9	1110	64.2	1529	-22.7	0
NORTH DAKOTA	86.8	138	59.4	130	-27.4	0
MASSACHUSETTS	85.8	808	61.3	1570	-24.5	0
MAINE	82.5	447	3.7	9	-78.8	1
ILLINOIS	80.1	2615	.8	89	-79.2	1
WEST VIRGINIA	72.6	377	73.0	374	.4	0
KENTUCKY	70.8	1308	70.5	1725	-.3	0
CONNECTICUT	69.4	978	3.0	76	-66.4	1

State Name	%ROP '74	#ROP '74	%ROP '87	#ROP '87	% Decrease	Determinate
IOWA	67.7	459	69.9	1395	-2.8	0
FLORIDA	66.6	2995	3.0	706	-63.6	0
WISCONSIN	66.4	674	20.2	499	-46.2	0
INDIANA	65.6	1202	2.9	89	-62.7	1
TENNESSEE	65.1	1070	92.8	2431	27.7	1
GEORGIA	64.8	2049	66.2	6723	1.4	0
NEVADA	64.7	211	56.7	1161	-8.0	0
OREGON	63.8	650	98.2	2905	34.4	0
ALABAMA	63.3	1324	52.1	1512	-11.2	0
SOUTH DAKOTA	61.9	153	66.9	358	5.0	0
NEW YORK	61.1	3985	82.4	13361	21.3	0
MARYLAND	60.1	2376	47.2	1916	-12.9	0
TEXAS	58.0	4796	66.8	21459	8.8	0
ARIZONA	56.8	385	22.6	833	-34.2	1
VIRGINIA	55.4	1088	69.1	3855	13.7	0
MISSISSIPPI	55.3	510	67.2	1497	11.9	0
DELAWARE	53.3	112	35.9	224	-17.4	0
OKLAHOMA	50.7	988	13.2	538	-37.5	0
LOUISIANA	49.8	742	40.4	1681	-9.4	0
MISSOURI	48.7	780	90.5	3923	41.8	0
ALASKA	39.5	79	13.0	77	-26.5	0
NEBRASKA	38.1	249	65.4	499	27.3	0
DC	29.7	685	42.9	763	13.2	0
SOUTH CAROLINA	22.2	561	49.6	1952	27.4	0
WYOMING	11.8	14	63.5	141	51.7	0
NORTH CAROLINA*			87.1	9023		1

* Data for North Carolina for 1974 were missing.

cases (split sentences) have been excluded from consideration in the table, in part because they may be used at times as a substitute for parole (where parole options are lacking) or as a way for a judge to bypass parole. (In either case, relative parole use is clouded by including split sentences in the denominator.)[7] Those states that have been characterized by Shane-DuBow et al. (1985) as determinate sentencing states as of 1985 are indicated in the far right hand column of Table 3.1.[8]

Several interesting findings are revealed in this table. In 1974 (before determinate sentencing), parole was not the modal form of release in six jurisdictions: Alaska, the District of Columbia, Missouri, Nebraska, South Carolina, and Wyoming. Except for Nebraska and the District of Columbia, where many offenders were released under supervision without parole (supervised mandatory release), these jurisdictions required that relatively high proportions of their offenders serve the maximum times (data not presented here). Nevertheless, all states had some releases on parole, and most states released the vast majority of their inmates to parole (median value across states of around 70 percent of nonprobation releases are parole releases; also, for the country as a whole, about 70 percent of all nonprobation releases were parole releases in 1974).

The predominant alternative to parole in 1974 was releasing offenders upon expiration of the maximum sentence, although nine states also had active supervised mandatory release programs: Delaware, Florida, Georgia, Illinois, Kentucky, Maryland, New York, Tennessee, and Wisconsin (again, data not presented here).

As Table 3.1 shows, by 1987 a general shift away from parole use is apparent—but not in every jurisdiction. Fifteen states released a higher proportion of offenders on parole in 1987 than in 1974; all the other states decreased. Of the fifteen states deemed determinate by Shane-DuBow et al. (1985), all but two (Colorado and Tennessee) showed a decline in relative parole use between 1974 and 1987. Some of these declines are substantial, as in Arizona, California, Illinois, Indiana, Maine, Minnesota, and Washington. Several states not characterized as determinate by Shane-Dubow et al. nevertheless curtailed relative parole use by more than one-third: Florida, Oklahoma, and Wisconsin. (Florida uses the equivalent of a sentencing guideline grid and thus could be counted as a determinate sentencing state. Wisconsin discharges a large proportion of its inmates under supervised mandatory release. In Oklahoma a major proportion are held until the expiration of their sentence.)

Overall, under half (43 percent) of the nonprobation releases were on parole for the country as a whole in 1987. No other type of release rivaled it, however, as a proportion of all releasees. Thus, even though there has been a widespread reduction in parole release, it remains the *modal* type of release among the states. Furthermore, if one state, California, is removed from consideration, parole release is characteristic of all nonprobation releases, accounting for 53 percent of such releases in the rest of the country. Nevertheless, determinate sentencing has had an effect on the domain of discretionary parole release, as reflected in the general decrease of its use from 70 percent to 43 percent between 1974 and 1987.[9]

It is apparent that parole release has been affected by the determinate sentencing movement. The exact nature of the effects are difficult, however, to assess empirically. Complexities exist in defining states as determinate, yet there is evidence of a sharp curtailment of parole release in those jurisdictions that have been identified as moving from indeterminate to determinate sentencing codes. Other states have also experienced reductions in proportionate parole use, although a substantial percentage of the overall reduction can be attributed to California. Despite inroads made by legislated determinate sentencing, parole release remains the modal type of release from prison.

The Development of Parole Guidelines

In response to dissatisfaction with indeterminate sentencing and unlimited discretion in granting or denying parole, a significant number of paroling authorities have attempted to make the parole release decision itself more rational (i.e., in harmony with explicitly stated goals). This is best revealed through the development and use of parole release guidelines during the past fifteen to twenty years. Guidelines are often defined as stated principles of the criteria by which the decision to release on parole should be made. Other definitions more narrowly confine guidelines to the use of statistical or actuarial tables in which numerical weights are assigned and time to be served established for individual cases (within ranges). The term *grid guidelines* may be usefully applied to the latter, while the former may be referred to as *guiding principles*.

Although this distinction is useful, it has not generally been made in the literature, nor is it consistently made among practitioners. Thus, for example, in the ACA Parole Task Force survey results, twenty-three (or 46 percent) of the parole administrators said that their board used "formal, structured guidelines" in making parole release decisions.

Only nine of the these twenty-three administrators, however, actually described grid guidelines (or a close approximation): Alaska, Florida, Georgia, Maryland, Missouri, Nevada, New York, Oregon, and Utah. At least four other states (Ohio, Pennsylvania, South Carolina, and Texas) have systems that could not be characterized from the information available as a grid system, but did involve assigning offenders scores based on characteristics of the offense and offender. It was unclear as to how those scores were used to guide the release decision.[10]

There are normally three components to most parole release guideline grids: time to be served, severity of presenting offense, and risk assessment. There are a variety of methods available to form risk instruments, which are then used to assign risk scores to offenders for parole release.

The most common is the traditional Burgess method of forming an additive scale, based on the presence or absence of various offender characteristics. Under Burgess' original formulation, for example, twenty-one items were used to differentiate offenders. He found that 98.5 percent of parolees were successful in the lowest risk category, while only 24 percent were successful in the high risk category (Bruce et al. 1928).

Ohlin and Duncan were later able to reduce the number of items needed to twelve (1949). Sheldon and Eleanor Glueck (1946) demonstrated that their scales, in which weights were assigned according to the failure rates associated with those items, could differentiate a high-risk group with a failure rate of 95 percent to a low-risk group with a failure rate of 29 percent.

Don Gottfredson helped develop base expectancy scales, eventually implemented in several states. The scales used multiple regression analysis to determine items that were useful for predicting recidivism and then totaled those items for each person (essentially using the Burgess method, although some items received more weight than others). The most widely known and used scale embracing this approach is the U.S. Parole Commission's Salient Factor Score (Gottfredson et al. 1978). Several states have adopted scales similar to some version of it (for an example, see Missouri's scale in the Appendix).

A somewhat different approach, called configural analysis, was developed by Glaser. Offenders were classified on seventy-one types of background variables that were coded as dichotomies. The item that was the "most differentiating" of parole failure was chosen to define two subpopulations. Then, the remaining seventy items were used to determine the best remaining predictor of parole failure. This procedure was repeated until several categories of offenders were defined, all varying in the likelihood of parole outcome (Glaser 1964). The Michigan Department of Corrections has developed configuration tables, one for property crime risk and one for violent felonies.[11]

In addition to variations in the statistical tools used to devise risk assessments, there are differences in the types of predictor items used to form risk scales. The risk assessment criteria are listed for several states in the Appendix. Although it is not possible here to describe in full how these

Table 3.2

Criteria Used in Parole Release Risk Instruments
(from Petersilia and Turner, 1987: 158)

Most Commonly Used Items (5)
(found in over 75% of instruments identified)

Number of parole revocations
Number of adult or juvenile convictions
Number of prison terms served
Number of incarcerations served
Current crime involves violence

Second Most Commonly Used Items (11)
(found in 50-74% of instruments identified)

Number of prior convictions
Number of previous felony sentences
Number of juvenile incarcerations
Number of jail terms served
Age at first incarceration
Commitment-free period shown
On parole at arrest
Victim injured
Current age
Drug use
Prison infractions

Third Most Commonly Used Items (15)
(found in 25-49% of instruments identified)

Number of adult or juvenile arrests
Age at first conviction
Repeat of conviction types
Length of current term
Total years incarcerated
Current crime is property crime
Current crime involved weapon
Current crime involved forcible contact
Educational level
Employment history
Living arrangements
Alcohol use/abuse
Program participation in prison
Parole release plan formulated
Escape history

scales are implemented, it is important to note that a wide variety of scale items are used in the various states.

Petersilia and Turner have compiled a list of the types of factors used in parole release decision making in twenty-eight jurisdictions (1987). These factors, classified into broad categories of use, are listed in Table 3.2. The most frequently used items on parole release instruments pertain to criminal career characteristics of the offenders: all five of the most commonly used criteria and most of the eleven second most used criteria as seen in Table 3.2.

The most common predictors measure the frequency of prior criminal or delinquent behavior (sometimes called anamnestic variables, as by Morris and Miller 1985), as well as prior action by the criminal justice system (e.g., imprisonment and revocations). Social factors, such as educational achievement, employment history, and living arrangements are not relied on as often, though they appear in over half of the instruments studied.

Although information on the use of prediction items over time is not available, it seems that the general tendency has been to rely increasingly on criminal career attributes for predicting risk. Conversely, less emphasis has been placed on social attributes. In part, this is because the criminal career variables are reasonably good predictors of recidivism. On a philosophical level, they are also more compatible with retributionist goals (e.g., a repeat offender is more deserving of punishment than a first time offender). Also, social characteristics may incorporate potentially discriminatory principles in the determination of punishment.[12] It appears that social factors are used less frequently in risk instruments, while criminal career attributes are more prevalent.

Predicting recidivism is one purpose of the risk instrument. Another purpose is to help establish a prescribed time to be served for individual offenders within the guidelines grid. The parole guidelines grid for one of the states, Georgia, is presented in Table 3.3. This is the most common general format for states using grid guidelines, with offense severity scores down the left-hand column (along with examples of offenses falling within the severity levels), and prognosis categories across the top. In Georgia the parole prognosis is determined mainly by criminal career factors: age at first commitment, number of prior convictions, number of prior incarcerations, parole and probation failure, heroin or opiate drug use, type of presenting offense, and employment in preceding six months (see Table 3.3).

Table 3.3 shows not only the risk assessment component of the grid (the parole prognosis), but the other two components as well: recommended time to be served, and the severity of the presenting

Table 3.3

Parole Decision Guidelines: Georgia
(Cell Values = Months)

CRIME SEVERITY LEVEL	Parole Prognosis:				
	Excellent 13-20	Good 11-12	Average 9-10	Fair 6-8	Poor 0-5
I (Bad checks)	4	6	8	12	18
II (Thefts under $5,000)	6	8	9	14	21
III (Burglary under $5,000)	8	9	12	15	24
IV (Burglary $5,000-10,000)	10	12	15	18	27
V (Aggravated Assault)	20	25	30	40	52
VI (Serious Drug Violations)	36	48	54	60	78
VII (Armed Robbery)	60	72	78	90	102

offense. Comparisons of offense definitions across states are difficult to make (because definitions of offenses and degree structure are quite complex and vary considerably from one jurisdiction to the next), so it is not possible to compare states directly in terms of the severity of the prescribed punishment times.

It is possible, however, to get an approximate idea of the extent to which discretion may be exercised within the guidelines by examining the range of allowable times to be served for a given offense type and offender prognosis. In the case of Georgia, no ranges are provided.[13] Most states with grid guidelines, however, specify ranges of time to be served within each cell of the grid. Alaska, for example, specifies a range for each cell with a ratio of approximately two to one (e.g., most severe number of months twelve, least severe six). Maryland's ratio is approximately three to two for most cell values involving the more serious offenses, with broader discretionary ratios available to the board for less serious offenses. New York's ranges vary as a function of both the severity and parole prognosis categories, but generally most cell value ranges are approximately two to one. Nevada's grid has ranges for moderately serious offenses and for less serious offenses, for offenders with high or very high risk. (Other cell values are specific values, not ranges.) The ranges vary from four to twenty months, increasing as a function of seriousness of offense and risk, but never does a range exceed three to two (i.e., no ranges are as broad as two to one).

One of the more complex systems is that of Oregon. Here there are "base ranges" with ratios of approximately three to two or four to three, but departures are allowed depending on the consensus of the board and the seriousness level of the offense: the more board votes to concur on more or less time, the more standard deviations of time from the base range are allowed. For example, an offender convicted of a level-six crime (seriousness), with an "excellent" risk assessment score may have his/her time reduced by twenty months if four board members agree to reduce the sentence by the four standard deviations of five months (four times five equals twenty) that are allowed under the grid rules.

Thus, there is flexibility built in the parole release grid guidelines, either in terms of ranges of permissible times to be served (commonly with ranges of two to one or three to two) or explicit numerical exception rules, such as in Oregon. Generally, the broader the range, the greater the possibility of discretion. Whether or not that discretion is exercised wisely is an open question.

Departing From the Guidelines

Grids are guidelines and do not strictly bind the release decision. Within the states that clearly use a standardized grid instrument of some type, exceptions to the release date ranges prescribed by the grid guidelines are allowed, such that boards retain some discretion over release dates even in these states. For example, in New York the following statement from the Guideline Application Manual of 1985 makes clear that departures from guidelines are possible:

> The time ranges devised are merely guidelines. Mitigating or aggravating factors may result in decisions above or below the

guidelines. In any case where the decision rendered is outside the guidelines, the detailed reason for such decision including the fact or factors relied on shall be provided to the inmate in writing (New York State Division of Parole 1985, 1).

The extent to which states with parole guideline grids actually implement them is unknown. What is clear is that states allow for mitigating and aggravating factors which may, in turn, preempt or alter the decision that would be made based on the grid alone. Missouri, for example, cites the following as reasons for departing from parole release guidelines: conduct violations while in prison, superior program performance, determination that an offender is dangerous or is a persistent offender, mental competency, and the parole release plan.

Alaska has an extensive list of "good cause" to depart from guideline ranges:

AGGRAVATING FACTORS:
- aggravated or sophisticated offense behavior
- substantial negative impact on the victim
- magnitude of the offense
- violation of position of trust, or vulnerable victim
- multiple offenses/counts/victims
- extensive prior record
- pattern of repetitive criminal behavior and/or violence
- repeated probation/parole failures
- failure on pretrial diversion or bond/bail/O.R. failures
- other verified criminal behavior
- lengthy history of alcohol/drug abuse
- failure to take advantage of alcohol/drug programming before
- poor institutional behavior
- failure to make restitution when able to do so
- well-reasoned negative recommendation of victim/judge/D.A. or other person or group

MITIGATING FACTORS:
- verified pretrial diversion compliance over substantial period of time under strict reporting/supervision conditions
- incident-free recent probation/parole history
- no prior criminal behavior
- exceptional institutional program achievement
- strong community support/resources available
- substantial cooperation with the government resulting in the conviction of equal or more serious criminals
- payment of substantial amount of restitution to the victim

- life-threatening medical problem
- substantial continuous period in jail on other charges

In Georgia, if the board's decision to depart from the guidelines recommendation would result in more than three years time served, the case would be reviewed at the guidelines-recommended time. There appear to be no jurisdictions where the board preempts its authority to decide a case based on the prescription of its guidelines. The extent to which boards depart from the prescribed release times is also generally unknown, as such information is not usually available. In Utah, however, about 61 percent of the cases departed from the guidelines in 1985-86, usually toward the more harsh punishment (Pray 1987, 8). Also, little is known about the ambiguities of determining the classification of offenders into the appropriate cell of the grid. Some states explicitly cite the parole board as the ultimate decision maker in ambiguous cases.

It should be noted that risk instruments are often used for parole release decisions, but not within the context of release guidelines. They are used for the determination of the level of risk of recidivism, but not to guide explicitly the choice of a release timeframe. According to results from the ACA Parole Task Force survey, 40 percent (or twenty) of the boards responded that they used a risk-assessment instrument to assist in making a release decision.[14] It is not clear how the risk instruments are used (presumably in conjunction with other criteria) to make a decision in the states with risk instruments but without guideline grids. Only twelve of the twenty states, however, claim to have validated their risk instruments; thus some states may be using instruments adopted from other states or the U.S. Parole Commission, without determining if such criteria represent valid predictors in their own state.

In summary, there are ample reasons parole boards may depart from the grid guidelines, in the states in which they exist. Nonetheless, in most of these states, it appears that the release decision is influenced by the guidelines. It also seems that risk assessment instruments without grid guidelines play a more limited role in determining release. In a loose sense, an offender's score on a risk assessment instrument influences the likelihood of release, but it is not as evident how these instruments are linked systematically with release decisions. Thus, it may be that an essentially clinical decision is made with or without the help of a risk assessment score, although the grid guidelines have a structuring effect on decisions. In the remaining states, a clinical approach to decision making forms the basis for granting or denying parole.

Opening the Release Decision Process

While there has been considerable movement toward standardizing parole release (by using parole release guidelines and risk scales) in the past two decades, there has also been an attempt to "open" the parole release process by allowing for input from victims, prosecutors, and judges. On the surface, this second movement seems to contradict the first: it represents yet another alternative to standardized release procedures as a basis for making the release decision. The actual use of input from victims and judges is probably quite limited, however. Permitting formal participation may only influence parole release decisions in a small proportion of cases. Nevertheless, allowing such input may help to legitimate the release decision.

In the ACA Parole Task Force survey, respondents were asked if their board had a "formal set of procedures for obtaining input from victims, prosecutors, and judges." Most states claimed to have such procedures for victims (thirty-eight states, or 76 percent) and for prosecutors (thirty-five states, or 70 percent), while just over half of the states (twenty-seven, or 54 percent) claimed to have such procedures for judges.

The definition of "formal set of procedures" seems to vary across respondents. It is important to distinguish whether or not a state solicits input or merely allows input. If a state solicits input, then it is more actively concerned with obtaining such input than if it is merely permitted. The survey results suggest that thirteen states actively solicit input from victims and judges. More states, however, solicit input from prosecutors (eighteen states). In other states where input is allowed from these sources, notifications of possible release may be sent, or sent only upon request.

The right to provide input to the board is not used very often by victims. Information on this subject is not available from all states. Thirty-two respondents in the ACA Parole Task Force survey answered a specific question about the percentage of cases in which victim input was actually provided. Victim input is seldom received (median value of 5 percent) in most states, although eleven states appear to get such input in more than 10 percent of the cases. One respondent commented that victims did not seem to want to get involved and that they take the attitude of "out of sight, out of mind."

The receipt of prosecutor input is more common, with a median value of 45 percent among the twenty-six states for which information was available. Input from judges was not as frequent, with a median value of 10 percent of cases among the twenty-one states for which information was available. Thus, it appears that victim input is relatively rare; that of judges

Figure 3.1

Parole Board Chairs' Average Ranking of Release Factors

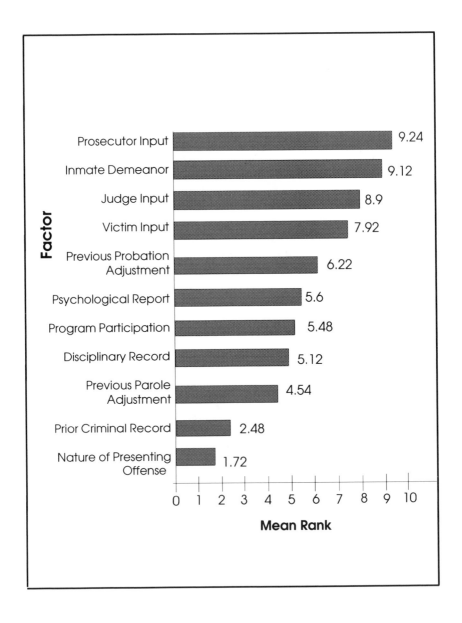

more common, but not characteristic of the process; while prosecutor input is quite common, occurring in as many as half of the cases.[15]

Regarding the significance of whatever input is received, relative to the release decision, parole board chairs were asked if they thought that "input of the [victim, prosecutor, judge] into the parole process offers valuable information on an offender's readiness for parole."

Roughly one-third (nineteen) of the board chairs thought that victim input was valuable, whereas about 43 percent (twenty-two chairs) saw judge input as valuable, and 46 percent (twenty-three chairs) defined prosecutor input as valuable (that is, they "strongly agreed" or "agreed").

The chairs' modal (most common) response was to disagree that valuable information came from the three sources of input. (It is possible, however, that "readiness" for parole was defined by board chairs in a more narrow sense of "rehabilitated," whereas the input from the three sources would probably address primarily the seriousness of the offender's criminal behavior for the presenting offense. If so, the answers to the questions would underreport the significance of the input.)

The parole board chairs were also asked to rank order the importance of eleven items of information in making parole release decisions (see Figure 3.1). Input from prosecutors ranked last, while input from the sentencing judge ranked ninth, and input from victims, eighth. (Interestingly, prosecutor input, which seems more common, is judged *least* important, and victim input, which seems least common, is judged slightly more important than prosecutor or judge input.) The factors that were considered more salient were (in order of importance): the nature of the presenting offense, prior criminal record, previous parole adjustment, the inmate's disciplinary record, institutional program participation, the inmate's psychological report, and previous probation adjustment. (The inmate's demeanor or disposition at the hearing was ranked tenth.)

Although the prevalence of input from victims, prosecutors, and judges varies across the states from quite rare to common, its importance, relative to other parole release criteria, appears to be small. Most parole board chairs do not view it as a valuable source of information for making release decisions.

Parole Release: Standardization With Discretion

Parole board members face many conflicting pressures when deciding to grant or deny parole. They are expected to make release decisions fairly, in general accordance with past release decision making. They may occasionally face pressure from victims, prosecutors, or judges to keep offenders longer, presumably due to the nature of the crime or the offender's role in it. At the same time, they must evaluate the offender's progress toward rehabilitation and decide when the threshold of acceptability is reached. Yet, they must avoid making the spectacular mistake: releasing an offender who commits a serious violent offense. Less spectacular mistakes, however, are at least tolerable in the sense that relatively high recidivism rates (at least as measured by revocation, rearrest, and reincarceration) are commonplace.[16]

Faced with the difficult task of addressing these crosscutting pressures, parole boards lost some of their legitimacy, or, in some jurisdictions, all of their domain. Statutory determinate sentencing and presumptive sentencing guidelines have limited who is eligible for parole or abolished discretionary parole release. In many states, however, parole boards have resisted attempts to dislodge them entirely from the process. Inmates still become eligible for parole in most states, although often only after serving a minimum period as determined by statute, guidelines, and the computation of good time.

Paroling authorities in many states have made tools available to themselves to make better decisions and to protect themselves from the ethical, legal, and political pressures. Once an inmate is eligible for parole, various means are available to assist with decision making. Risk assessment instruments and guideline grids help standardize the release process. However, parole boards preserve some measure of discretion: they reserve the right to depart from parole release guidelines where mitigating or aggravating factors seem salient. Opening release decision making to input from victims, prosecutors, and judges is yet another avenue for the exercise of discretion.

Parole release has become a more complicated and at times sophisticated process than it was twenty years ago. In some jurisdictions, parole boards have sought to further their legitimacy by mechanisms such as risk assessment instruments, grid guidelines, and formalization (allowance or encouragement) of input from outside sources. Boards have been required to make the process more rational and have responded by attempting to lessen the seemingly capricious nature of the release decision. Nevertheless, parole boards reserve ultimate authority to release, if specific circumstances occur that cannot be incorporated into its more standardized procedures.

Notes

1. In indeterminate states, offenders who are incarcerated generally serve some "minimum time" not necessarily defined by statute, but nevertheless normatively defined by parole boards as being "necessary time" before release will be considered.

2. Indeterminate states may also have good-time credits, and states with mandatory proportions with deductible good-time credits may vary considerably in how those credits are applied across offenders. Sometimes, good-time credit may be assumed to be automatic; at other times, it is earned through program participation or work within the prison.

3. Additional variations in sentencing and parole eligibility are introduced by special punishment requirements for certain offenders. Habitual offender laws may be invoked for some chronic offenders, adding further time to the expected minimum to be served. Also, in many states, there is "enhancement time" to be served, if, for example, guns were involved in the crime, or drug sales were involved, or drugs were in possession within a school zone.

4. Plea and charge bargaining may further the differential between what an offender did and what he/she is convicted of. To the extent that plea bargaining varies across states, any attempt to compare states as to their punitiveness would be risky.

5. Of course, parole release and determinate sentencing are not mutually exclusive since both may be used within a given state.

6. It should be kept in mind that "because of the absence of standardized administrative and record-keeping practices from state to state, the data for admissions and departures are not always entirely comparable across jurisdictions" (see BJS 1988b, 730).

7. For varying reasons, some states use split sentences more than others. Rather than incorporate these cases into the denominator, we have chosen to exclude them.

8. Also, states combine determinate sentencing with parole release; therefore, it is not possible to identify the number of offenders within states who served time under determinate sentences versus indeterminate ones.

9. It is important to note some of the limitations of Table 3.1, relative to more general issues of determinate sentencing and parole release. Plausibly, the length of time served for those sentenced under determinate sentencing laws is simply longer. Prison crowding may in part reflect lengthier times served by some offenders. The limited data that are available for some states on the median time served for general offense categories such as violent offenses, property offenses, and drug offenses, however, suggests that there is very little difference, if any, between determinate sentencing states and indeterminate ones (BJS 1988b, 410).

   Data on mean or median length of time served should be treated with caution, however, since it is quite probable that the distribution of time served is bimodal, and the mean or median values do not adequately reflect this distribution. That is, in determinate sentencing states, there may be a subgroup of offenders who serve very long times and another who serve relatively short times. The resulting median or mean may be the same as for indeterminate sentencing states, where such bimodality may not exist or be less accentuated. Ideally, statistical accounts of time served should include measures of variance and skewness. Without such information, it is not possible to ascertain the general impact of determinate sentencing on time served.

10. Parole administrators from twenty states said they used risk-assessment instruments for making parole *release* decisions, while the use of such instruments for supervision classification purposes is more widespread: forty-three states.

11. Using what is known as the Automatic Interaction Detection program, researchers were able to identify several factors that allowed for the differentiation of offenders into risk groups varying from 2 percent to 40 percent failures for violent felonies and from 15.1 percent to 39.5 percent for nonviolent felonies.

12. Other items used in various states include the following: number of address changes during past twelve months client was in the community (Maine and Minnesota); attitude toward change, accept responsibility or authority (Kansas, Minnesota); associates with delinquent others (Illinois, Kansas); and releasee rejected social service agency help (Illinois, Kansas).

    In so far as blacks are less well educated and less likely to have steady employment, use of those factors to determine punishment may result in discrimination. Research by Petersilia and Turner, however, suggests that the fear of this impact may be unfounded.

13. Note that for offense categories VI and VII, the board is expected to use the number of months in the cells of the grid or one-third of the sentence length, whichever is greater.

14. Eighty-four percent, however, use risk instruments for determining the *level* of supervision.

15. We are not sure, however, of the extent to which the prosecutor input that is being reported is from a recommendation made at sentencing, as opposed to one made at the parole hearing.

16. Recidivism rates vary depending on the sample studied, on the definition of recidivism used (e.g., arrest, conviction, reimprisonment), and on the length of the follow-up period. A number of studies have found approximately 70 percent failure rates among those who have served time (see Gottfredson and Gottfredson 1988; Petersilia et al. 1985). Nonetheless, the meaning of recidivism is not self-evident. See Chapter 6 for a detailed discussion of this issue.

Chapter 4

Prison Crowding and Parole

When the first national census of federal and state prisoners was conducted in 1850, it showed that the nation housed 6,737 inmates (Austin and McVey 1988). The rate of incarceration was 29 per 100,000 population.[1] Through the end of the nineteenth century until the start of the 1970s, the incarceration rate increased somewhat but hovered for the most part between 75 and 125 prisoners per 100,000 (Austin and McVey 1988). Thus, despite some fluctuation for well over 100 years, the rate of imprisonment exhibited a fair amount of stability.

The situation has changed dramatically in a very short time. In 1970, just under 200,000 individuals were housed in state and federal facilities throughout the country. The rate of incarceration was 96 per 100,000 (Blumstein 1988, 232). By 1980, a total of 329,821 inmates were confined behind prison walls, and the incarceration rate stood at 139 per 100,000. Five years later, the nation's prison population had grown to just over 500,000.

Prior to this major growth surge, it had taken forty-seven years (between 1927 and 1974) to double the total prison population (BJS 1986). Yet in the short span of ten years, from 1975 to 1985, the prison population more than doubled from 240,593 to 502,507 (BJS 1990).

This extraordinary growth has continued unabated. At the end of 1989, the prison population stood at a record high of 710,054, while the imprisonment rate jumped to 274 per 100,000 (BJS 1990). Six months later, the prison population had grown by more than 80,000 persons to a historically unprecedented 755,425 inmates and a record-setting incarceration rate of 289 per 100,000 (see Table 4.1).

According to the director of the Bureau of Justice Statistics, this latest increase (recorded as of 30 June 1990) represented "the largest growth in sixty-five years of prison population statistics" (USA *Today*, 9 September 1990). Current projections suggest that the prison population will continue to grow, perhaps even more dramatically, well into the 1990s (Austin and McVey 1989; Blumstein 1989).[2]

The enormous jump in the rate of imprisonment has been accompanied by unparalleled increases in expenditures for corrections. For some time, the costs associated with corrections have been increasing at a significant rate relative to per capita spending by state and local governments for such functions as education, public welfare, hospitals, highways, and police protection. In fiscal year 1987, the fifty states spent nearly $12 billion on corrections. During fiscal years 1988 and 1989, these expenditures grew even more, from $13.9 billion to $14.5 billion (National Association of State Budget Officers 1989).[3]

Though parole release remains controversial, the concern with managing finite correctional resources within a severely constrained budgetary environment has tempered the rush to abolish discretionary release. Especially during the past decade, the incessant growth in the number of inmates confined, combined with escalating correctional expenditures, has exerted enormous pressure on paroling authorities to serve as de facto managers of prison population levels.

Parole boards have been called on to manage prison population pressures in many ways, including adjusting parole guidelines and establishing quotas for releasing inmates relative to new prison admissions. The next section will focus on the best-known and most widely criticized method used by paroling authorities to regulate prison populations: emergency powers acts or their equivalents.

Emergency Powers Acts and Parole Boards

During the 1970s and 1980s, at the same time that states struggled to cope with severe crowding in many of their correctional

Table 4.1

Prison Population in the United States on 30 June 1990

State	Total	State	Total
Alabama	14,742	Missouri	15,091
Alaska	2,610	Montana	1,408
Arizona	13,940	North Carolina	18,102
Arkansas	6,660	North Dakota	491
California	93,810	New Hampshire	1,286
Colorado	6,878	New Jersey	20,806
Connecticut	10,190	New Mexico	2,881
District of Columbia	10,569	New York	54,648
Delaware	3,556	Nebraska	2,509
Florida	42,733	Nevada	5,408
Georgia	21,608	Ohio	32,148
Hawaii	2,523	Oklahoma	11,889
Idaho	1,984	Oregon	6,708
Illinois	27,295	Pennsylvania	21,876
Indiana	12,764	Rhode Island	2,355
Iowa	3,842	South Carolina	16,767
Kansas	5,669	South Dakota	1,319
Kentucky	8,824	Tennessee	10,286
Louisiana	18,353	Texas	48,078
Maine	1,558	Utah	2,447
Massachusetts	8,008	Virginia	17,251
Maryland	17,129	Vermont	953
Michigan	33,234	West Virginia	1,535
Minnesota	3,201	Washington	7,403
Mississippi	8,161	Wisconsin	6,944
		Wyoming	1,093

Source: USA Today. 9 September 1990. *Prison population at record level.*

facilities, federal courts across the country began to declare that certain levels of prison crowding were unconstitutional (Thomas 1988; Dilulio 1990a). A recent report notes that at least one institution in thirty states is operating under a court order or consent decree due to crowding, while such orders or decrees affect the entire prison system in another ten jurisdictions (National Prison Project 1988).[4]

Due in part to the impact of judicial intervention, numerous jurisdictions were confronted with the option of either increasing their prison capacity quickly or greatly reducing the number of offenders incarcerated. The dramatic expansion of prison bedspace is both costly and time-consuming, requiring on average three to five years to move from the initial authorization to build to the design, construction, staffing, and actual operation of a new correctional facility. Given the sizable costs, inevitable delays, and continuous judicial pressure, a number of jurisdictions chose to reduce their prison population by relying on statutory procedures for emergency release.

In 1981, Michigan became the first state to enact a statutory mechanism permitting emergency release.[5] By 1988, twenty-one jurisdictions had enacted such legislation, formally acknowledging that extreme measures were necessary to address serious prison crowding. According to the ACA Parole Task Force survey and the findings of other researchers (Modley 1985), those jurisdictions that have, or have had, emergency release legislation are Alaska, Arizona, Arkansas, Connecticut, the District of Columbia, Florida, Georgia, Idaho, Iowa, Michigan, Mississippi, Montana, New Jersey, North Carolina, Ohio, Oklahoma, South Carolina, Tennessee, Texas, Utah, and Washington.

Although there are unique features associated with the emergency powers acts in each jurisdiction, their general framework largely follows the basic structure adopted in Michigan. The acts were designed to be temporary, short-term, and infrequently used options to enable a state to "buy time" to construct additional prison capacity or develop and expand community-based alternatives to divert offenders from prison.

As a matter of definition, emergency powers acts are formal, statutorily authorized devices that, when triggered, provide for the orderly release of eligible inmates when the prison population exceeds the available capacity for a specifically defined period of time (Modley 1985). When a prison's population exceeds its capacity for a given period (usually thirty to sixty days), a designated body or individual informs the governor that an emergency exists. The governor is ultimately responsible for invoking the act, though the discretion to do so varies considerably from state to state.[6]

Once an emergency powers act is triggered, the minimum sentences of offenders are automatically reduced by a specific amount of time. In some states, how much time is granted is defined by statute. In other jurisdictions, the governor may determine the exact amount of time to be deducted. This reduction, in turn, advances the mandatory release dates or parole eligibility dates for those affected. With respect to the latter, the parole board then reviews the newly created pool of parole-eligible inmates for early release. The decision to grant parole is based on normal administrative and statutory criteria.

Invoking an emergency powers act does not result in the wholesale release of inmates to the community. Though the actual number of inmates that may be released is generally not specified, the "rollbacks" are typically for ninety days. If the act's initial implementation fails to end the emergency, another emergency declaration may follow.

It is important to note that not every state with an emergency release statute has invoked it. Moreover, in a number of jurisdictions, the original statute has expired (e.g., New Jersey). Between 1980 and 1985, seventeen states enacted emergency powers acts, though only seven actually triggered their use. Four more states passed emergency release legislation in the next three years. During this same period, according to the ACA Parole Task Force survey, four states invoked their emergency release powers. Thus, a total of eleven jurisdictions have at some time invoked their emergency powers act.

The ACA Parole Task Force survey also indicates that, of those jurisdictions furnishing information, one state invoked its emergency release statute eight times, another six times, one state five times, and six other states three times or less. Two states said that they did not use their emergency powers procedures. Of those states reporting the use of emergency early release by their parole boards, two states responded that they had released nearly 1,000 inmates, one state had released 231, one state, 96, and one state, 20.

Emergency powers acts are designed to serve as an infrequently used option to address serious prison crowding. In those states under court order, they are also intended to be responsive to prison population "caps" and deteriorating conditions of confinement. In states where they have been used with some frequency (e.g., Michigan, South Carolina, and Washington), there has been a notable reduction of inmates in the prison system. Nonetheless, emergency powers acts are not a panacea for resolving prison crowding. In fact, they have proven problematic for several reasons.

Emergency early release offers immediate relief from the pressures associated with prison crowding by reducing the number of inmates confined. Such reductions give the jurisdiction in question an opportunity to build and/or expand prison bedspace to comply with court orders or to expand alternatives to incarceration. Yet if crowding persists, there is a tendency to trigger the act with some frequency, an action that undermines the intent of the legislation. Of equal significance, there has been no state that has been able to resolve its lack of prison capacity through the use of emergency release mechanisms. At best, invoking such mechanisms achieves a reduction in the extent of growth in the inmate population for a limited time.

The frequent triggering of emergency powers acts also places immense pressure on all aspects of the parole process. Although the parole board is not directly involved in several states' emergency release procedures (e.g., Arkansas), it is in the majority of jurisdictions. In states where the board is authorized to release inmates under an emergency declaration, the workload increases dramatically. There are more parole hearings, more case summary preparations, and in some states, more administrative reviews. The invocation of such acts does not result in the sudden release of every offender who is confined. Nonetheless, significant pressure is placed on the parole board to grant release dates earlier than expected to a certain percentage of offenders who would not otherwise be eligible at that time.[7]

In addition, major amounts of time credits have been awarded in several states following the frequent declaration of such acts. In Texas, inmates confined in the department of corrections during a recent two-year period received a sentence reduction of twenty-one months through the awarding of time credits under emergency early release (Jackson et al. 1987).

The relative advantages and shortcomings associated with emergency powers acts are illustrated by the Michigan experience. As this example illustrates, the use of an emergency powers act often represents a politically troublesome issue for the governor, who in most states must ultimately invoke the act and advance the date of release for large numbers of offenders. The following scenario describes the rise and fall of emergency early release in the very state that conceived the concept.

The Emergency Powers Act and Parole in Michigan[8]

During the 1970s, Michigan's prison population began to rise steeply. The state reacted by adding 4,000 new prison beds and 2,000 preparole community placement beds. The total capital cost of this construction was $52 million. The crowding crisis continued, however. Additional inmate housing was created using classrooms, dayrooms, and gymnasiums. At the same time, state-sentenced inmates were housed in county jails for a longer time prior to their transfer.

In 1980, a federal court issued a decision requiring that the department of corrections reduce the population in its correctional facilities to a level in line with available prison capacity. In November of that same year, the voters were asked to approve a bond issue authorizing a major prison construction program. The measure failed by a margin of two to one. In response, the state passed the nation's first emergency powers act in January 1981 (Boyd and Padden 1984).

Though the constitutionality of the act was challenged immediately, it was eventually upheld by the state Supreme Court. Under the act, a five-member corrections commission appointed by the governor was to certify that the inmate population exceeded the rated design capacity of the prison system for thirty days. The commission was also asked to determine if all available administrative options had been pursued to reduce the prison population. If so, the governor was then authorized to declare a prison crowding state of emergency.

Upon a declaration of emergency, the minimum sentences of all inmates with established minimum terms were to be reduced by ninety days. If this action failed to reduce the prison population to 95 percent of rated capacity, the minimum sentences were again to be reduced by an additional ninety days following the same process.

The reduction of established minimum sentences created a new pool of parole-eligible offenders. These cases were then processed in accordance with the existing screening procedures and criteria governing normal parole release. The actual discretion to release these offenders was retained by the parole board, which was allowed to deny parole to any inmate considered to be an unreasonable risk to the community.

Michigan's emergency powers act was triggered on eleven occasions between May 1981 and November 1984. While it was never intended to provide a long-term solution to prison crowding, it did enable the state to maintain its correctional population below 95 percent of capacity as required by law. Approximately 2,000 to 3,000 inmates were paroled earlier than they would have been otherwise. Nonetheless, prison crowding remained a serious problem. When asked to invoke the act again, the governor refused to do so. In a letter dated 14 December 1984, he wrote, "I am notifying you that I do not intend to declare a prison overcrowding emergency now or in the near future. I am convinced that the Corrections Commission and the Department of Corrections can and must find alternative housing to prevent the system from prematurely releasing dangerous felons onto Michigan streets" (Michigan Department of Corrections 1985).

The governor's unwillingness to go any further pushed the legislature into authorizing $16 million to construct five new prisons and renovate the Detroit House of Corrections. Though the act was revised in 1985, the statute was eventually repealed. At the time, the prison system was operating at 124 percent capacity (BJS 1986).

With respect to parole, the frequent invocation of the state's emergency powers act placed enormous pressure on the board, both by accelerating the pace of hearings and requiring an inordinate amount of advance case preparation. In the early stages, the average number of monthly hearings rose from 450 a month to roughly 800 a month (Mathias and Steelman 1982). Supervision caseloads were also affected, increasing initially by as much as 25 percent. Though the caseloads eventually stabilized, these releasees were eligible for early discharge by field officers if they met certain criteria. Two members of the parole board were required to vote on such cases.

On those occasions when the emergency powers act was used, the parole board reviewed the expanded pool of parole-eligible inmates and selected appropriate nonviolent inmates for release. The act became increasingly less effective as the board expressed reluctance to release additional offenders even though they fell into the pool of eligibility. Though a sizable number of inmates were granted parole release earlier than they would have been in the absence of such an act, parole release policy in Michigan was not altered in a significant fashion as a means to maintain the prison population below a prescribed level.

Parole Boards and Prison Population Control: Other Strategies

The use of emergency powers or prison management acts seems to have subsided in recent years, even though the majority of states with such acts still retain the statutory authority to use them under extraordinary circumstances. Regardless of the presence of emergency statutes, paroling authorities have also been called on to help manage prison populations in other ways.

Some parole boards have received legislative authority and direction to control the prison population through the explicit use (and adjustment) of parole guidelines. Other paroling authorities have been requested informally, either by the legislature, the governor, or the director of the department of corrections, to find additional candidates for release who might not be immediately eligible under the normal release criteria. In several states, the parole board that was abolished at one point has been restored primarily to address serious prison crowding.

Florida represents a pertinent illustration. In 1983, the parole commission was abolished, retaining jurisdiction only over those inmates sentenced before the effective date of the legislation. In view of unrelenting prison population growth and the need to comply with a court-imposed "cap," a Crime Prevention and Law Enforcement Study Commission recommended and the legislature subsequently enacted a Controlled Release Authority. This authority (whose membership is the same as that of the former parole commission) must screen all inmates within ninety days of their admission to the prison system and establish a "controlled release date" for those who do not pose a serious threat to society. The Controlled Release Authority offers a way to ensure that scarce correctional resources are reserved for inmates who, if released, would be likely to commit new crimes (*Criminal Justice Newsletter* 1990).

Throughout the 1980s, parole boards have been called on with increasing frequency to serve as the formal regulators of prison population levels. In Georgia and Texas, parole boards have been expected by policy makers and others to assist in managing prison populations that seem to be spinning out of control. Certain policy quandaries arise from this development.

Georgia: An Active Partnership

The Georgia Board of Pardons and Paroles became involved in managing the state's prison population in an incremental and informal fashion (Moore 1989). The board's participation became more formalized as the crowding crisis escalated and federal court intervention became a reality. The initial reliance on the parole board began in 1967. However, due to relentless growth over time, the parole board's involvement has since become firmly institutionalized under an initiative now known as the Governor's Emergency Release Program.

In 1967, then Governor Lester Maddox became distressed at the crowded conditions he observed during a visit to the Georgia Industrial Institute for young offenders. He asked the parole board informally to expedite the release of short-term inmates serving nonviolent offenses. The first group to be released was taken to Atlanta and addressed by the governor. At this point, those released were confined to one institution. Moreover, the motivation for taking such a step was rooted in humanitarian concern. Governor Maddox made a second request, which was honored in 1970. These requests set the stage for the criteria that were to be adopted in the years to follow: offenders eligible for early release were to be nonviolent inmates serving sentences of two years or less.

The next stage of parole board involvement in determining suitability for early release occurred under Governor Jimmy Carter. In 1974, he directed a committee of criminal justice professionals and legislators to review the prison population crisis. The committee and the governor expressed concern over crowding and noted the growing interest of the federal courts in the conditions of confinement in many of the state's prisons.

In response, the parole board developed a program for special early release that considered three categories of inmates: those within six months of sentence completion, those who had been denied parole by a three to two vote, and those serving time for property offenses who had completed one-fourth but not one-third of their sentences. Approximately 600 inmates were released under this initiative, thus lessening the crisis.

Nonetheless, in October 1975, then Governor George Busbee, citing an "atmosphere of tension and potentially explosive violence" in the state's prisons and jails, once again asked the parole board to intervene. With the governor's support, the board issued a commutation order that reduced by one year the sentences of thousands of inmates serving time for nonviolent offenses.[9] This action resulted in the immediate discharge of 327 inmates. It also created earlier discharge and parole eligibility dates for 5,026 others (Moore 1989, 2).

The language of the commutation order is significant. In its order, the parole board deplored the "need to employ immediate, short-term responses to long-term problems," but pointed out that a "drastic and immediate crisis demands drastic and immediate action and that the hazards in taking such action must be viewed in relation to the dangers involved in failing to act." The board stressed the need to provide time in which the governor and General Assembly could "address themselves to the crisis, examine the priorities of Georgia's correctional system, and seek significant long-range remedies." The board's reluctance and resolve signaled that the management of the state's prison population was now part of its operational responsibilities.

The early release effort in 1975 brought a measure of temporary relief. But in 1978 the crowding crisis reasserted itself and the board was asked to assist once again. Roughly 900 inmates were released during the summer by reconsidering those cases that had been denied by a three to two vote and those scheduled for discharge within six months.

This was followed by further involvement in 1980 as a result of a request for assistance from corrections officials and county sheriffs. The latter were facing federal court intervention (which had already occurred in several counties). Stating that it had a responsibility to avoid a "powder-keg situation" and "federal receivership of state and county institutions," the board agreed to consider all inmates for early release who were within six months of discharge. From 1980 to mid-1982, 8,819 inmates were released through special paroles, reprieves, and sentence commutations. In its 1981 annual report, the board expressed hope that the General Assembly would adopt measures that would provide a more lasting solution.

In 1982, the General Assembly enacted a Prison Management Act. Though patterned after the Michigan Plan, the statute was never invoked. This was due, in part, to the board's continued emphasis on expedited early releases. In addition, then Governor Busbee conveyed his conservative view of the legislation in a letter to the chair of the board. The governor wrote that he did not intend to implement the law "unless and until" he was "positively convinced that the state has exercised every feasible action and utilized every possible resource to house the inmates we are legally bound to house (Moore 1989, 2)." In that same letter, he requested that the board provide more special releases of inmates serving time for nonviolent offenses.

At this point, the board took a major step in expanding its responsibility as the sole manager of the state's prison population level. The governor pointed out in his letter that existing state law authorized exceptions to the one-third rule for parole eligibility. Citing this provision as one possibility for relief not yet exhausted, he asked the board to waive the statutory minimum when appropriate. With the governor's explicit approval, the board for the first time began making exceptions to the one-third rule of parole eligibility for a substantial number of inmates. The practice continues today.

In 1983, the next governor, Joe Frank Harris, renewed the request that the parole board assist in monitoring and controlling prison and jail crowding. At this stage, however, the board implemented a new approach to achieve this purpose. It chose to revise its Parole Decision Guidelines, which had been in use since 1979. The guidelines were altered to permit increased releases, a measure that avoided for a time the need to grant additional emergency releases.

From 1983 until 1986, aided by prison expansion and a downturn in the state's crime rate, prison and jail crowding was kept within manageable limits. In 1984, in an action that was to eventually exert a significant impact, the system of "earned time" for calculating prison release was eliminated. Inmates found that they were no longer to be released early for good behavior during confinement. Prior to this development, earned time, which was administered by the Department of Corrections, had reduced by nearly one-half the amount of time served for inmates without life sentences. The board supported the repeal of this measure, expecting that it would result in a corresponding reduction in court-imposed sentence lengths. Such reductions were not forthcoming.

Due to serious crowding in the county jails in 1987, sheriffs across the state again called on the board to provide immediate relief. The board thus faced a major crisis, given the elimination of earned time and the fact that prison population growth was fast outpacing prison construction. In response, from June 1987 to October 1988, the board commuted the sentences of 6,700 inmates to time served. These offenders were selected from a pool of inmates serving two years or less, as well as those revoked for violations of probation. Yet the prison crowding crisis did not abate.

Early in 1989, the governor announced a major new initiative called the Governor's Early Release Program. The program was designed to expedite (or place on a "fast track") designated nonviolent offenders through the prison system until sufficient prison capacity could be created. At that time, the governor requested funding to expand the prison system by more than 8,000 beds. This initiative is currently in effect and has served to avert federal judicial intervention.

These efforts have placed the parole board squarely in the role of prison population regulator. They have also affected the board's overall operations, most notably with respect to supervision and revocation policy. To ensure effective supervision, the Governor's Emergency Release Program provided for a significant expansion in the number of parole officers to maintain caseloads at an adequate level. Nonetheless, the severity of prison crowding has reduced the ability of parole officers to respond to rule violations with arrest and temporary jail time. Likewise, the option of pursuing parole revocation for any but the most serious public safety violations (generally, new crimes) has been eliminated. The revocation and return of a parolee to prison requires that the board release an inmate who is currently confined. This situation is not unique to Georgia.

Texas: The Creation of a Quota System

The Texas Board of Pardons and Paroles became actively involved in maintaining the state's prison population within judicially prescribed limits as a result of the well-known case *Ruiz v. Estelle*, 503 F. Supp. 1265 (S.D. Tex. 1980), aff'd, 679 F.2d 1115 (5th Cir. 1982), cert. denied, 460 U.S. 1042 (1983).[10] The *Ruiz* case unfolded over the course of a nine-year legal battle between the plaintiff, David Ruiz, the Department of Corrections, and the federal district court (DiIulio 1990a). Though the prison crowding problem became apparent during the litigation, for a period of time the state was able to house a large number of inmates in temporary tents without resorting to emergency release mechanisms. When the court found in favor of the plaintiff and imposed prison population limits, however, it became apparent that such a solution was no longer acceptable or constitutional.

Early in 1981, the parole board was asked by the governor's office and corrections officials to assist in reducing the prison population. The ongoing legal maneuvering in *Ruiz* provided the actual impetus to show the court that the state was making a good-faith effort to reduce crowding, a major complaint of the plaintiffs. As a result of the request, the board developed a "conditional parole" program that provided an early review for nonviolent offenders who were serving short sentences and were within six months of their scheduled release. The inmates selected for release under this program were transferred to halfway houses for up to ninety days. This initiative only offered short-term relief.[11]

To some extent, this was due to then prevailing parole eligibility requirements mandating that inmates serve at least one-third of their sentence. This requirement, coupled with the state's good-time statute, placed some limitations on when and who the board could consider for release. These restrictions, as well as the rapidly escalating growth in the correctional population and the conditions imposed by the *Ruiz* case, caused the legislature to enact a Prison Management Act in 1983.

The act defined the procedures that were to be implemented by the governor when the prison population exceeded 95 percent of rated capacity. Modeled after Michigan's emergency powers act, the Texas plan advanced additional good-time credits to eligible inmates. The inmates thus affected were, in turn, either discharged from their sentence or made immediately eligible for parole. The act itself was to be triggered when the Corrections Board (a lay board overseeing the department of corrections) determined that the rated capacity was exceeded. Once this determination was made, the department of corrections closed its doors to new admissions until the parole board could review and grant additional releases.

In 1983, the board was called on with some frequency to release inmates earlier than it might have otherwise. During a two-month period, it conducted special reviews and selected nearly 1,000 nonviolent offenders for early release. On this occasion, however, there was no requirement that they be released to a halfway house. Later in 1983, the board was again asked to provide two additional special reviews, selecting releasees from a pool of inmates who had been reviewed previously and denied parole.

By the end of 1984, following several special reviews during the year, the board's overall approval rate for those considered for parole exceeded 45 percent. Prior to its involvement in early-release decisions, its rate of approval was roughly 40 percent (Jackson et al. 1987). However, the number of inmates admitted to prison continued to far outdistance the number who were released.

Redoubling its pursuit of options for releasing additional inmates, in 1985 the legislature adopted a preparole program. Under this initiative, the board was given the authority to release inmates to a halfway house up to 180 days prior to their eligibility for parole. Although they were placed on parole supervision in halfway houses under contract with the board, these offenders were still classified as inmates. They could be returned to custody for violating parole conditions or the rules of the halfway house.

The preparole program nonetheless enabled the state to add additional prison bedspace and to relocate inmates from correctional facilities to residential placements through expedited decisions made by the parole board. The board now served as the primary manager of the state's entire correctional capacity, from jails and prisons to postrelease community centers.

Since 1986, the parole board has been undertaking ongoing special reviews to release as many inmates as can be managed as quickly as possible. The net effect of such reviews and subsequent releases has been a significant reduction of inmates eligible for parole or mandatory release. Though the data are incomplete due to changes in record-keeping, between October 1985 and August 1987, approximately twenty-three special reviews were conducted by the board. Nearly 27,000 cases were reviewed, resulting in 6,000 favorable release decisions (Jackson et al. 1987).

During 1987, as a result of court-imposed population limits and the requirements of the Prison Management Act, the department of corrections closed the prison doors to admissions more than twenty times. By the end of 1988, the pool of nonviolent, short-term inmates was largely depleted. The legislature responded to these developments by authorizing substantial funding and prison construction bond issues to expand the prison system's capacity by more than 10,000 beds.

Yet the pressure on the parole board has continued to mount. The frequent refusal of the department of corrections to accept new admissions has exacerbated already serious jail crowding. Moreover, the lengthy backup in the county jails has resulted in a growing number of felony offenders becoming eligible for parole prior to their transfer to the prison system. The outcome has been the creation of an expanded parole consideration program to large numbers of inmates confined in the 254 county jails located throughout the state.

Regardless of the program relied on, the continuous selection of nonviolent, short-term-sentenced inmates served to reduce the number of parole candidates considered acceptable risks to the community. By the end of 1989, however, the overall rate of parole approval stood at more than 60 percent. Nonetheless, the pressure on the prison system became so intense that the governor's office imposed a quota system on the parole board to balance admissions with releases. Each day the board was expected to release 150 inmates to make room for a comparable number of new admissions.

During this period, the parole board was placed in the position of having to select unacceptable candidates for parole release. Inmates who had been reviewed earlier, often several times, were frequently granted parole, as were those with poor disciplinary records. The absence of any real screening, coupled with a discernible lack of suitability for parole release, has created special problems for those responsible for parole supervision.

The most serious problem confronting field service agents is the lack of recourse for sanctioning or revoking parolees who refuse to comply with the conditions of supervision. The volume of those released through special reviews has likewise contributed to ever-larger caseloads. Parole detention centers were recently established for the short-term confinement of parole violators. These facilities, however, have since been filled to capacity and are currently being used as preparole centers for some of the more violent offenders that are being released from prison.

For eight years, the parole board has played a major role in keeping the prison system open and under the population limits imposed by the court in *Ruiz*. It has been called on to release as many inmates as are admitted and to continuously adapt parole release policy to rapid prison population growth. When it first began conducting special reviews in 1981, the process was viewed as a unique aberration from the board's traditional release and decision-making policy. At the time, only 34 percent of those inmates initially eligible were granted parole. During fiscal year 1987, 70 percent of those considered initially eligible were approved for parole (Jackson et al. 1987). In view of a recent reorganization of the criminal justice system in Texas, it is likely that the board's role as an active participant in prison population control will continue in the years ahead.

Parole Boards and the Management of Prison Populations: A Policy Quandary

Although the philosophical underpinnings of parole, especially as they were developed during the Progressive Era of criminal justice in the 1920s and 1930s, are devoid of any reference to prison population management, parole release has long served as a safety valve for the correctional system. Rothman (1983) reports that during the first three decades of the twentieth century, the wardens (who dominated parole board decision making at the time) found parole release a useful device when necessary to reduce prison crowding.[12] Informally, this practice has continued to the present (Garry 1984).

The extraordinary level of growth in the nation's prison population, however, has forced many paroling authorities into a far more active and formal role than ever before in managing a jurisdiction's overall correctional capacity. If incessant prison population growth has curtailed the movement to abolish parole in a number of states, it has also imposed on many paroling authorities the expectation that they serve as de facto managers of the prison population. As Burke notes:

> There is no longer any question of whether paroling authorities will become involved in population issues, but rather...when. If this issue is not met head on, it will sooner or later be thrust upon a paroling authority, either in the form of emergency powers legislated as a responsibility of a paroling authority, as a formal or informal mandate of the governor, or in the form of legislatively mandated guidelines (1988, 31-32).

Michigan, Georgia, and Texas offer examples of states where the responsibility has been thrust on the parole board to play active, albeit different, roles in prison population control. Very few parole boards have been completely immune from pressures within their respective jurisdictions to assume such responsibilities. In terms of parole board chairs, there is a wide range of opinion on how significant this pressure actually is with respect to release decision making. There is, however, a rather substantial consensus on whether this responsibility belongs to parole.

The ACA Parole Task Force survey asked parole board chairs to respond to the following statement: "The main problem parole boards face today is the pressure to release offenders as soon as they are eligible for parole." Thirty-one (61.7 percent) of the respondents disagreed with this statement. Another fifteen chairs (29.4 percent) expressed some measure of agreement. The remaining five were uncertain.

Regardless of the pressure to release, most parole board chairs surveyed by the Task Force do not believe that the "management of prison population levels should be an important responsibility of parole boards." In fact, while thirty-four (68 percent) of the respondents disagreed with this statement, within this group a majority of chairs (N = 18) strongly disagreed. Only nine parole board chairs agreed that prison population management should be an important responsibility of their agency. Not a single chair expressed strong agreement on this matter. This response suggests that while some chairs acknowledge the pressure to release (caused presumably by prison crowding), the majority do not feel that managing prison population levels should be one of their more important responsibilities.

There are a host of policy quandaries that reside underneath the misgivings expressed by the parole board chairs with respect to this issue. These quandaries cut across the entire parole continuum. As the experiences in Michigan, Georgia, and Texas show, it is nearly impossible to resolve prison crowding through emergency or accelerated parole release.

The reductions achieved, even through the frequent use of emergency powers acts or special reviews, are at best temporary. Even where the state relies on or develops new community-based options (e.g., probation, electronic monitoring/house arrest), correctional population growth eventually requires that the parole board accelerate the release of additional groups of offenders.

When population growth drives release policy, whatever rationale the board uses to determine suitability for release is compromised. Many paroling authorities consider some combination of risk to the community, the nature of the conviction offense, an acceptable parole plan, postrelease employment, and positive prison behavior in deciding whether to grant or deny parole. Where crowding drives the decision to release, these factors assume secondary importance, if they are considered at all.

Accelerated parole or early release also affects postrelease supervision. Larger average caseloads are often the outcome. Several states (e.g., Georgia) have expanded the number of parole officers to accommodate this often unplanned increase in the parole supervision population. Moreover, some jurisdictions have expanded community resources such as halfway houses, work release centers, house arrest/electronic monitoring, and intensive supervision to monitor those offenders who are granted early release. Not all states have, however, been able to do so. In these jurisdictions, the prison population crisis is simply transferred from the correctional (or institutional) component to the postrelease (or community supervision) component.

In some states, the continuing escalation in prison populations has had another, albeit unanticipated, effect on the ability of parole officers to revoke parole for anything other than serious criminal violations. In Georgia and Texas, parole officers have experienced difficulty in revoking parolees for technical violations of the conditions of supervision, even when there are indications of deteriorating behavior on the part of the parolee. In 1984, approximately 52 percent of those revoked in Texas represented technical violators (Texas Board of Pardons and

Paroles 1985). In 1988, this figure fell to less than 5 percent (Herrick 1989). Though the state subsequently created Intermediate Sanction Facilities, operated by the parole board, for technical parole violators, this sort of initiative represents an exception to the rule.

Paroling authorities are in an advantageous position to assist a state in managing its limited correctional resources through the judicious and infrequent use of emergency early release mechanisms. Nonetheless, emergency powers acts and expedited parole releases do not address the front-end factors that drive prison crowding; namely, the politicization of crime control policy, determinate sentencing reform, mandatory minimum terms, and enhanced sentences. In the absence of addressing these factors, the expectation that parole alone can resolve prison crowding is similar to the adage that rearranging the deck chairs on the *Titanic* would have saved the ship.

Notes

1. Rothman (1983, 636) points out that prior to 1850, there was a notable lack of prison crowding due to a commitment to provide each inmate with a single cell. In this way, prison officials could avoid the contamination that would invariably follow were inmates permitted to associate with one another while confined in their cells.
2. The need to expand prison capacity was one of the major concerns voiced by governors across the country in their 1990 annual State of the State addresses (National Criminal Justice Association 1990). Governor Wallace G. Wilkinson of Kentucky requested a $96 million general fund increase during the next two years to expand the state's available bedspace by 26 percent. The increase, he stated, is necessary to accommodate the growth that is anticipated through 1994 (National Criminal Justice Association 1990, 6).
3. California offers an illuminating example. In 1979, the state's prison population stood at 22,500. In January 1990, it totaled more than 86,000, an increase of over 400 percent (California Blue Ribbon Commission on Inmate Population Management 1990). According to estimates developed by a blue ribbon commission, there will be more than 136,000 inmates by 1994 in a prison system able to house only 72,000 despite further construction. By 1994-95, the corrections budget will exceed $4 billion (California Blue Ribbon Commission on Inmate Population Management 1990).
4. The number of states operating prisons under court order to remedy conditions of confinement or serious crowding has since increased to forty-one (National Prison Project 1989).
5. In at least one jurisdiction (Alaska), provision for emergency release was a matter of executive order, not formal legislation.
6. In some states (Arizona, Georgia, Iowa, Montana, and North Carolina), however, the governor is not involved. In these states, the department

  of corrections notifies the paroling authority and the two agencies establish the procedures for securing emergency releases (Modley 1985).

7. The frequent use of such acts also results in a significant diminution in the pool of inmates eligible for future consideration. This problem is exacerbated in states that have narrowly defined the criteria of eligibility for emergency early release. Since nonassaultive, low-risk inmates are normally eligible, those inmates who remain represent a more problematic group of offenders to manage during their confinement.

8. This discussion draws, in part, from an earlier article written by one of the authors on emergency powers acts and parole (see Rhine 1986).

9. The Georgia Board of Pardons and Paroles has the constitutional power to commute sentences, including death sentences.

10. For three different perspectives on *Ruiz*, see Dilulio (1990a), Chapters 2-4.

11. During the last four months of fiscal year 1981, the board conducted thousands of special reviews resulting in the granting of an additional 1,564 "conditional paroles." This program of accelerated release was funded by a grant from the Criminal Justice Division of the governor's office in response to *Ruiz*.

12. The introduction of parole in California in 1893 resulted eventually in its use as a means to control the size of the prisoner population (Messinger et al. 1985).

Chapter 5

Postrelease Supervision: Managing the Offender in the Community

Although policy makers and others have focused on prison crowding during the past decade, for the past several years the fastest growing component of all adult correctional populations has been parole or postrelease supervision. Between 1983 and 1988, the prison population grew 39 percent, from 437,248 to 606,810; the probation population, 49 percent, from 1,582,947 to 2,356,483; and the jail population, 54 percent, from 221,815 to 341,893. The parole population, however, increased 65 percent, from 246,440 to 407,977 (BJS 1988a, 1989a). Table 5.1 illustrates the extent of growth among the four adult correctional populations from 1983 to 1988.

Nonetheless, there is significant variation in the pattern of growth and the number and rate of adult offenders on parole by region and jurisdiction. From the end of 1987 to the end of 1988, seventeen states

Table 5.1

Growth of Adult Correctional Populations 1983-88 (in thousands)

Correctional Populations	1983	1984	1985	1986	1987	1988	% Change
Probation	1,583	1,741	1,969	2,115	2,247	2,356	48.8
Jail	222	233	255	273	294	342	54.1
Prison	437	448	488	526	563	609	38.7
Parole	246	267	300	326	355	408	65.5
Total	2,488	2,684	3,011	3,239	3,460	3,713	49.2

Source: BJS 1988a, 1989a.

reported increases of 10 percent or more.[1] During this same period, thirteen states reported a decline in their parole population.[2] The largest parole populations were found in Texas (77,827), California (49,364), Pennsylvania (46,466), and New York (33,962). The smallest parole populations (excluding Maine) were found in Nebraska (447), Rhode Island (442), Connecticut (371), Vermont (182), and North Dakota (163) (BJS 1989a).

The northeast, which in 1987 showed the smallest growth in the number of offenders on parole, experienced the largest percentage increase in 1988 (BJS 1988a, 1989a). It also had the highest ratio of parolees to residents: 272 per 100,000 adults. The ratios for the remaining regions were 253 in the south, 201 in the west, and 115 in the midwest (BJS 1989a). Five jurisdictions exceeded the highest regional rate, including the District of Columbia (824), Texas (657), Pennsylvania (508), New Jersey (314), and Washington (311).

The continuing growth and institutional pressures associated with prison crowding will likely contribute to significant increases in the number of offenders under postrelease supervision in the years ahead. Regardless of the method of release—whether supervised mandatory release or a discretionary parole board decision—the responsibility for supervising ever larger caseloads falls under the jurisdiction of parole field services. Often independent of the parole board, this agency represents the other major component of the parole process.

101

Paroling Authorities, Parole Field Services, and the Conditions of Supervision

Just as parole boards have become increasingly autonomous from departments of corrections, the administration of parole field services has become more independent of paroling authorities. In fact, as shown in Figure 5.1, since 1966 there has been a pronounced trend away from the parole board itself administering postrelease supervision.

In 1966, thirty-one boards had administrative responsibility for parole supervision. By 1972, the number had dropped to eighteen; by 1979, to twelve (Carlson 1979). This trend toward independent parole field services has remained stable for more than a decade. According to the results of the ACA Parole Task Force survey, the parole field service agency is housed under a separate agency in thirty-eight jurisdictions (74.5 percent), usually the department of corrections. Responsibility for supervising parolees is under the parole board in only thirteen states (25.5 percent).[3]

Though parole field service is administratively separate in most jurisdictions from the parole board, these agencies share common goals and objectives. In granting parole, the board is expressing its judgment that it is appropriate to continue an inmate's sentence outside prison walls. Moreover, by setting the conditions of release—some tailored to meet the needs of individual cases—the parole board is prescribing the goals it expects to be met during supervision (e.g., risk management). The responsibility for achieving these goals, however, resides with the parole field service agency. Thus, in carrying out the supervision function, the field service agency is, in effect, implementing the release decision-making goals established by the parole board (McGarry 1988).

The period of community supervision is generally designed to provide assistance to parolees, control their activities, and monitor their adjustment during the demanding and often problematic transition from confinement to the community (Clear and Cole 1990). How these objectives are to be accomplished is addressed through the setting of parole conditions. Parolees (and mandatory releasees) must agree to comply with various conditions of supervision that place restrictions on their movement and liberty. The violation of these conditions may result in a formal revocation and return to prison.

The conditions of parole fall into two categories: standard and special. Though they display wide variation in number and scope, standard conditions of parole are those that are uniformly imposed on every releasee within a given jurisdiction. They are designed to reduce the likelihood of new criminal behavior. Thus, movement and travel may be limited, association with known felons prohibited, and the use of alcohol

Figure 5.1

Administration of Parole Field Services

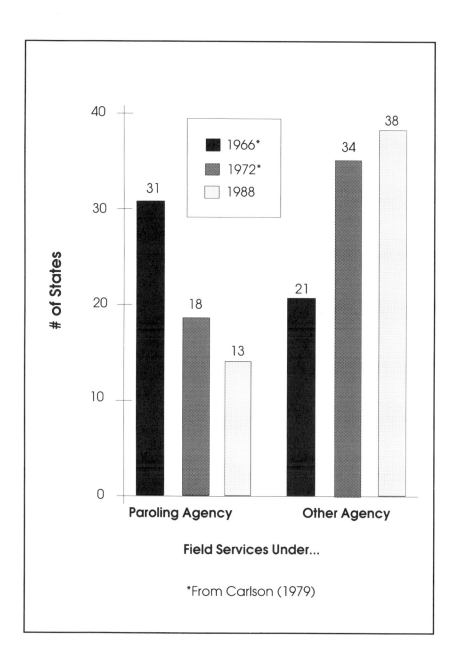

Field Services Under...

*From Carlson (1979)

or drugs explicitly forbidden. Special conditions are those added to individual cases either to deter a certain behavior or to assist in the reintegration process. The parole certificate that parolees must sign in New Hampshire, for example, lists the following special conditions, one or more of which may be required depending on the needs of the case:

1. I will participate regularly in Alcoholics Anonymous to the satisfaction of the Probation/Parole Officer.
2. I will secure written permission from the Probation/Parole Officer prior to purchasing and/or operating a motor vehicle.
3. I will participate and satisfactorily complete the following program: _____.
4. I will enroll and participate in mental health counseling on a regular basis to the satisfaction of the Probation/Parole Officer.
5. I will not be in the unsupervised company of (female/male) minors at any time.
6. I will not leave the county without permission of the Probation/Parole Officer.
7. I will refrain totally from the use of alcoholic beverages.
8. I will submit to breath, blood, or urinalysis testing for substance abuse at the direction of the Probation/Parole Officer.

Paroling authorities have long been criticized for the number and thus the unenforceability of the conditions that are often imposed (Arluke 1956, 1969). There is some evidence, however, that parole boards have begun to restrict the number of standard conditions and to focus more on crime control matters rather than the social activities of parolees (Travis and Latessa 1984, 598).[4]

Recognizing the diversity in parole conditions, the ACA Parole Task Force survey provided respondents with a list of fourteen preselected parole conditions and asked them to indicate which ones applied to parolees within their jurisdiction. Previous research on this topic requested each jurisdiction to forward a list of their standard conditions of parole (Arluke 1956, 1969; Travis and Latessa 1984). The list of conditions given by the Parole Task Force was not exhaustive. It did not ask if parolees were expected to report immediately upon release, or whether parolees were expected to submit regular reports to their supervising officers, waive extradition, or agree to be searched at any time. A review of the parole certificates that were received along with the surveys indicates that these conditions are frequently imposed.

The results of the ACA Parole Task Force survey show that of the fourteen conditions of parole, the average number imposed across all jurisdictions was 8.9. Of these conditions, states varied in the actual number they required, ranging from as few as four to as many as fourteen. Table 5.2 illustrates the number and percentage of jurisdictions requiring these conditions.

According to Table 5.2, 90 percent or more of the field service agencies require that the parolee obey all laws (federal, state, and local), report when directed and answer all reasonable inquiries, refrain from carrying a firearm or other dangerous weapon, and remain within the jurisdiction of the sentencing court, reporting any change in residence to the parole officer. In forty states (78.4 percent), parolees are expected to maintain gainful employment. In another nineteen states (37.3 percent), parolees must pay supervision fees.[5] Although it is used in probation, community service may be ordered as a condition of parole in only seven jurisdictions (13.7 percent).

The conditions of supervision convey the parole board's expectations to those parole officers responsible for supervising individual offenders. Within broadly defined limits, they define the officer's range of discretion when dealing with parolees. Nonetheless, these conditions constitute at best the outer parameters of an officer's work. More important, how supervision is performed, as well as the frequency and type of contact between parolees and parole officers, reflects the approach of the field service agency to classification and case management.

Classification and Case Management in Parole

Until well into the 1970s, offenders under community supervision were monitored largely according to the priorities for supervision established by their probation or parole officer (Stanley 1976; Studt 1978). If it existed at all, agency policy regarding how individual officers were to manage their caseloads left them with nearly unlimited discretion and thus de facto authority to determine their own approach to supervision. Though offender classification was a well-established practice at other stages involving criminal justice decision making (Gottfredson and Tonry 1987), very few community supervision agencies had a formal system for classifying or managing offenders falling under their jurisdiction.

This situation has changed dramatically, due in large measure to the impact of the Model Probation/Parole Classification and Case Management Project sponsored by the National Institute of Corrections during the 1980s (Burke et al. 1990c). The Model Project was designed to

Table 5.2

Selected Conditions of Parole in Effect in Fifty-one Jurisdictions in 1988

Condition of Parole	Number of Jurisdictions	Percent
Obey all federal, state, and local laws	50	98.0
Report to the parole officer as directed and answer all reasonable inquiries by the parole officer	49	96.1
Refrain from possessing a firearm or other dangerous weapon unless granted written permission	47	92.2
Remain within the jurisdiction of the court and notify the parole officer of any change in residence	46	90.2
Permit the parole officer to visit the parolee at home or elsewhere	42	82.4
Obey all rules and regulations of the parole supervision agency	40	78.4
Maintain gainful employment	40	78.4
Abstain from association with persons with criminal records	31	60.8
Pay all court-ordered fines, restitution, or other financial penalties	27	52.9
Meet family responsibilities and support dependents	24	47.1
Undergo medical or psychiatric treatment and/or enter and remain in a specified institution, if so ordered by the court	23	45.1
Pay supervision fees	19	37.3
Attend a prescribed secular course of study or vocational training	9	17.6
Perform community service	7	13.7

help probation and parole agencies respond effectively to escalating caseload growth and dwindling resources. It was also responsive to increasing demands for accountability regarding the effective management of offender supervision.

Drawing on innovative efforts that were coming to fruition in Wisconsin (Baird et al. 1979), the National Institute of Corrections proposed a new and systematic approach to classification and case management. This approach recognized that systems of classification provide a rational decision-making structure to improve case management. Moreover, offenders are not equal in their need for supervision. Different offenders require various uses of agency resources or amounts of officer time. In terms of effective case management, they may and should be classified into different levels of supervision according to priorities established by the field service agency.

Between 1981 and 1986, the National Institute of Corrections awarded thirty-seven grants totaling more than $775,000 to forty jurisdictions. The recipients included eleven probation agencies, four parole field service agencies, and twenty-two agencies with responsibility for both probation and parole supervision (Burke et al. 1990c). According to a recent evaluation of this undertaking, the Model Project exerted a significant impact on the supervision practices of the participating agencies (Burke et al. 1990c). Though the supervision case management model that was disseminated included four basic components, its influence was most notable with respect to the first and best-known component: the classification of offenders based on a structured assessment of risk and needs.[6]

As Clear and Gallagher (1985) observe, most classification systems begin with a formal, instrument-based assessment of risk. A number of risk instruments have been developed recently to identify those probationers and parolees who represent the greatest threat to public safety (Klein and Caggiano 1986; Gottfredson and Tonry 1987; Clear 1988). These assessments place such offenders in a group with a known probability of committing a new crime or violating the conditions of supervision.

A formal needs assessment, on the other hand, provides a standardized means for discerning the problem areas that may have contributed to an offender's being placed on supervision. Those with pronounced needs for assistance and service may very well require a greater investment of officer time and agency resources.

The structured assessment of risk and needs produces separate scores which, in turn, allow probationers and parolees to be assigned to one of several levels of supervision. The intensity of supervision and the frequency of contact between the supervising officer and offender varies according to the actual classification of the case as maximum, medium or minimum or other comparable designations.

The ACA Parole Task Force survey included a series of questions addressing parole field services' classification systems. The respondents were asked whether they used a formal classification system, and if so, to specify the supervision levels and associated contact standards for each level. Additional questions focused on the issue of risk and needs assessments and reassessments of parolees, as well as the timeframes for conducting such assessments. The findings show striking similarity to those reported by Burke et al. 1990c.

According to the survey results, forty-five (or 92 percent of) parole field service agencies use a formal classification system. Of the remaining four respondents (8 percent), two indicated that they were planning to develop such a system in the next twelve months, while one other agency said it was considering such a step. (Two jurisdictions were missing.) These results, illustrated in Figure 5.2, suggest that the concept of classification is a widely accepted component of regular parole supervision.

The vast majority of jurisdictions that have adopted classification systems rely on risk and needs instruments. Of those field service agencies with systems of classification, forty-three (86 percent) use risk instruments for initial classification. (One state was missing.) An initial assessment of a parolee's needs is conducted in thirty-seven states (74 percent), while thirteen (26 percent) reportedly do not rely on such assessments. Another seven states said that they use agency-developed criteria for classification. Only six jurisdictions indicated that they did not use anything at all.

If a state conducted risk and needs assessments at initial classification, it was also likely to conduct instrument-based reassessments of risk and needs at specified intervals. Thus, with one state missing, forty-one jurisdictions (82 percent) indicated they engaged in formal risk reassessments, while thirty-six (72 percent) reported the use of needs reassessments. Both risk and needs reassessment tools place more of an emphasis on the parolee's adjustment after release and thus enable them to reduce their classification level for satisfactory behavior during supervision.[7]

The ACA Parole Task Force survey also asked how much time was normally allowed for initial classification to be completed. Forty-one (80.4 percent) of the respondents stated that initial classification was completed within thirty days, while three (5.9 percent) indicated that they did so within thirty-one to ninety days. Recall that six (13.7 percent) agencies do not have a classification system.

Figure 5.2

Classification in Parole Field Services

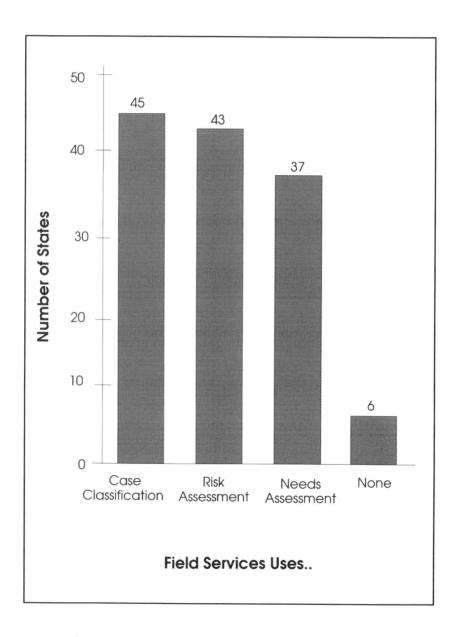

Table 5.3

Contact Standards by Supervision Level for Five Parole Field Service Agencies

MAXIMUM/INTENSIVE SUPERVISION

- One face-to-face contact and one collateral contact monthly.
- Monthly report; one home visit; one face-to-face (in addition to home visit); one employment verification; one special condition.
- Two face-to-face contacts monthly; one collateral contact monthly; one home visit every forty-five days.
- Four face-to-face contacts monthly; one collateral contact monthly; one home call within thirty days of placement on caseload and within two weeks after each reported move; verification of residence every three months; criminal history check after first year of supervision.
- Two face-to-face contacts monthly, one of which must be in the field; two collateral contacts per month.

MEDIUM/MODERATE SUPERVISION

- One face-to-face contact monthly and one collateral contact per quarter.
- One home visit (per quarter); one monthly report; one residence verification; one face-to-face contact; one employment verification; one special condition, if applicable.
- One face-to-face contact and one collateral contact monthly; one home visit every ninety days.
- Two face-to-face contacts monthly with unemployed offenders; one contact if verified full-time employment/training; one collateral contact per month; home call within thirty days of placement on caseload and within two weeks after each reported move; verification of residence every three months and employment/training monthly; criminal history check after first year of supervision.
- One face-to-face contact per month; one collateral contact monthly; one field visit every three months.

MINIMUM SUPERVISION

- One face-to-face semi-annual contact and collateral contact quarterly.
- One home visit, as needed; one monthly report; one face-to-face (per quarter); one employment verification (per quarter).
- One face-to-face contact monthly, unless quarterly reporting.
- One face-to-face contact monthly; verification of residence once every three months.
- Mail-in report monthly; one face-to-face contact every three months; one collateral contact every three months.

Classification reassessments show more variation in the average timeframes. While six agencies (10.9 percent) conduct such reassessments at either two- or three-month intervals, most jurisdictions (N = 31 or 67.4 percent) do so every six months. Nonetheless, one parole field service agency (2.2 percent) reported that classification reassessments occur at nine-month intervals, and another seven agencies (15.2 percent), every twelve months.

If classification systems are tools to enhance case management, they also serve to realize an agency's philosophy of supervision. They do so by distributing offenders into different groups to provide greater (or lesser) monitoring and control and greater (or lesser) service delivery and treatment (Clear and Gallagher 1985). To some extent, these choices are reflected in the number of supervision levels and the associated contact standards for supervision.

The ACA Parole Task Force survey revealed considerable variation in the levels of supervision and the contact standards required by parole field service agencies. Excluding those states without classification systems or for which data were missing (N = 7), eighteen reported using three levels of supervision. Another seventeen indicated that they used four supervision levels, with most of these using an "intensive" or "close" level as the addition. (Those states with separate Intensive Supervision Programs, in contrast to those reporting an intensive level of supervision as part of the classification system, will be discussed.) Finally, seven states classify parolees into five supervision levels, while two others use six levels.

The contact standards for each level of supervision also display wide variation. Among the jurisdictions reporting, notable differences are found in the required number of contacts both within and between classification levels. Table 5.3 provides examples drawn from five jurisdictions illustrating the number of face-to-face or personal contacts that are required on a monthly basis. The standards also include reference to collateral contacts with employers, family members, and others.

The extent to which individual parole officers are able to comply with an agency's supervision standards is dependent, in part, on their average caseloads. Numerous reports have long recommended that supervision caseloads be limited to an average of thirty-five cases or less (e.g., The President's Commission on Law Enforcement and Administration of Justice 1967).[8] Though research suggests that there is no ideal caseload size (Banks et al. 1977; Byrne et al. 1989), it is also evident that where caseloads exceed 75 to 100 parolees it is difficult, if not impossible, to maintain anything but superficial and infrequent contacts.

The ACA Parole Task Force survey asked for the average caseload statewide for adults on parole. Reported averages ranged from twenty-five in one state to 307 in another state, with pronounced variation in between. Five jurisdictions reported average caseloads of fifty or less, while nineteen reported caseloads averaging between fifty-one and seventy-five. In eighteen states, the average caseload ranged from 76 to 100. Finally, four states had average caseloads between 101 and 125, while one state reported an average caseload of 162, and another, 307. These findings are shown in Figure 5.3.

While assignment to a particular classification level influences the quantity of supervision a parolee receives, the quality or content of supervision is shaped, to a large extent, by the presence of case planning and the existence of specialized caseloads. Thirty jurisdictions (61.2 percent) stated they use some form of case planning, while another nineteen (38.8 percent) do not. (Two states were missing.)

Specialized caseloads are reportedly used to supervise certain types of offenders in twenty-five (50 percent) of the states. Such caseloads have been created for sex offenders in fourteen states. Twelve states have established special drug offender caseloads. Another ten jurisdictions have created specialized caseloads for those offenders who suffer from mental disabilities, while five assign "career criminals" to special caseloads. Two states noted that they have specialized caseloads for violent offenders.

In a number of states, classification systems and specialized caseloads are increasingly being supplemented by initiatives that reflect a more general movement toward surveillance and control in community supervision (Clear and O'Leary 1983). These initiatives include the development of intensive supervision programs, the growing use of

Figure 5.3

Parole Field Services: Average Adult Caseloads

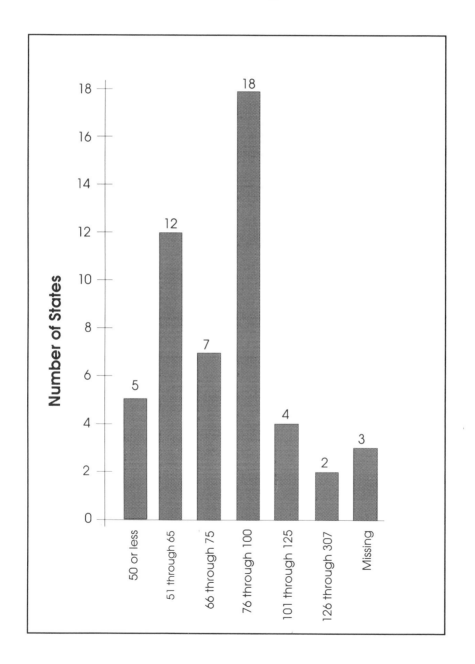

electronic monitoring,[9] and reliance in some states on home confinement (or house arrest).[10] The growth of intensive supervision, however, provides the most visible evidence of an evolving trend.

The Intensive Supervision Movement in Parole

The prison crowding crisis of the 1980s, coupled with heightened concerns over public safety, has been primarily responsible for the birth of a surveillance-oriented style of community corrections that has been referred to as the "new intensive supervision movement" (Clear and Hardyman 1990, 42). In one state after another, intensive supervision programs have emerged "in response to both the *demand* for alternatives to crowded institutions and the *need* for more control over offenders who are supervised in community settings" (Byrne et al. 1989, 2).

A recent survey indicated that forty-five states either had, or were in the process of establishing, intensive supervision programs (Herrick 1988). More than 25,000 offenders were enrolled in such programs that, in turn, were operated mainly under departments of corrections or circuit courts. Given the rapidity of their growth, it is not surprising that the programs display considerable variety in the types of offenders considered suitable for participation and their strategies for case management (Byrne et al. 1989, 11-16). Nonetheless, the one element they share is an aggressive approach to supervision.

This point is not lost on the advocates and administrators of these programs, who often present them as tough and demanding intermediate sanctions between prison and probation. Offenders placed under intensive supervision are held strictly accountable for their actions through the rigorous enforcement of program conditions. In most of these programs, the requirements for supervision include several weekly face-to-face contacts, unannounced home visits, random curfew checks, drug and alcohol monitoring, community service, and restitution.

To date, most research has centered on the intensive supervision movement in probation (Erwin 1987; Pearson 1987; Petersilia 1987; Lurigio 1990). These programs generally function as front-end, intermediate sanctions. Intensive supervision programs are also being used, however, as back-end, early release mechanisms (Byrne et al. 1989, 5). For the past several years, there has been a notable, but less recognized, trend toward the development of intensive supervision programs in parole.

One question on the ACA Parole Task Force survey asked whether the parole field service agency operated a special intensive supervision program for parolees. Twenty-eight jurisdictions (54.9 percent) indicated that they had such a program, while another eleven (21.6 percent) stated that they were considering or planning to implement an intensive supervision program during the next twelve months. The remaining eleven jurisdictions (21.6 percent) stated that they did not have and were not planning to develop such an initiative. (One state was missing.)

Nonetheless, closer examination of the materials provided by the respondents reveals that an intensive supervision program (separate from the formal classification system) is found in only fifteen (29.4 percent) of the reporting jurisdictions. In the remaining thirteen states with such a program, intensive supervision appears to be part of the regular classification system.

As with intensive supervision programs in probation, those in parole display considerable diversity in goals and purposes, the target population, intake procedures, the methods or conditions of supervision, and program capacity or enrollment. With respect to goals, many of these programs are designed to accelerate the release of offenders under highly structured conditions of supervision, thus providing an alternative to continued incarceration without jeopardizing community safety. Many of these same programs are also intended to provide an alternative to reincarceration for technical violations of the rules or misdemeanor convictions.

Though exceptions are to be found, the target populations most often involve offenders who might not otherwise be released upon reaching parole eligibility given their level of risk or need for services. Such offenders may have moderate- to high-risk scores on an objective-based risk instrument, a record of chronic substance abuse, a documented history of mental illness, a complete absence of marketable skills coupled with illiteracy, or a criminal record involving sexual acts.

There are three main avenues of referral to intensive parole supervision programs. In all jurisdictions surveyed, the parole board is responsible for referring appropriate cases. Another source of entry is through the sentencing or circuit court. Finally, parole (and probation) officers may refer cases for consideration, especially where the parolee is facing possible revocation for continued noncompliance with the conditions of supervision.

The following programs illustrate the various goals that are served through intensive supervision at the back end of the corrections system. They also reveal the extent of diversity that exists in terms of the target populations and the methods or intensity of supervision. Though most intensive supervision programs in parole are operated by the field service component under the department of corrections, in some states the paroling authority has administrative responsibility for the program (e.g., Massachusetts, Pennsylvania).

Alaska. An Intensive Supervision/Surveillance Program (ISSP) is administered by Adult Probation and Parole within the Department of Corrections. The program, which began in 1988, is designed to provide close surveillance and supervision to selected felony offenders, either as an alternative to incarceration or in lieu of revocation. Staffing for ISSP consists of intensive supervision teams of two officers with a maximum of twenty-five cases. High-risk offenders (as determined by an objective risk assessment score) are excluded from the program, as are those who have a chronic substance abuse problem, lack motivation to change, or evidence repeated failure in treatment programs. Offenders are placed in ISSP by the Parole Board.

The program requires each offender to pass through four phases of supervision lasting twelve months. During the first and most restrictive phase, which extends for a minimum of ninety days, the standards of supervision include twenty contacts per month, at least twelve of which are face-to-face; four employment verification checks each month or daily verification of employment-seeking for those unemployed; a 10:00 p.m. to 6:00 a.m. curfew, with four random checks for compliance monthly; arrest record checks every ninety days; sixteen hours of community service per month; and participation in treatment programs as required. Offenders who successfully complete ISSP are transferred to a regular parole supervision caseload.

Idaho. An Intensive Supervision Program (ISP) for parolees is operated by the Division of Probation and Parole under the Department of Corrections. The Commission for Pardons and Paroles may impose participation in the program, as can an Intensive Supervision Screening Committee, based on risk and needs assessments. Participants sign an intensive supervision contract and are held strictly accountable for compliance with the conditions.

The program is divided into two phases that together may last up to six months. During Phase I, the Intensive Supervision Team makes seven face-to-face contacts per week, four of which involve home visits. Weekly employment verification checks are conducted, random curfew checks are made four times per week, biweekly checks of arrest records are made, regular drug and alcohol tests are conducted (which the parolee must pay for), travel is restricted, and a minimum of fifty hours of community service must be completed (followed by another thirty hours in Phase II). Upon successful completion of ISP, the parolee will again be given a risk and needs assessment and classified under regular parole supervision according to the score.

New Jersey. The Bureau of Parole under the Department of Corrections operates an Intensive Surveillance/Supervision Program. First implemented in 1986, the program is designed to provide an alternative to incarceration for hard-to-manage or high-needs offenders who would otherwise not be released by the state parole board. Public safety and offender reintegration are emphasized through strict enforcement of program conditions. Recently, the program was expanded to include inmates with established parole dates released to electronically monitored home confinement and parolees facing revocation for technical violations during supervision. ISSP officers supervise caseloads of twenty-five.

The requirements for supervision include a minimum of one positive home visit every two weeks, weekly face-to-face contacts and two collateral contacts, the development of case plans targeting specific behavioral objectives, weekly monitoring of parolee compliance with any treatment that has been ordered, and random testing for alcohol and drug use. If, after six months, the parolee's adjustment has been satisfactory, the case will be transferred to a regular parole supervision caseload.

Pennsylvania. In 1988, the Board of Probation and Parole began a Special Intensive Supervision Drug Program for parolees considered high risk due to a history of drug abuse. The program is located in and targets parolees residing in Philadelphia and Pittsburgh. It is designed to reduce new offense recommitments and meet the parolees' service needs through close monitoring and supervision and enhanced treatment intervention. Offenders may be released to the program after an evaluation and recommendation to the Board of Probation and Parole by a Department of Health service provider.

The program consists of three phases that involve increasingly less restrictive requirements. The first phase, which lasts for at least six months, involves two office contacts per week, four field contacts per month, two weekly collateral contacts (one of which must be with the police), six urine tests per month, an evening curfew, limitations on travel, electronic monitoring on a selective basis, and compliance with special conditions requiring treatment. To move to the next phase, the parolee must be sanction-free or free of program violations for the preceding three months. Upon successful completion of the final phase, the parolee is transferred to a regular supervision caseload.

Virginia. The Division of Adult Community Corrections under the Department of Corrections administers Intensive Supervision Programs for probationers and parolees in several districts across the state. The programs, the first three of which were implemented in 1985, are designed "to provide more custody than regular supervision and greater treatment than incarceration" to "moderate- to high-risk offenders with low to high services needs." While a district screening committee determines participants' acceptability for ISP, there are three main sources of referral: circuit court referrals, parole board referrals, and caseload referrals (as an alternative to incarceration for technical violations and/or misdemeanor convictions). The ISP caseloads average twenty cases.

The program consists of two phases. Phase I lasts a minimum of three months and includes one to five face-to-face contacts weekly, two monthly home contacts with a family member, employment verification one to four times monthly for three months, verification of full-time enrollment in educational or vocational programs one to four times monthly (as a substitute for employment), monthly collateral contacts with treatment/referral agencies, arrest record checks on a weekly basis, and monthly collateral contacts with law enforcement officials. The supervision requirements are relaxed somewhat during the second phase, which extends from three to twelve months. Upon successful completion of Phase II, the screening committee reviews and assigns the case to regular supervision. Continuity of contacts and aftercare is provided for three to six months thereafter through placement in Level I supervision.

Though the movement toward intensive supervision in parole reflects the impact of prison crowding, it also underscores a more general concern with the efficacy of community supervision. In fact, intensive supervision programs in parole (as well as probation) reflect an implicit acknowledgement that in many cases regular supervision may not be sufficient to achieve the goals of public protection or offender control.

The Status of Postrelease Supervision

Although parole boards in some states have experienced serious challenge, if not outright abolition, the vast majority of inmates who are released from prison remain subject to a period of postrelease supervision. Since 1977, more than 80 percent of those offenders released each year have been granted some form of conditional release (BJS 1989a). This category, however, includes both discretionary parole and supervised mandatory release.

As shown in Table 5.4, discretionary parole release has diminished dramatically over the past decade or so. In 1977, nearly 72 percent of all releases from prison resulted from a discretionary decision of the parole board. In that same year, roughly 6 percent were mandatory releases. Just over a decade later, 40.3 percent of those released reflected discretionary parole, while almost 31 percent were the result of supervised mandatory release. What this striking change reveals is that mandatory and discretionary releases are approaching parity in terms of conditional releases more generally.

Inmates who leave prison as supervised mandatory releasees do so when the calendar time they have served plus the accrual of good-time credits equals their maximum sentence. They are not on parole, though they are generally supervised by a parole officer. In contrast to regular parole, mandatory releasees usually remain under supervision only for a period equal to the amount of good time deducted. During this time, they may be subject to revocation by the parole board for noncompliance with the conditions of supervision.

Though parole supervision has been abolished in at least three states (Florida, Maine, and Washington),[11] most jurisdictions recognize that a period of postrelease supervision enables the state to monitor the offender's behavior, as well as to provide assistance in managing the transition back to the community. Though some research suggests that mandatory releasees do not fare as well as those under parole supervision (Breed 1984), the importance of supervision generally was highlighted in a recent study that reached this conclusion:

Table 5.4

Trends in Methods of Release From State Prison 1977-88 (Percent)

Type of Release	1977	1988
Discretionary Parole	71.9	40.3
Supervised Mandatory Release	5.9	30.6
Probation	3.6	4.1
Other	1.0	6.0
Total Conditional Releases	82.4	81.0
Unconditional Releases	17.6	19.0
Total All Releases	100.0	100.0

Source: BJS 1989a

|although| there is no firm evidence concerning the impact of incarceration, |we| found evidence indicating that supervision after release from confinement is a critical component of corrections efforts. Offenders released without supervision after serving their full sentences tended to have much higher rates of recidivism than offenders placed under any form of supervision (Genevie et al. 1986, 53).

Nonetheless, research on the efficacy of parole supervision is equivocal (Clear and Cole 1990). In part, this is due to the absence of a commonly accepted definition of recidivism (Maltz 1984; Hawkins and Alpert 1989, 198-299; Champion 1990, 289). It also reflects, however, state-by-state variations in revocation policy and practice.

Regardless of the verdict on the efficacy of parole supervision in recidivism prevention, it seems unlikely that supervision will diminish in importance over the next decade. In fact, given the seeming success and popularity of intensive parole supervision, it is likely that traditional parole supervision will continue to grow, increasingly adopting some of the former's programmatic features.

Notes

1. The states reporting such increases during 1988 included Alabama, Alaska, California, Indiana, Kansas, Louisiana, Maryland, Michigan, Minnesota, Missouri, New Jersey, North Carolina, North Dakota, Oregon, Pennsylvania, South Dakota, and Texas.
2. The states showing a decline include Arkansas, Connecticut, Delaware, Florida, Idaho, Iowa, Mississippi, Nebraska, New Mexico, Oklahoma, Vermont, West Virginia, and Wyoming.
3. As was pointed out in Chapter 2, since the completion of the survey, Texas transferred parole supervision from the Board of Pardons and Paroles to the Department of Corrections under a general reorganization of criminal justice. Thus, twelve parole boards currently have jurisdiction over parole field services.
4. Travis and Latessa sent letters to all paroling authorities in the United States requesting copies of the conditions of parole. They found that in 1982 a total of 139 different standard conditions of parole were reported across all jurisdictions, with a mean of 16.48 standard conditions and a median of 14.83. States ranged from a low of six to a high of twenty-three conditions (1984, 593).
5. According to a recent report, forty-eight states authorize the collection of correctional fees to offset the costs of supervision, service, or treatment (Parent 1990).
6. The other components include the adoption of client management classification to assist in case planning and the setting of behavioral

objectives, the use of a management information system as an enhancement to planning and evaluation, and the implementation of a workload deployment as opposed to a caseload system to equalize the distribution of work within the agency (Burke et al. 1990c).

7. Burke et al. found that the most commonly used risk and needs instruments were those associated with the Wisconsin model, even though they were often modified in practice (1990c).

8. Recall that one of the four components of the Model Project was a workload versus a caseload approach to staffing and supervision. With respect to this issue, 81 percent of the jurisdictions participating in the project reported moderate to full use of a workload deployment system (Burke et al. 1990c).

9. According to the ACA Parole Task Force survey, fifteen jurisdictions (29.4 percent) supervise parolees with the assistance of electronic monitoring. However, eight states indicated they were planning to implement an electronic monitoring program during the next twelve months, while another nine jurisdictions stated the issue was under consideration.

10. Home or residential confinement is only slightly less common than electronic monitoring. Twelve jurisdictions (23.5 percent) reported they use home confinement, while thirty-nine (76.5 percent) do not. Of the latter, thirteen indicated they were either planning to implement such a program or the issue was under consideration.

11. Parole supervision has been partially restored in Washington.

Chapter 6

The Revocation of Parole

The revocation of parole—the decision to return a parolee to prison for violating the terms of conditional release—is one of the major responsibilities of every paroling authority across the country. In the 1970s, debates over parole revocation generally centered around the provision of constitutional due process to ensure fair and impartial hearings. During the ensuing decade, very little attention was devoted to the topic. More recent developments, however, suggest that parole revocation is becoming an issue of growing importance to the criminal justice and corrections system.

The renewed focus on parole revocation is evident within the broader debate over the problem of prison crowding (as the experience of California suggests, where a surprisingly large number of admissions to prison are due to the return of parole violators). In addition, the importance of parole revocation is evident in that several jurisdictions have adopted explicit policies to structure or guide parole revocation decision making (e.g., South Carolina, Tennessee). To varying degrees, these jurisdictions have begun to rely on an array of intermediate sanctions for handling parole violations—options that lie between parole and reimprisonment. Finally, concerns have been expressed during the past few years over unacceptably high rates of parolee recidivism. Though the interpretation of such rates (e.g., is parole revocation a success or failure of "the system"?) has yet to be adequately addressed, how this matter is resolved carries enormous implications for the entire parole process.

Prison Crowding and Parole Revocation

The most pressing factor driving the concern about revocation practices today is the tremendous growth in the nation's prisons during the past decade. As prison populations continue to spiral upward, administrators have begun to examine every possible avenue for relief.

Prison admissions have been increasing at the front end of the system. Runaway growth in prison populations continues to burden state correctional systems. This growth appears unlikely to abate in the foreseeable future (Blumstein 1989). Although the population dynamic is a complex one, changes in sentencing practices at the front end of the system have contributed significantly to this growth.

What is less understood is the degree to which parole revocation is also fueling prison population growth. Admissions have been increasing noticeably at the back end of the system as offenders are reincarcerated for violations of parole conditions. The National Council on Crime and Delinquency reports that between 1977 and 1987, the number of admissions to prison nationwide resulting from parole violations increased by 284 percent (Austin 1989).[1] This far exceeds the rate of growth (97 percent) in court admissions for the same period. With respect to California, this report notes that

> the criminal justice system is spending more resources on recycling prisoners released to parole than on new offenders being sentenced directly by the courts. In 1987, there were 62,729 prison admissions in California. Of this number, 31,581 (or 50.3 percent) were parole violators (Austin 1989).

Though the situation may not be as dramatic in other states, the trend is clear. As the correctional system absorbs more offenders, each point at which discretion is exercised can have a significant impact on the other components of the system. It is becoming apparent that this includes even the relatively unexplored decision regarding revocation. Thus, as one possible avenue to ease the crowding crisis, parole boards are coming under increasing pressure to examine their handling of violation behavior.[2]

A second factor in the emphasis on parole revocation: the discretionary role of paroling authorities in initial release decision making is diminishing. As a proportion of all decisions made by paroling authorities, revocation decisions are growing in significance. Thus, parole boards are beginning to focus an increasing amount of attention on them.

During the past fifteen years, the discretion exercised by paroling authorities with respect to release decision making has decreased. Although postrelease supervision has been widely retained, discretionary parole release has been abolished in some jurisdictions and narrowed in others through the adoption of greater determinacy in sentencing structures. At the same time, the adult offender population under parole supervision has grown dramatically because of the overall growth in correctional populations. This population increased by 65 percent between 1983 and 1988, making it the fastest-growing element of the entire correctional system.

Not only is the parole population growing, but offenders are joining this population increasingly as a result of mandatory release provisions, rather than through discretionary parole board decisions. Regardless of the method of release, for offenders under supervision, the paroling authority is ultimately responsible for formal revocation resulting from violations of the conditions of their release.

These changes suggest that discretionary parole release has diminished at the same time that the role of revocation decision making has grown in importance. Moreover, within the context of prison crowding, the impact of paroling authorities' decisions has increased relative to revocation and the reincarceration of parole violators.

Nonetheless, how parole revocation decisions are made and what procedures are followed takes place within a well-defined constitutional framework. It is notable that until prison crowding became a critical issue, it was only within a legal context that parole revocation was usually discussed. Some of the legal and constitutional issues are considered in the next section.

The Supreme Court, Due Process, and Current Revocation Practices

Inmates do not have an inherent constitutional right to be released on parole before the expiration of their lawful sentence. Nor, according to *Greenholtz v. Inmates of the Nebraska Penal and Correctional Complex*, 442 U.S. 1 (1979), do they enjoy constitutional protections in the determination by the parole board to grant or deny parole.[3] Once inmates are released and placed under supervision, however, their parole may only be revoked by using procedures that accord them adequate due process.

The procedural protections surrounding parole revocation have not always been present. Through the 1960s, parolees had virtually no legal standing to question the actions of a parole officer who pursued revocation or those of a parole board that returned them to prison, whether for new criminal conduct or for technical parole violations. The situation, however, has changed dramatically over the past twenty years, largely as a result of the landmark Supreme Court decision handed down in 1972, *Morrissey v. Brewer*, 408 U.S. 471.

Rooted in the "prisoners' rights movement" in correctional law (Jacobs 1983; Thomas 1988),[4] the decision in *Morrissey* determined for the first time what procedural guarantees were applicable in parole revocation proceedings. In its ruling, the Supreme Court found that even though the liberty interest of parolees is conditional, it enables them to do most things open to persons who enjoy the benefits of unqualified liberty. Thus, they may be gainfully employed, carry on normal family relations, and form enduring attachments with friends and others. In light of these considerations, the Court determined that the revocation of parole would inflict a "grievous loss" upon the parolee.

Having found a protected liberty interest, the Court turned next to the issue of what due process safeguards were required. It established that the revocation of parole is not a stage of a criminal prosecution and thus does not represent an adversarial proceeding.

Nonetheless, neither the state nor society at large has a justifiable interest in summary action in the absence of due process, because "fair treatment in parole revocations will enhance the chance of rehabilitation by avoiding reactions to arbitrariness" (*Morrissey* 1972, 485). In coming to this conclusion, the Court ruled that the revocation of parole must incorporate two distinct stages.

The first stage requires that a reasonably prompt preliminary hearing be held by an impartial decision maker to assess if there is probable cause to believe that the parolee has violated the conditions of parole. If probable cause is found, in a second stage, a full revocation hearing must be convened. At this hearing, the parolee must be accorded the following due process protections:

- a written notice of the alleged violation
- disclosure of the evidence of the violation
- an opportunity to be heard in person and to present evidence as well as witnesses

- an opportunity to confront and cross-examine adverse witnesses (unless good cause can be shown for not allowing this confrontation)
- judgment by a detached and neutral hearing body (such as the parole board or hearing officers)
- a written statement of the reasons for revoking parole, as well as of the evidence used in arriving at the decision

Though *Morrissey* did not extend the right to representation during a parole revocation hearing, the issue was addressed one year later in *Gagnon v. Scarpelli*, 411 U.S. 778 (1973). *Gagnon* reviewed what due process should be provided during probation revocation.[5] In its ruling, the Court considered whether legal counsel should be extended to indigent probationers or parolees facing possible revocation. Balancing the various interests at stake, the Court ruled that:

> the decision as to the need for counsel must be made on a case-by-case basis in the exercise of the sound discretion by the state authority charged with responsibility for administering the probation and parole system (*Gagnon* 1973, 790).

In a recent review of liabilities of parole personnel for a variety of actions, including revocation, del Carmen and Louis note that:

> *Morrissey* is the only major case decided thus far by the Supreme Court on parole revocation. It is, in fact, one of the few cases ever decided by the Court that specifies the constitutional rights of parolees (1988, 42).

While *Morrissey* stands as the constitutional benchmark against which revocation practices are currently measured, there have since been numerous legal challenges to revocation decisions (Merritt 1980). These challenges have targeted the timeliness of the hearing, the composition of the hearing body, the need for a probable cause and final revocation hearing, and parole board liability with respect to revocation (or failure to revoke). Although most have been unsuccessful, the following decisions illustrate how these issues have been resolved since *Morrissey*.

Although *Morrissey* requires a timely hearing, the Court eased this requirement to some extent in *Moody v. Dagett*, 429 U.S. 789 (1976). *Moody* involved a parolee who was convicted of a new crime after his release by the U.S. Parole Commission. The plaintiff/parolee was sentenced to a term of imprisonment. A revocation warrant that had been issued before his conviction was not rescinded. The Court determined that a revocation hearing was not required until the intervening sentence had been served.[6]

In *Blackwell v. Commonwealth of Pennsylvania*, 516 A.2d 856 (Pa. Cmwlth. 1986), a parolee contended that he had not been afforded a "neutral and detached" revocation hearing (as required by *Morrissey*) because at the time his parole was revoked, the parole officer who had written the original violation report was a member of the parole board making the decision. The court held that the offender had indeed been denied the impartial hearing required. This case illustrates how a parolee's right to a detached or neutral hearing body may be violated.

Another challenge to revocation has been the claim that a preliminary revocation hearing is required in all cases to determine if probable cause exists to proceed to the final hearing. In a number of states, parolees may waive their probable cause hearing. There is, however, some ambiguity concerning the need to hold a final revocation hearing if the parolee has been convicted of a new crime.

In a decision handed down in 1977, the Ninth Circuit Court of Appeals ruled in *U.S. v. Lustig*, 555 F.2d 751 (1977) that parole may be revoked without a final hearing, as a criminal conviction is considered sufficient to establish a violation of parole. In contrast, a more recent case involving the Court of Criminal Appeals in Texas, *Mathis Carl Williams v. State* (1987), resulted in the overturning of a revocation order because there was no final hearing, even though the parolee had been convicted of a felony (del Carmen and Louis 1988, 47). At the time, the Texas Board of Pardons and Paroles' rules allowed for revocation without a hearing if the parolee was convicted of a felony offense and sentenced to prison. The Supreme Court refused to hear the case on appeal.

In still other instances, injured third parties have filed suit against paroling authorities alleging that injuries caused by a parolee would not have happened had the individual's parole been revoked and had he/she been reincarcerated. The rulings in these cases have generally affirmed that when making parole revocation decisions, members of the parole board are acting in a "judge-like" capacity and thus enjoy absolute immunity (del Carmen and Louis 1988, 45-46).

The central constitutional concern with respect to revocation proceedings involves the provision of due process to parolees to ensure a fair and impartial hearing. Although subsequent cases have addressed various issues that are implicated in such proceedings, the ruling in *Morrissey* remains the central Supreme Court decision on what process is due within the context of hearings that may result in the revocation of parole.

Although the requisites of procedural due process are relatively well established, very few studies have examined the extent to which these requirements are adhered to in practice. To address this topic, a series of questions on the ACA Parole Task Force survey asked the respondents for information on their compliance with the *Morrissey* guarantees.

According to the survey, every paroling authority has established formal procedures governing the revocation process. Moreover, these procedures appear to be firmly grounded in state statutes or administrative rules. Forty-nine jurisdictions (96 percent) reported that their revocation procedures are founded in statutes, administrative rules, or both. One state's procedures are established by case law, and another's, by case law and administrative rules.

Several questions on the survey focused on determining what procedural protections were provided to parolees during the preliminary or probable cause hearing and during the second stage or final revocation hearing. The results indicate that forty-six (90.2 percent) of the jurisdictions conduct a preliminary hearing to determine probable cause. Each of the fifty-one jurisdictions (100 percent) provide a final or second stage revocation hearing. Parole officers (not involved in the case), field

Table 6.1

Procedural Due Process Routinely Provided at Parole Revocation Hearings

Due Process Protection	Preliminary Hearing		Final Hearing	
	#	%	#	%
Written Notice of Alleged Violation	45	88.2	51	100.0
Disclosure of Evidence of Violations	42	82.4	51	100.0
Opportunity to Confront & Cross-examine Adverse Witnesses	44	86.3	47	92.2
Representation by Counsel	31	60.8	40	78.4
Opportunity to be Heard in Person & to Present Evidence & Witnesses	43	84.3	51	100.0
Written Statement of Reasons for the Decision	45	88.2	48	94.1

service supervisors, and hearing officers (or their equivalent) generally conduct preliminary hearings. Hearing officers and board members usually conduct the final revocation hearing.

Table 6.1 presents the responses of jurisdictions with respect to which due process protections are routinely accorded parolees during the preliminary and final revocation hearings.

Forty-five jurisdictions conduct preliminary hearings. Nearly all accord parolees the due process to which they are entitled. The provision of due process is even more substantial at the final hearing. Every paroling authority stated that it provides parolees with written notice of the alleged violation, disclosure of the evidence against them, and the opportunity to be heard in person and to present evidence and witnesses. Compliance with the remaining due process safeguards is also very high, with the possible exception of representation by counsel. Forty states (78.4 percent) responded that they offered the assistance of counsel to parolees.[8]

The opportunity to appeal a revocation decision is not a *Morrissey* guarantee. If parole is revoked, of fifty jurisdictions for which information was available, the ACA Parole Task Force survey indicates that parolees are entitled to appeal the decision in only twenty-four jurisdictions (48 percent). They are not given an opportunity to appeal in twenty-six states (52 percent).

One of the survey questions asked for an estimate of the timeframe between the initiation and completion of a revocation action. According to the forty-seven jurisdictions responding, the average amount of time between the start and finish of revocation ranges from ten days in one jurisdiction to more than sixty days in eleven states. Five of those eleven states reported that they averaged more than ninety days. While Table 6.2 illustrates the extent of variation, it also shows that thirty-six (76.4 percent) of the jurisdictions reporting complete the revocation process within two months.

The results of the ACA Parole Task Force survey suggest that most paroling authorities have in place a fully developed set of revocation procedures that comply with the requirements of due process. Firmly institutionalized procedural machinery exists to establish probable cause that a violation has occurred, as well as to reach a subsequent determination of guilt or innocence.

The emphasis on procedural fairness has served to focus attention almost exclusively on the fact-finding aspect of the revocation process. The issue of what disposition to impose has evoked little, if any, attention. As will be explained, this reflects the fact that most parole boards have not developed formal policy to guide the eventual disposition. It also reflects a narrow definition of the term *revocation*. In corrections, revocation is often understood to mean that the parole board either finds the parolee not guilty of the alleged violation and restores the offender's parole status, or it revokes parole and returns the offender to prison. The concept of revocation is thus reduced to a dichotomous "in/out" decision. Paroling authorities, however, typically have a wide range of options at their disposal after a formal revocation hearing.

Clearly, revoking parole and returning the parolee to prison represents the ultimate sanction a parole board can impose for violations of the conditions of supervision. Yet even if parole is revoked, the parolee may remain in the community under supervision. The ACA Parole Task Force survey provided paroling authorities with a list of nine possible outcomes following parole revocation and asked them to check as many as applied to them. Table 6.3 summarizes the findings.

Table 6.3 reveals, not surprisingly, that in forty-seven states (92.2 percent), if parole is revoked, the parolee may be returned to custody to serve the duration of the original sentence. In thirty-eight jurisdictions (74.5 percent), parole boards may choose to restore the offender's parole status or modify the conditions of supervision. Parolees who receive an out-of-state sentence may be required to serve that sentence concurrently or consecutively to their term of revocation in twenty-two jurisdictions (43.1 percent). In twenty-one jurisdictions (41.2 percent), the parolee may be kept on parole but the term may be extended. With less frequency, the revocation of parole may result in an extended term (N = 18) or confinement to serve a new term (N = 16).

Although a variety of dispositions or outcomes are possible whenever parole is revoked, the issue of what constitutes the most

Table 6.2

Average Time Between the Start and Finish of the Revocation Process

Jurisdictions Reporting:	Number	Percent
Less than 45 days	17	36.2
45 to 60 days	19	40.2
More than 60 days	11	23.6
Total reporting	47	100.0

appropriate sanction to impose has been largely overlooked by the courts and paroling authorities. As has been indicated, the courts' concern with procedural fairness has served to focus attention almost exclusively on the fact-finding aspect of the revocation process. Once a violation of parole is sustained, the decision concerning what disposition to impose is often unstructured. It is rarely addressed as a matter of agency policy.

The concentration on due process, though essential if parolees are to receive fair and impartial hearings, has thus served to deflect concern from an equally important aspect of the revocation process: the disposition. As prison populations continue to spiral and parole violation admissions increase at a rate faster than court admissions, some states are beginning to recognize that a more structured approach to revocation is necessary. This approach, which must incorporate a range of appropriate responses or intermediate sanctions, is essential to the effective management of limited correctional resources.

Table 6.3

Possible Outcomes Following the Revocation of Parole

Outcome of Parole Revocation	Number of Jurisdictions	Percent
Incarceration for Original Term	47	92.2
Restore to Parole Status—No Change	38	74.5
Restore to Parole Status—Modify Conditions	38	74.5
Serve Out-of-state Sentence Concurrently to New Sentence	22	43.1
Serve Out-of-state Sentence Consecutively to New Sentence	22	43.1
Restore to Parole Status—Extend Term	21	41.2
Incarceration for Extended Term	18	35.3
Discharge From Parole	17	33.3
Incarceration for New Term	16	31.4

Structured Decision Making, Intermediate Sanctions, and Revocation

In every jurisdiction across the country, if a parole violation is upheld—whether for new criminal convictions or technical violations—the parole board is authorized to revoke parole. Though prison crowding and court-ordered prison population caps constrain the parole board's ability to return parole violators to custody in some states; in others, most individuals found guilty of a parole violation are normally reimprisoned, regardless of the nature of the violation. In a number of states, there is a standard length of time until the next hearing and thus, until the first possibility of rerelease. In other jurisdictions, the decision about the length of reincarceration is largely discretionary and is guided only by the full term of the sentence.

At present the parole board's response to rules violations in most jurisdictions is completely unstructured. Moreover, substantial discretion to act exists at numerous points in the revocation process before the case even reaches the parole board:

- the discretion of the officer in initiating a violation report
- the discretion of a supervisor in "staffing" such a report
- the discretion of a hearing officer in disposing of a case at a preliminary hearing
- the discretion of the board or other decision maker regarding the final disposition

As this suggests, the authority that parole boards have with respect to revocation is shared with the parole field service staff: mainly, parole officers and their supervisors. The decision to write a violation report, issue or seek permission to issue a warrant, take an offender into custody, and initiate formal revocation action is a significant one.

In many states, the circumstances under which a violation report should be issued and a warrant pursued are often loosely defined, by both the field service agency and the parole board itself. Such language as "violation in a significant respect" is often the only formal guidance a parole officer has in determining when and how to exercise the power to violate. As earlier studies have found, inconsistent and uneven responses to parole violations are often the result (e.g., Stanley 1976; McCleary 1978).

The decision to revoke parole rests ultimately with the paroling authority. The responsibility for developing appropriate policy regarding responses to revocation short of reincarceration rests primarily with the parole board. This responsibility may be shared with the parole field service agency, especially where it is independent of the board. As seen in California, the absence of formal policy governing the use of appropriate intermediate sanctions for responding to parole violators may carry significant consequences in terms of exacerbating already serious prison crowding.

In response to these concerns, several parole boards have begun to develop explicit policy to structure or guide revocation decision making.[9] Through technical assistance from the National Institute of Corrections, paroling authorities in the District of Columbia, Massachusetts, New York, South Carolina, and Tennessee have implemented or are considering the adoption of formal policy to govern responses to parolee violations of the rules (Burke et al. 1990a). Revocation is only one—albeit the most serious—of a number of possible responses to violation behavior.

The types of options that are most often considered are viewed as cost-effective alternatives to incarceration, as well as more appropriate responses to the behavior underlying the decision to initiate revocation.[10] In fact, they represent intermediate sanctions lying between the continuation of regular parole supervision and reimprisonment (Morris and Tonry 1990). These sanctions may include changing the level of supervision and thus requiring more frequent reporting; increasing the intensity of urine monitoring, electronic monitoring, or home confinement; and placement in a residential program or halfway correctional facility.

In 1989, the South Carolina Department of Probation, Parole, and Pardon Services and the Parole Board piloted a set of revocation guidelines prescribing specific responses for specific types of violations. The policy that was adopted separates violation behavior into categories and defines the range of responses appropriate to the various violations that are possible. The policy also indicates what responses may be taken at each level of the paroling authority: parole officer, parole supervisor, hearing officer, and the board.

It is apparent that the range of responses to parole violations implicates policy issues beyond the simple decision to revoke parole and return the offender to prison. Through their linkage with field supervision agencies, paroling authorities are in a position to continually reevaluate whether an offender should remain in the community. They may impose various intermediate sanctions that are both cost-effective and more responsive to the nature of the parole violation and the needs of the parolee. It is within this framework that

> parole can be seen as part of a larger picture of postrelease
> discretion that governs the movement of offenders among
> various population groups—prison, levels of supervision,
> specific programming, intensive supervision, residential
> placements, and back into prison (Burke et al. 1990a, 28).

The trend toward structured parole revocation decision making and greater reliance on intermediate sanctions brings to the fore the importance of defining parolee "success" and "failure." It also raises the question of the effectiveness of parole supervision in relation to the utilitarian concern with crime control.

Parolee Recidivism, Violations of Parole, and Crime Control

An examination of revocation as an integral component of the parole process leads invariably to the question of whether the act of revoking parole should be interpreted as a success or a failure for the offender or for the parole system.

On the one hand, the authority to revoke gives parole officers the leverage they need to intervene and prevent the very behavior communities fear: violent, predatory crime. On the other hand, such a "successful" response on the part of system is often regarded as a "failure" regardless of the type of behavior that resulted in official action.

The confusion over how to interpret parole revocation is compounded by the tendency to treat the failure rates of parolees as synonymous with parolee recidivism. In recent years, a number of studies have been published highlighting the apparent extent of parolee (and probationer) recidivism (BJS 1984, 1985, 1987b, 1987c, 1989b; Petersilia et al. 1985; Klein and Caggiano 1986; Lunden 1986, 1987b).[11] The findings from these reports seem to confirm unacceptable levels of parolee recidivism. The conclusion to be drawn is that convicted felons under community supervision are clearly high risk and recidivism prone. A closer look at some of these studies suggests that the "facts" do not speak for themselves; the frequency and meaning of parolee recidivism is not self-evident.

In one of its earliest reports, the Bureau of Justice Statistics (1984) examined the recidivism rates of parolees released from fourteen states during a three-year follow-up period. It found that the highest risk of recidivism (defined as return to custody) occurred during the first twelve months. Specifically, the results indicated that 15 percent of the inmates released were returned to prison within the first year, 26 percent within two years, and just under 32 percent within three years.

In a subsequent study assessing the Recidivism of Young Parolees (BJS 1987b), the authors found that 69 percent of those released from prison were rearrested for a new offense, 53 percent were convicted, and 49 percent were returned to prison. The study was based on a sample of 3,995 parolees drawn from a larger pool of 11,347 persons who were released from prison in twenty-two states in 1978. The parolees were between the ages of seventeen and twenty-two. Of the failures that occurred during a six-year period, however, the report notes that only an estimated 37 percent of the parolees were actually rearrested while still on parole. For the remainder, supervision had ended.

Similarly, a 1986 Rand study found that within a cohort of 1,023 inmates released from prison in California, Michigan, and Texas, 63 percent were rearrested within thirty-six months of their release, often for serious crimes; of these, 46 percent were reconvicted, and 41 percent were returned to custody (Klein and Caggiano 1986). Nonetheless, a subsequent reanalysis of this study determined that among all three states, only one-quarter, or 24.5 percent of the total sample, were incarcerated for public safety crimes, including homicide, rape, kidnapping, assault, robbery, burglary, and attempts to commit these crimes (Fischer 1986).[12]

Finally, two studies were conducted by Massachusetts Parole Board staff examining recidivism among parolees in that state (Lunden 1986, 1987b). Using a twelve-month follow-up period, the most recent of these studies found a combined recidivism rate of 36 percent, drawing on a sample of 241 state and county parolees released in 1985 (Lunden 1987b, 3).[13]

The studies cited defined parolee recidivism as a return to prison mainly for behavior resulting in a new arrest and/or conviction. Several, however, included technical violations of parole as well. This serves to highlight the well-known but unresolved issue of how to measure and whether to include technical parole violations in determining the level of recidivism. While some parolees who are returned to custody for technical violations have, in fact, committed new crimes, many are revoked for failure to comply with the conditions of supervision.

The 1984 BJS study cited earlier found that "technical violations can compose as many as half or more of the total number of recidivists in a releasee cohort" (1984, 3). A more recent survey supports this statement. Drawing on the responses from forty-six states, this study reported that there were 365,823 persons on parole in 1987. Of these, 89,000 were discharged; 78,000 were revoked. Roughly 21 percent of those on parole in the responding jurisdictions were revoked (Herrick 1989). Of the latter, 42 percent were revoked for committing a new crime, while 55 percent were revoked for violating the conditions of parole.

The survey listed the most frequent reasons why parole was revoked, excluding new criminal involvement. The reasons that were most often cited included the failure to participate in a stipulated treatment program, leaving an assigned area without permission, failure to report to a parole officer, alcohol or drug abuse, and the parolee's failure to secure or hold employment.

In contrast, Lunden's (1987b) research in Massachusetts revealed that only 13 percent of the parolees were returned to prison for technical parole violations; 79 percent of the state and 87 percent of the county parolees were returned for a new arrest. Eight percent of the state parolees absconded and were counted as a failure.

The studies discussed here suggest that there is significant variation in the frequency and type of behavior included under the label *recidivism*, in the types of offenders sampled, and in the length of the follow-up period. They also demonstrate that the revocation of parole is not synonymous with parolee recidivism.

While there is some overlap, the former includes a large percentage of noncriminal violations of the conditions of parole. Moreover, as other research has shown, the decision to initiate proceedings against parolees for technical infractions of the rules often reflects the revocation policy of the field service agency, as well as parole officer discretion (McCleary 1978; Maltz 1984; Clear and Cole 1990).

In terms of the goal of crime control and public policy, the findings illustrate the need to clearly define what can be reasonably expected of a system of parole release and supervision. If the effectiveness of parole is measured by reference to an arrest or return to custody for those crimes involving violent or predatory behavior (i.e., public safety crimes), then a 24.5 percent parolee recidivism rate is unacceptably high (Fischer 1986). So also is a 36 percent return rate for new arrests within the first year of release (Lunden 1987b).

What might constitute an acceptable level of parolee recidivism or rate of parole revocation is less easy to define. Herrick's survey (1989) shows that although 21 percent of those under parole supervision in 1987 were revoked, the majority of cases involved technical violations of parole. The findings of this survey parallel those of an earlier study conducted, again, by the Bureau of Justice Statistics (1987c). The BJS study reviewed the records of 159,247 offenders who were released in thirty-three states in 1984. Of this group, 21.2 percent were returned to prison or jail with a new sentence, for technical violations, or to await a parole revocation hearing. The remaining 75.6 percent completed their term successfully.

Though some studies point to rather high rates of parolee recidivism, these findings suggest that nearly three-quarters of those on parole complete their term without incident. With respect to crime control, the system of parole may be held accountable for specific deterrence, that is, for reducing the amount of subsequent criminal behavior among those who fall under its jurisdiction. As a matter of public policy, however, what constitutes a tolerable level of revocation will depend far more on community norms, the nature or amount of crime in a given jurisdiction, shifts in public opinion, and changing political expectations of crime and punishment.

What is perhaps most salient about the general discussion of the failure of parole is the lack of standard definitions of what constitutes failure. Until such definitions are widely accepted, it will be difficult to ascertain accurately the comparative efficiency of parole supervision versus nonparole release or to compare the effects of varying levels of supervision within parole.

Even if acceptable and operational definitions of individual failure were agreed upon and implemented, additional information would be needed about parole supervision enforcement to determine, for example, if a jurisdiction has a low failure rate due to parolee success, or parole officer failure to detect or report failure.

Parole revocation will be hotly debated in the 1990s. Prison crowding, the rising rates of people on parole and of revocations to prison, as well as the development of alternatives to prison for parole failures, all point to its growing importance within the criminal justice system. As that system grapples with even larger issues, such as what constitutes appropriate punishment, and are there alternatives to prison that will prove effective, parole revocation will be a substantial component of that debate.

Notes

1. According to Byrne et al. (1989, table 2), the number of new admissions returned as parole violators increased by 33.8 percent between 1979 and 1983.
2. The importance of this issue has been recognized at the federal level. In early 1990, the National Institute of Corrections funded a program of technical assistance for paroling authorities in the area of parole violations and revocation. A total of $180,000 was allocated to support a limited number of parole boards interested in developing a range of intermediate sanctions and alternative policy responses to violation behavior. Though fifteen parole boards applied for assistance, five were eventually selected to participate in the eighteen-month project.
3. *Greenholtz* drew a distinction between the liberty interest at stake in a parole revocation proceeding and the desired liberty of an inmate who, though eligible, has yet to be released on parole. However, it also established that if the statute governing parole creates an expectation of release unless certain conditions are present, due process protections must be afforded the inmate during the hearing. This decision was again affirmed in *Montana Board of Pardons v. Allen*, 41 CrL 32581 (1987).
4. *Morrissey* represents one of the more notable decisions in a series of Supreme Court rulings establishing that the reach of the Constitution

extends across the prison walls. The increased willingness of the courts to intervene in prison administration represents a decisive turning point in the history of corrections. For an incisive account of this topic, see Thomas (1988).

5. According to the Court's ruling in *Gagnon*, the revocation of probation, like parole, represents a grievous loss, and thus a probationer is entitled to a preliminary and final revocation hearing, under the conditions specified in *Morrissey* (1972, 782).

6. Del Carmen (1988) notes that state courts have decided the issue of what constitutes a "timely" hearing in different ways. Some states have established time limitations governing the hearing process once a parolee is returned to custody. Where state courts have reviewed these timeframes, in some jurisdictions they have been found to be discretionary; in others, mandatory.

7. In one such case, *Nelson v. Balazic*, 802 F.2d 1077 (8th Cir. 1986), the plaintiff charged that injuries caused by a parolee would not have occurred had the parolee been revoked and returned to custody for earlier violations of his parole. While these violations were pending, the parolee had kidnapped, raped, and sodomized three women. The federal district court dismissed the case after concluding that the parole board and parole officer's actions fell within the bounds of their immunity. The Eighth Circuit Court of Appeals affirmed the decision of the lower court.

8. The survey did not ask if counsel was provided to indigent parolees who requested it. Though some states do, in fact, guarantee counsel to assist indigent parolees who may be subject to revocation (e.g., New Jersey), the survey did not query how many actually do so.

9. Initial work in this area focused on "revocation guidelines" following the U.S. Parole Commission's matrix model. A matrix approach seeks to distill all aspects of the parole decision into a single format that weighs such factors as desert, risk, time served, and aggravating/mitigating circumstances. The current trend is toward the development of a "sequential" policy model, which explains the different components and options that form the basis for the revocation decision (Burke et al. 1990a, v).

10. Markley (1989) reports that prison crowding was the driving force behind the creation of Texas' Intensive Supervision Parole program in 1987. He notes that the "initial objective of the program was to reduce revocation of releases by providing more effective methods of supervision...[as] the revoking of any release for anything less than a new felony conviction was virtually unheard of" (1989, 53).

11. As is evident, most research during the past decade has been conducted by the Bureau of Justice Statistics within the National Institute of Justice and by the Rand Corporation. With few exceptions (e.g., Maltz 1984), the concept of recidivism has received very little attention from criminologists during the past fifteen years. *Criminology*, the official publication of the American Society of Criminology, has

included only three articles explicitly addressing the topic in the past five years.

12. The author of this review played a central role in the development of the Iowa Model, which was criticized in the Rand report for its inability to predict parolee recidivism.

13. The recidivism rate from the earlier study was virtually identical at 36 percent, though the period of follow-up ranged from sixteen to twenty months (Lunden 1986).

Chapter 7

Canada: A National Parole System

This chapter describes the parole system in Canada to provide a comparative context for understanding parole in the United States. There are several features of the Canadian system that distinguish it from parole in the fifty states.

One, unlike the states where parole is administered by state-level jurisdictions, parole in Canada is best described as organized at the national level, with offenders under federal jurisdiction if sentenced to two years or more. Two, although prisoners' rights are well recognized in the United States, they seem to enjoy an even higher priority in Canada. Three, Canada, unlike some states, has resisted the temptation to abolish parole and has attempted to integrate the various goals associated with both parole release and supervision. Four, parole supervision in Canada is characterized by relatively low rates of recidivism.

The British North America Act of 1867, renamed the Constitution Act in 1982, is Canada's constitutional legislation and contains the Charter of Rights and Freedoms. The federal government is given exclusive jurisdiction to legislate substantive and procedural criminal law, which applies to the entire country; thus Canada has one criminal code. The act sets out the division of power and authority between the federal government, the ten provinces, and the two territories.

When dealing with criminal offenders, the division of powers between the federal and provincial levels is defined by the length of sentence imposed by the judge. Offenders sentenced to terms of incarceration of two years or more are under federal jurisdiction; all others come under provincial jurisdiction. The provinces enforce the criminal code within their municipal jurisdiction, create police forces, maintain provincial courts and jails, and exercise exclusive jurisdiction for the administration of probation.

The federal Parliament has established a system of federal courts for the administration of the laws of Canada. The involvement of the federal government in the criminal justice system is administered by the Department of Justice and the Ministry of the Solicitor General of Canada. Under the authority of the Solicitor General, the Correctional Service of Canada manages federal penitentiaries. The National Parole Board has exclusive authority concerning conditional release in federal penitentiaries and, in those provinces without a conditional release system, all releases to parole.

Early History of Parole

Until the turn of the century, clemency was unconditional. Only the "royal prerogative" was employed as an early releasing mechanism, and no conditions were set. In 1899, the Canadian Parliament passed the Ticket-of-Leave Act, establishing conditional release and a system of supervised freedom. The act created an indeterminate sentencing code with maximum terms set by the judge. There were no statutory limits defining parole eligibility. Conditional release could be granted to anyone by the governor general of Canada (Bottomley 1990, 333). Such release was generally viewed as a method "to bridge the gap between the control and the restraints of institutional life and the freedom and responsibilities of community life" (Miller 1976, 379).

Two years later, in 1901, what is now referred to as case management was established when the position of "dominion parole officer" was created to interview inmates and assess their release plans. The administration of the Ticket-of-Leave Act and the system of aftercare was handled by officers of the Department of Justice, which subsequently formed the Remission Branch in 1913. The branch became the Remission Service, the forerunner of the federal parole system.

By the 1930s, penal reformers had already begun to question the punitive orientation of the penitentiary system when a series of riots led to demands for reform. In 1936, a royal commission was appointed to investigate the penal system of Canada. The report issued in 1938 by the Archambault Commission recommended that rehabilitation become the purpose of incarceration. The commission attributed high levels of recidivism to the absence of any serious attempt to address the reformation of inmates during their confinement (Archambault 1938). Several of the commission's recommendations were later implemented during the mid-1940s. Vocational training and education courses were developed in prisons, and community services were increased.

In 1956, a federal Committee of Inquiry into the Remission Service released the Fauteux Report. The report recommended the creation of the National Parole Board. To the committee, parole represented "a logical step in the reformation and rehabilitation of a person who has been convicted of an offense and is undergoing imprisonment" (Fauteux Report 1956, 51). While providing a transitional stage for moving from confinement to the community, parole was also considered a control mechanism, given the provision for supervision and the possibility of revocation for violation of parole conditions.

The Parole Act, which became effective in 1959, created the National Parole Board as an independent administrative body within the Department of Justice. It gave the board (whose members were appointed by the Governor-in-Council—the Canadian Cabinet) the authority to grant, deny, terminate, or revoke conditional release. Seven years later, the board (as well as what is now the Correctional Service of Canada) was placed within the Department of the Solicitor General, which was created under the Government Organization Act of 1966.[1]

Initially, the board consisted of five members located in Ottawa and was supported by a regional field staff known as the National Parole Service. In 1977, the latter became part of the Correctional Service of Canada. At the same time, the board's membership increased to twenty-six. In 1986, the board's fulltime membership was expanded to its present level of thirty-six.

The Shifting Goals of Parole

Ten years after the creation of the National Parole Board, a federal government report on corrections (Ouimet 1969, 1) reaffirmed that rehabilitation was the major purpose of conditional release. The report stated that the most important aspect of parole was its efficacy in assisting the successful reintegration of the offender into society. It concluded that "one cannot learn to live in freedom without experiencing freedom" (Ouimet 1969, 331).[2]

Nonetheless, as the 1970s unfolded, other concerns were voiced, focusing on the need for greater fairness and due process in parole (and criminal justice) decision making (Hugessen 1973; Goldenberg 1974). The emphasis placed on ensuring safeguards in parole was part of a general trend toward legislation to protect civil rights and provide greater due process in the decision-making activities of all government bodies, particularly independent administrative agencies.[3]

The adoption of various procedural safeguards contributed to a decade of organizational change designed to ensure that the discretionary authority of the National Parole Board was not exercised in an unfair or capricious manner. With respect to parole, due process protections were implemented providing inmates with the right to the information to be used in deciding whether to grant or deny conditional release, written notice as well as an opportunity for an in-person hearing, written reasons in the event of parole denial, an internal review of any decision to deny release, and the right to an assistant at any panel hearing.

Since 1976, the concern with procedural due process has been coupled with a growing emphasis on public protection and offender control. This shift was sparked in part by the "nothing works" debate in the United States, which criticized the seeming inefficacy of treatment programs for offenders (Martinson 1974). It also reflected the Canadian public's desire to "get tough" on those convicted of crimes. The change in direction was expressed in the National Parole Board's 1976-77 annual report, which stated: "The board's policies and procedures continue to be reviewed and modified to increase the protection of the public against violence by parolees or inmates released under mandatory supervision."

Deterrence and punishment—not the treatment or the rehabilitation of offenders—came to be viewed as the principal purposes of criminal sanctioning in the late 1970s. The mood of the public was incorporated in the overall thrust of the Peace and Security Package legislation, which, following the abolition of the death penalty, increased the minimum parole eligibility period for offenders convicted of homicide.

Recent National Parole Board and government initiatives suggest that the emphasis on public protection as the primary goal of conditional release has become even more pronounced in the 1980s. In 1982, the board began to detain a small number of inmates who were regarded as a serious threat to public safety at the time of their release to mandatory supervision. These inmates, who were notified in advance and offered the assistance of counsel, were arrested under warrant as they left prison and were returned immediately to confinement.[4]

This practice was ruled illegal by the Supreme Court of Canada in May 1983. Nevertheless, an amendment to the Parole Act in July 1986 restored to the board the authority to detain or place under strict residential conditions certain inmates eligible for release on mandatory supervision.

In 1988, the board issued a formal document explaining its newly revised prerelease (parole) decision policies (National Parole Board 1988). According to the report, the board's primary objective is to contribute to societal protection "through facilitating the timely reintegration of offenders as law-abiding citizens" (National Parole Board 1988, 3).

As a matter of policy, the risk an offender presents to the community represents the fundamental consideration in all conditional release decisions. Therefore, any limitations imposed on those released must be necessary and reasonable to societal protection and to facilitate the offender's successful transition from confinement. Finally, a period of supervision is viewed as essential to ensuring both public safety and community reintegration (National Parole Board 1988, 4).[5]

Shortly after the adoption of these changes, several major studies were undertaken focusing on the future of sentencing and parole practices. The first of these was published in 1987 by the Canadian Sentencing Commission. This was followed by a report issued under the auspices of the Canadian Bar Association, as well as another report by the Daubney Committee, both in 1988. The findings and recommendations of each in relation to the future of parole in Canada will be discussed in the final section of this chapter.

The Organization of Parole

The National Parole Board is an administrative tribunal. Although the board chair reports to the Solicitor General on management and operational matters, the board is independent of external control in the exercise of its decision-making power. The Parliament, however, retains the ultimate authority to restrict or expand the board's jurisdiction through legislation.

As indicated earlier, the board's powers derive from the Parole Act and Regulations for parole matters. Other statutes that confer jurisdiction on the board include the Penitentiary Act for temporary absence, the Prisons and Reformatories Act, and the Criminal Code of Canada.[6] Federal parole legislation provides for the creation of provincial parole boards to exercise parole jurisdiction in accordance with the Parole Act and its attending Regulations.

Only three provinces—British Columbia, Ontario, and Quebec—have their own provincial parole boards. Thus, the National

Parole Board has jurisdiction over all federal offenders (except some in provincial institutions), provincial inmates in seven of the ten provinces, and inmates in two territories. The Governor-in-Council (the Canadian Cabinet) appoints full-time board members for fixed, five-year terms that may be renewed (ACA Parole Task Force Survey 1988). Part-time members are appointed for fixed, three-year terms, which may also be renewed. The Solicitor General appoints community board members for two years with renewable terms. Board members are drawn from the fields of criminology, psychology, social work, law, corrections, law enforcement, journalism, and other community-related fields. In conjunction with the Solicitor General, the National Parole Board has established a board member profile, which includes recommended qualifications and describes the nature of the work required of the board members.

Under the Parole Act, up to thirty-six full-time board members (senior, regular, temporary, community) can be appointed. The chair of the board serves as the chief executive officer. The chair is supported by a vice-chair, an executive director, director general, executive secretary, and director of communications. Board members and staff, located in the five regional offices, are each directed by a senior board member and a regional director.[7]

The duties of regular or full-time members are defined by statute (the Parole Act and the Criminal Records Act). When acting under the Parole Act, each member has full discretion in decision making; when acting in clemency matters, the member's vote constitutes a recommendation to the Solicitor General. The primary duty of community board members, however, is to vote on the conditional release of inmates serving life and indeterminate sentences and dangerous offenders.

The executive committee of the board, in consultation with board members, is responsible for the development and promulgation of board policies. The Governor-in-Council appoints board members to the executive committee under the recommendation of the chair to the Solicitor General. The present composition of this committee includes the chair, vice-chair, and the senior board member for each region as well as the Appeal Division. Regular members contribute to major board initiatives through regional or general board meetings.[8]

Conditional Parole Release

Programs and Eligibility

The board provides offenders with a range of programs to demonstrate that they are able to reside in the community in a law-abiding fashion. Four programs contribute to this goal; to be granted any form of release, however, inmates must be able to show that the risk they present to public safety is manageable outside prison walls.

There are four types of conditional release programs: temporary absence (escorted and unescorted), day parole, full parole, and mandatory supervision.[9] Offenders become eligible for the various release programs at different points in their sentence. The board regards these periods of ineligibility, defined by the Canadian government and placed in the parole regulations, as the period of denunciation of any sentence.

A temporary absence, with or without escort, is often the first release an offender may be granted. Temporary absences are intermittent leaves granted for medical, rehabilitative, or humanitarian reasons. Except for certain categories of inmates (e.g., those serving life or indeterminate sentences), escorted temporary absences are under the authority of the Correctional Service of Canada. Unescorted temporary absences are under the authority of the board.

Nevertheless, for most offenders serving sentences of less than five years, the board has delegated this authority to the wardens. The board has no authority over such releases for provincial offenders. Table 7.1 highlights the eligibility criteria for unescorted temporary absences.

Day parole provides offenders an opportunity to participate in approved community-based activities. Offenders on day parole are usually required to return nightly to a correctional facility or a community halfway house. It is normally granted for transitional purposes, to permit the offender to participate in programs not available in the institution, or to take part in community service projects, educational studies, or seasonal work such as forestry or harvesting. These releases also provide an opportunity to obtain a controlled assessment of risk. Table 7.2 provides an overview of the eligibility for day parole.

Full parole is the conditional release of an inmate for the remainder of the sentence in the community. Though offenders released on full parole are subject to supervision, the conditions that are imposed are limited to those deemed necessary to manage risk. Some conditions are standard to all inmates, while special conditions are tailored to individual needs.

Supervision is intended to provide individualized assistance and control. If there is evidence that the level of risk to society has increased and cannot be controlled by supervision or by the imposition of special conditions, a person designated by the board chair takes appropriate action to suspend the release. The offender is, in turn, reincarcerated, pending a review of the situation.

Inmates who serve a definite sentence are generally eligible for a full parole review after serving one-third of their sentence, or seven years,

Table 7.1

Eligibility and Voting Requirements: Unescorted Temporary Absence

Length of sentence	Time to be served before eligibility	Number of votes required for review/Number of votes required for decision
0 to 2 years less a day	N/A	
2 to 5 years	If entered penitentiary before March 1, 1978, 6 months after entrance; on or after March 1, 1978, 6 months after sentencing or 1/2 time before PED*, whichever is longer.	2 votes required for review 2 votes required for decision where authority has not been delegated
5 to 10 years		
10 years or more excluding life sentences		
Life as a maximum punishment (for crimes other than 1st and 2nd degree murder)	If entered penitentiary before March 1, 1978, 6 months after entrance; on or after March 1, 1978, 3 years before PED.	2 votes required for review 2 votes required for decision no CBM votes required
Preventive detention (a habitual or dangerous sexual offender)	1 year	
Detention for an indeterminate period (since Oct. 15, 1977 as a dangerous offender)	3 years	
Life for murder before Jan. 4, 1968	3 years after entered penitentiary	4 votes (including 2 CBM votes) required for review** 3 votes required for decision
Life for murder Jan. 4, 1968 to Jan. 1, 1974		
Life: death commuted before Jan. 1, 1974		
Life for murder, Jan. 1, 1974 to July 26, 1976	3 years before PED	
Life: Death commuted by Jan. 1,1974 to July 26, 1976		
Life: Death not commuted by July 26, 1976		
Life for 1st degree murder on or after July 26, 1976		
Life for 2nd degree murder on or after July 26, 1976		

*PED refers to full parole eligibility date. It is calculated from sentencing date except for lifers, where it is calculated from date of arrest, but does not include any period when the offender is on bail.

**CBM—Community Board Members

Table 7.2

Eligibility and Voting Requirements: Day Parole

Length of sentence	Time to be served before eligibility	Number of votes required for review/Number of votes required for a decision
0 to 2 years less a day	1/2 time to PED*	2 votes required for review 2 votes required for decision
2 to 5 years	For 2 to 12 year sentences, 6 months or 1/2 time to PED, whichever is the longer. For sentences of 12 years or more, 2 years before PED.	2 votes required for review 2 votes required for decision
5 to 10 years		
10 years or more excluding life sentences		
Life as a maximum punishment (for crimes other than 1st and 2nd degree murder)	5 years	2 votes required for review 2 votes required for decision
Preventive detention (a habitual or dangerous sexual offender)	1 year	4 votes (including 2 CBM votes) required for review** 3 votes required for decision
Detention for an indeterminate period (since Oct. 15, 1977 as a dangerous offender)	3 years	
Life for murder before Jan. 4, 1968	3 years before PED	
Life for murder Jan. 4, 1968 to Jan. 1, 1974		
Life: death commuted before Jan. 1, 1974		
Life for murder, Jan. 1, 1974 to July 26, 1976	3 years before PED	
Life: death commuted by Jan. 1, 1974 to July 26, 1976		
Life: Death not commuted by July 26, 1976		
Life for 1st degree murder on or after July 26, 1976		
Life for 2nd degree murder on or after July 26, 1976		

*PED refers to full parole eligibility date. It is calculated from sentencing date except for lifers, where it is calculated from the date of arrest, but does not include any period when the offender is on bail.

**CBM—Community Board Member

whichever is less. Eligibility dates for other categories of offenders vary considerably. For example, persons convicted of first degree murder are not eligible for full parole consideration for twenty-five years. They are eligible for unescorted temporary absences and day parole three years before their full parole eligibility date.

Full parole eligibility for persons convicted of second degree murder is determined by the sentencing judge, on recommendation of a jury, at between ten and twenty-five years of the sentence. Second degree murderers become eligible for unescorted temporary absences and day parole three years before their full parole eligibility date.

Inmates designated as violent conduct cases are not eligible for full parole until they have served one-half their term of imprisonment, or seven years, whichever is less. Life-sentenced inmates and dangerous offenders are so defined by the courts at the time of sentencing, but the board may establish eligibility dates beyond the normal one-third for offenders who have particular previous criminal histories involving acts of violence. Table 7.3 illustrates the range of eligibility for full parole.

The Parole Regulations allow inmates to be paroled (excluding those serving indeterminate or life sentences) before their parole eligibility date only in exceptional circumstances (related to severe health problems, excessive hardship, satisfaction of court-ordered programs, deportation, or extradition). The discretion to grant release by exception is exercised only in rare instances and must be based upon statutory criteria related to risk assessment.

Mandatory supervision, the fourth program of conditional release, was created by an amendment to the Parole Act in 1970. Originally proposed by the Fauteux Commission (1958) and subsequently endorsed by the Ouimet Report (1969), this method of release provides a period of mandatory parole supervision equal to the time earned through earned remission.[10] It is designed to offer a degree of control and assistance comparable to that received by parolees. Bottomley (1990, 336) notes that the primary objective of mandatory supervision is to ensure that every offender released from prison is subject to a period of monitoring and surveillance to reduce the risk of reoffending.

The Hearing Process

The responsibility for conducting conditional release hearings or reviews is decentralized. Regional offices review all federal cases within their geographical area of responsibility. The board conducts interviews (panel hearings) with federal and, where applicable, provincial offenders. The interviews are regarded as an essential feature of justice and an important forum for assessing risk. Federal offenders are automatically entitled to a panel hearing for first review at day- and full-parole eligibility,

Table 7.3

Eligibility and Voting Requirements: Full Parole

Length of sentence	Full parole	Number of votes required for review/Number of votes required for decision
0 to 2 years less a day	1/3 of sentence	2 votes required for review 2 votes required for decision
2 to 5 years	1/3 of sentence or 7 years, whichever is less except, if violent conduct (described in the Parole Act and Regulations) is involved, then it is 1/2 of sentence or 7 years, whichever is less.	
5 to 10 years		
10 years or more excluding life sentences		
Life as a maximum punishment (for crimes other than 1st and 2nd degree murder)	7 years	2 votes required for review 2 votes required for decision no CBM votes required
Preventive detention (a habitual or dangerous sexual offender)	1 year	4 votes (including 2 CBM votes) required for review* 3 votes required for decision
Detention for an indeterminate period (since Oct. 15, 1977 as a dangerous offender)	3 years	
Life for murder before Jan. 4, 1968	7 years	
Life for murder Jan. 4, 1968 to Jan. 1, 1974	10 years	
Life: death commuted before Jan. 1, 1974		
Life for murder, Jan. 1, 1974 to July 26, 1976	10-20 years; Judicial review possible at 15 years	
Life: death commuted by Jan. 1, 1974 to July 26, 1976		
Life: Death not commuted by July 26, 1976	25 years; Judicial review possible at 15 years	
Life for 1st degree murder on or after July 26, 1976		
Life for 2nd degree murder on or after July 26, 1976	10-25 years; Judicial review possible at 15 years	

*CBM—Community Board Members

then to a review hearing every two years after reaching full parole eligibility.

Provincial offenders under the board's jurisdiction must apply for review and are given in-person interviews. Offenders sentenced to less than two years are not under the jurisdiction of the board with respect to granting temporary absences, nor are they subject to mandatory supervision or the detention provisions of the Parole Act.

Various other board decisions (e.g., reviews for unescorted temporary absences, or a variance in the conditions of release as recommended by the Correctional Service of Canada) are usually conducted by a review of the file, if the offender has already been seen once by the board. An offender may elect not to be seen by the board and may request a file review instead of a panel hearing.

Case preparation occurs prior to the board's formal review. Correctional staff submit case documentation, which includes the offender's criminal background and score on the recidivism prediction tool, information on institutional performance, professional assessments,[11] the results of the community investigation and the release plan, and comments from the police and the original sentencing judge (if available). Correctional staff also provide a recommendation to the board and share relevant information with the offender.

The board also considers victim input during the decision-making process, especially lingering fears and any long-term harm caused by the crime. Victims may request assistance from board staff to prepare their presentation. If the inmate consents, the victim may observe the panel hearing.[12]

Parole hearings represent a nonadversarial forum in which inmates can present their case and respond to information relied upon by the board. In fact, inmates are provided with a comprehensive summary of the information the board will consider, as well as possible decision outcomes, at least fifteen days before the hearing. If they choose, they may also have assistance in presenting their case. At each hearing, board members ensure adherence to the standard procedural safeguards. Each hearing is recorded on audio cassettes.

Board members conduct hearings in the institutions. Correctional staff from the case management team generally attend the hearing. Representatives from the community and the institution who have worked with the offender address any questions that may arise during the interview, especially those pertaining to institutional performance and the release plan.

After a private discussion among board members, offenders are informed immediately of the decision and the reasons therefor. Written notification is provided within fifteen days of the hearing. All board members have an equal vote. The length of the sentence determines the number of votes required. Any board member, however, may request in advance of a review or hearing, and the chair may approve, that more than the minimum number of members vote on a particular case.

In most cases, the vote of two regular members is required. Four members, two of whom must be community board members, must vote on parole or unescorted temporary absence cases that involve inmates serving life or indeterminate sentences. Two votes are necessary for parole or mandatory supervision revocation and for day and full parole or temporary absence termination. Potential detention cases referred by the Correctional Service of Canada require three votes.

Federal offenders and provincial inmates subject to the board's jurisdiction are entitled under the Parole Act to have certain decisions reviewed. These include the denial or termination of day or full parole, the revocation of mandatory supervision, and the imposition of detention or residency as a condition of such supervision. The onus is on the individual to request a review within forty-five days of being notified of a decision.

The Appeal Division reexamines the decisions. This division is composed of four board members designated by the chair. Three members of the Appeal Division constitute a panel and can affirm, modify, cancel, or reverse the original denial of parole (except for offenders serving life or indeterminate sentences) or order a new hearing. Regardless of the outcome, reasons must be provided in writing to the inmate.

Supervision Practices and Procedures for Revocation

Legislation sets forth the mandatory terms and conditions of supervision for all offenders granted conditional release. Like most paroling authorities in the United States, the board may impose special conditions, if they are related to particular behavior that might otherwise increase the probability of an offender's committing a crime while under supervision.

The board, however, does not exercise direct control over the actual supervision of offenders. The Correctional Service of Canada is responsible for supervising inmates released on parole and on mandatory supervision. In addition to the conditions of release imposed by the board, the offender is expected to comply with any instructions issued by the supervising officer. The type of conditional release granted determines what supervision is provided and the frequency with which the parolee is expected to report.

According to the ACA Parole Task Force survey, there are three classification levels for supervision: intensive (requiring one face-to-face contact every fifteen days); active (requiring one face-to-face contact every twenty-one days); and periodic (requiring one face-to-face contact every thirty days). A formal needs assessment is done during the first sixty days of initial intake and classification. At the time of the survey, the average adult caseload for parole officers was twenty-five to thirty parolees. A total of 8,618 parolees were currently under supervision.[13]

In the event of an actual or suspected violation of release conditions, involvement in a police investigation for new criminal activity, or the judgment that continued release would entail a risk to society, the supervising officer is authorized to suspend the release and report the case to the board. The offender is then returned to custody and an investigation is begun. Offenders may request a hearing following the suspension of a day parole, full parole, or mandatory supervision release. During the course of the hearing, they are given an opportunity to present their case for the board's consideration.

A suspension may be canceled by a designated officer of the Correctional Service of Canada within fourteen days, if it is determined that the reasons for the suspension are not of continuing concern. When a case is referred to the board, several decisions are possible, including canceling the suspension, modifying the release conditions, or terminating (or revoking) the release. As a matter of stated policy, the focus of decision making is on the assessment of the offender's continuing risk to the community.

Release Outcomes

Figures 7.1 and 7.2 show the outcomes of federal inmates released on full parole and mandatory supervision during the five fiscal years from 1979-80 to 1983-84. The analysis is based on a follow-up period that extended through 31 March 1989.

As illustrated by Figure 7.1, nearly 70 percent of the 8,202 inmates released over the five-year period successfully completed their supervision. Another 5.5 percent were still under supervision at the end of the period. Just over one-quarter of those released during this time were returned to an institution. Thirteen percent were revoked for a new offense, and 12.4 percent were reincarcerated for a technical violation of parole.

Figure 7.2 shows that 54.5 percent of the 12,674 inmates granted release on mandatory supervision successfully completed their term of supervision. Another 45.5 percent were returned to custody, though 20 percent of these were returned to an institution following a revocation for a new offense. The other 25.5 percent were reincarcerated for a technical violation. Generally, the length of supervision on a mandatory supervision release is shorter than the period of supervision on a full parole release.

Figure 7.1

Outcome of Full Parole Releases (Canada)

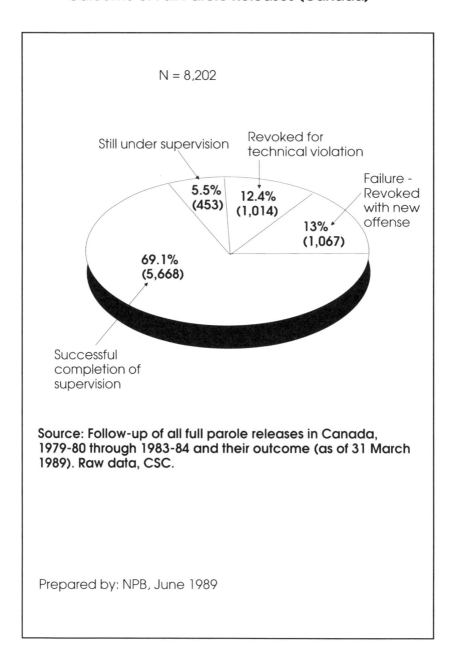

N = 8,202

Still under supervision

Revoked for technical violation

Failure - Revoked with new offense

5.5% (453)

12.4% (1,014)

13% (1,067)

69.1% (5,668)

Successful completion of supervision

Source: Follow-up of all full parole releases in Canada, 1979-80 through 1983-84 and their outcome (as of 31 March 1989). Raw data, CSC.

Prepared by: NPB, June 1989

Figure 7.2

Outcome of Mandatory Supervision Releases (Canada)

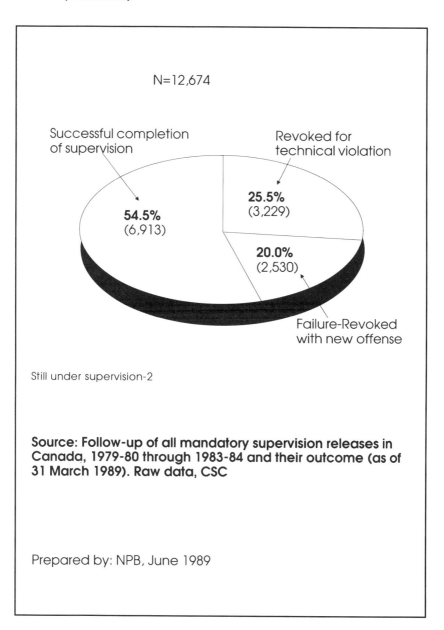

N=12,674

Successful completion of supervision

Revoked for technical violation

25.5% (3,229)

54.5% (6,913)

20.0% (2,530)

Failure-Revoked with new offense

Still under supervision-2

Source: Follow-up of all mandatory supervision releases in Canada, 1979-80 through 1983-84 and their outcome (as of 31 March 1989). Raw data, CSC

Prepared by: NPB, June 1989

Parole in the Provinces

The provinces have jurisdiction for the administration of probation, the enforcement of the criminal code, and for local law enforcement, provincial courts, and jails. As indicated earlier, offenders sentenced to terms of incarceration of two years or less come under provincial jurisdiction. Three provinces have established parole boards: British Columbia, Ontario, and Quebec.

Ontario

The Ontario Board of Parole is the largest and the oldest of the three provincial boards. It was established in 1910 as the Ontario Parole Commission, with powers limited to advising federal authorities on early release during the indefinite portion of sentences served by provincial offenders. Subsequent to the passage of the Federal Parole Act in 1959, the Ontario board was given the authority to grant rather than simply recommend release.

In 1978, when legislation was passed creating provincial parole boards, full authority for parole decisions regarding all provincial offenders was delegated to the Ontario Board of Parole, a mandate that it pursues to the present time.

The Ontario Board of Parole is a decentralized organization with responsibility for five geographical regions. Located in Toronto, its membership is composed of a chair, executive vice-chair, and three administrative staff. Five vice-chairs are responsible for the board's regional offices, while twelve full-time members conduct parole hearings and case reviews.

The Ontario board also has 106 community part-time members who are appointed from various walks of life and professional backgrounds. The community members participate in each parole hearing. The members of the board, both full-time and community part-time, are appointed by the Lieutenant Governor of the province through an Order-in-Council. Community members are employed and paid on a per diem basis.

The board itself is an administrative tribunal in which the chair reports to the Minister of Correctional Services. The board, however, relies on the Ministry of Correctional Services for administrative and professional staff support to carry out preparole community investigations, gather required documentation for hearing purposes, and provide community supervision and monitoring of parolees.

Parole decisions are normally made by a quorum consisting of two community part-time members and one full-time member who chairs the hearing. By statute, the board may grant or deny parole in the absence of the offender; however, as a matter of policy and practice, in-person hearings are held with each offender at one of the province's forty-six correctional institutions prior to reaching a decision.

The hearing process consists of two stages. During the first stage, the quorum reviews material on the offender's criminal history, the nature and extent of the current charges, behavior while incarcerated (including misconduct reports and progress in available institutional programs), social background information, the offender's current family situation, and release plans including residence, employment, and relevant treatment programs.

The second phase consists of the actual hearing, which usually occurs on the same or next day after the case file review. During this stage, the offender is interviewed and questioned by the three quorum members. The hearing affords the offender the opportunity to provide additional information and clarify matters for the board.

Once the hearing is completed, the offender leaves the interview room while the quorum discusses the case and arrives at a decision. The decision to grant or deny parole need not be unanimous; a majority vote is sufficient. If parole is granted, special conditions are established as needed. The offender then returns to the room and is told of the decision. Written notification is provided subsequently.

The Ontario board conducts roughly 9,000 institutional hearings and approximately 1,500 case review meetings annually. Parole is denied about as frequently as it is granted. For those who are paroled, 82 percent to 85 percent complete their terms successfully.

British Columbia

The British Columbia Board of Parole was established in 1949 with a mandate to release young adult offenders during the indeterminate portion of a definite/indeterminate term of imprisonment. Following the repeal of such terms (and amendments to the Parole Act of Canada in 1977), the board was reconstituted by the provincial government with a new mandate to exercise parole jurisdiction over all inmates in provincial correctional centers.

The main philosophical underpinning of the board is reflected in the principle that parole decision making represents the community's participation in the justice process. In 1989, this principle was established in law with the passage of the British Columbia Parole Act.

The provincial parole act takes its authority from the Federal Parole Act. All members of the board, except for the chair, are community members who serve for one four-year term. Board members reside in all regions of the province and are selected on the basis of specific criteria, including decision-making skills, participation in community affairs, and interest in and knowledge of the criminal justice system.

When the board conducts a parole hearing, the information it relies upon is furnished by the corrections branch of the Ministry of the Solicitor General. The board has a contractual agreement with the branch to prepare community and institutional assessments and to supervise those on parole. Normally, parole hearings are convened within six weeks of receipt of a parole application. Cases are reviewed at or near their statutory parole eligibility dates at the correctional center in which the applicant is incarcerated.

Inmates must apply for parole if they wish to be considered. Parole hearings are conducted by a panel of two board members. Offenders are accorded procedural protections, including the provision of a hearing upon application, the disclosure of the information upon which the decision will be based, the opportunity for representation at the parole hearing, timely receipt of the decision and reasons for the decision in writing, and the opportunity to request a reexamination of the decision.

During the past ten years, the British Columbia Board of Parole, the smallest of the Canadian boards, has conducted 13,645 parole reviews. Parole was granted in 6,495 of the decisions, while another 4,600 decisions resulted in parole denial.

Those on parole are held accountable for their behavior in the community through the terms of the Certificate of Parole. Less than 10 percent of those on parole were revoked in 1988-89. Of these, over half were revoked and returned to custody for technical violations of parole conditions. Through cooperation with the National Parole Board and the provincial boards of Quebec and Ontario, parolees are, with permission, able to relocate anywhere in Canada. Conversely, those under suspension can be dealt with, when apprehended, in any province or territory.

Quebec

The Quebec statute, passed in 1978, adopted the guiding principles of the Federal Parole Act, as well as other procedures and regulations. It reflects the board's belief that even though parole changes the circumstances under which a sentence is served, it is mainly a means to enforce a term of imprisonment. The fundamental mission and statutory mandate of the board is to protect the public and facilitate offender rehabilitation. Its main task is to grant or refuse parole to any inmate who has served at least six months in a provincial correctional institution.

The Quebec Parole Board has two administrative offices, one in Montreal and the other in Quebec City. The board's staff is composed of seven full-time members, including the chair, and forty-nine community members. It also has an executive director and other administrative and support staff.

By statute, the parole board must review an inmate's case at the full parole eligibility date, which is generally after one-third of the sentence of imprisonment has been served. Inmates may notify the board in writing that they do not wish to be granted parole. They do not have to request a hearing.

Inmates are entitled to be present at their hearings and to be represented or assisted by a person of their choice, with the exception of an inmate from another correctional institution. Hearings in the twenty-three correctional institutions in Quebec are held by two board members, one full-time and one part-time, referred to as community board members.

The decision to grant or deny parole is based on a majority vote. The inmate is advised of the decision orally and subsequently in writing. The Quebec Parole Board rendered 4,077 decisions in 1988. Of the 23,673 inmates interviewed over a ten-year period, 50.6 percent were denied parole, while 49.4 percent were granted parole.

Six mandatory and standard conditions are imposed when parole is granted. In certain cases, special conditions may also be imposed. A return to criminal activity or breach of these conditions may result in parole suspension or revocation.

Supervision of parolees is the responsibility of the probation branch, which provides information and assistance and exercises the required control over the activities and behavior of parolees.

Since 1984, 86 percent of parolees have successfully completed their sentence in the community; only 14 percent had their parole revoked for failing to meet the conditions of release or for returning to criminal activity. The success rate with respect to nonrecidivism is 92 percent.

The provincial parole systems must balance their discretionary powers as administrative tribunals with the growing emphasis on accountability for decisions, both to the public and to those offenders whose parole cases are heard. The boards have followed policies adapted from federal legislation, as well as a set of standardized decision-making procedures.

However, there has been ever-increasing pressure to articulate more thoroughly the process leading to the final decision, from the information relied upon at the hearing through the quorum's eventual decision. This pressure is not due to court challenges or to concerns regarding the exercise of discretion, but is mainly a result of the enactment of the Canadian Charter of Rights and Freedoms.

The provincial boards, as well as the National Parole Board, also continue to face concerns on the part of the public that parole represents an "easy way out" for dangerous criminals. This perception, along with several recent initiatives concerning sentencing reform, resulted in wide-ranging calls for reform (and abolition) of parole at both the federal and provincial level.

The Future of Parole in Canada

In 1987, the criminal justice system in general, and parole in particular, became major foci of attention, due mainly to several incidents involving violence by offenders on conditional release. A series of reports were issued reviewing the fundamental purpose and rationale for parole, the balance between rehabilitation and control in the parole process, and the question of whether parole should be abolished or retained. A variety of proposals were made to modify the system of parole, as well as to abolish it altogether.

Perhaps the best known of these reports was that issued by the Canadian Sentencing Commission in 1987. The nine-member commission was formed to conduct a thorough assessment of the structure of sentencing. It eventually proposed a comprehensive set of recommendations modeled after a just deserts sentencing framework.

According to this approach, the sentence imposed should be proportionate to the gravity of the offense and the culpability of the offender. It also should ensure equity and predictability in sentencing outcomes. The Canadian Sentencing Commission added that the structure of sentencing should be understandable to the public and offenders alike, while the use of incarceration should be restrained (Canadian Sentencing Commission 1987).

Within the framework proposed by the commission, a presumption for or against incarceration was to be established for each offense, though judges could depart from the presumption if they provided reasons for doing so. Following the lead of several jurisdictions in the United States (e.g., Minnesota, Washington), it recommended that a permanent sentencing commission be created to promulgate presumptive sentencing guidelines for all offenses.

The Canadian Sentencing Commission called for the abolition of parole. It argued that because discretionary parole is essentially based on a rehabilitation model, the selection of offenders for release invariably violates the principle of proportionality in punishment. It also noted that offenders sentenced to the same term of imprisonment may be released to one of several forms of conditional release (e.g., day parole, full parole) or granted mandatory supervision if they are refused parole, all at different points in their sentence. This creates a good deal of uncertainty in sentencing.

Finally, the commission observed that parole transfers the sentencing decision from a judge to an executive branch agency, thus usurping a properly judicial function. How much time an offender serves in prison should, it argued, be determined by a judge at the time of sentencing (Bottomley 1990).

The Canadian Bar Association subsequently challenged the recommendation to abolish parole. In 1988, a special committee wrote:

> This committee remains skeptical about the likelihood of real change in the absence of an understanding about the nature of imprisonment, and we therefore continue to advocate a system of parole or conditional release. It is the committee's view that parole is a necessary part of the checks and balances which must exist in order to give meaning to the principle of restraint under prevailing conditions of imprisonment.

The committee also urged that sentencing policy within the criminal justice system shift from its current reliance on imprisonment to an array of community-based alternatives, including probation and halfway houses.

This view was given further support by a committee of the House of Commons that was formed to study sentencing and conditional release. Chaired by David Daubney, the committee issued a sweeping report in 1988 entitled *Taking Responsibility* (Daubney Committee 1988). It concluded that "public protection will be enhanced by preparing inmates for release into the society while they are still incarcerated and then providing offenders with the requisite degree of supervision and assistance once they are released into the community" (Daubney Committee 1988, 187-88).

The committee went on to recommend that conditional release be retained with some modifications. Two of the major changes proposed were that the period of ineligibility for release of offenders convicted of certain violent offenses be set at one-half rather than the current one-third of the sentence and that the board's decision-making criteria be incorporated into law.

At the same time, the Solicitor General sponsored several proposals that expressed the federal government's support for a system of parole in which public safety is restored as the primary goal. In the 1988 session of Parliament, the Solicitor General proposed legislation referred to as the parole initiatives. The various amendments to the Parole Act, however, were tabled just before the Parliamentary elections. The initiatives that were suggested signal reforms that may shape the future of parole in Canada in the years ahead. Several of the proposals are as follows:

- to significantly reduce (or eliminate) the automatic two-third release for good-time served—called mandatory supervision
- to move the first full parole eligibility date from one-third to one-half of federal sentences for some categories of offenses, namely, violent offenders and those who constitute a real risk to public safety
- to restrict day parole eligibility
- to coordinate institutional and community programming with parole decisions more effectively

Newscasters, print journalists, and the public currently show great interest in the subject of conditional release. Though Canadians significantly overestimate parole grant rates, they continue to express strong concerns for their safety. This is due in large part to the occurrence of serious crimes committed by a relatively small number of offenders on conditional release and to the intensive media coverage surrounding the incidents.

Some of these cases ended up in court; others brought about inquests and inquiries. Nonetheless, the inquests that have followed have not called for the abolition of parole. Rather, they have urged that the parole system reexamine its function, adequacy, and the completeness of reports relied upon for assessment purposes.

The policies that guide decision making—both in the process of granting release, called the prerelease decision policies, and in the processes of supervision and revocation, called the postrelease decision policies—will remain under close scrutiny for years to come. Even so, the system of parole will likely continue as a major component of the criminal justice and corrections system. This contrasts sharply with the future of parole in the United States, a future that will be shaped by how well parole boards respond to the twin pressures of prison crowding and determinate sentencing reform.

Notes

1. Today, the Department of Solicitor General also includes the Secretariat, the Canadian Security Intelligence Service (CSIS), the Inspector General of CSIS, the Public Complaints Committee (RCMP), the External Review Committee (RCMP), and the Correctional Investigator. From its inception, it has included the Canadian Royal Mounted Police.
2. The Ouimet Committee report recommended the abolition of indeterminate sentences in Canada, a recommendation that was

adopted in 1977 (with the only exception pertaining to legislatively defined "dangerous offenders").

3. The Canadian Human Rights Act became effective in March 1978. It stated that individuals were entitled to know what records the government had that could be used in decisions directly affecting them and to be informed of any use of those records after the act's date of enactment.

4. A former chair of the National Parole Board who signed the first "gating" warrant noted recently that doing so was perhaps the most difficult decision of his term of office (Outerbridge 1990, 14-15).

5. A validated risk prediction instrument is used to assist in parole release decision making (ACA Parole Task Force Survey 1988).

6. Other statutes that provide a framework for the operations of the board include the Canadian Charter of Rights and Freedoms, the Financial Administration Act, the Public Service Employment Act, the Official Languages Act, the Privacy Act, the Access to Information Act, the Canadian Human Rights Act, and the Auditor General's Act.

7. There are currently six senior board members, one in each regional division of the board and one in the appeal division. These members serve as spokespersons for the regions and the appeal division and also provide guidance and direction to members.

8. NPB headquarters is in the national capital, Ottawa, Ontario. Five regional offices operate out of Moncton, New Brunswick, for the Atlantic provinces: Montreal, Quebec; Kingston, Ontario; Saskatoon, Saskatchewan, serving the Prairie region and the Northwest Territories; and Abottsford, British Columbia, serving the Pacific region and the Yukon.

9. The Criminal Records Act empowers the board to administer the processing of applications for the granting of a pardon and gives it the authority to make recommendations to the Solicitor General. Upon receipt of a pardon application, the board initiates inquiries, which are conducted by the Royal Canadian Mounted Police. Board members of the Appeal Division review the information and make a recommendation to the Solicitor General, who in turn refers favorable recommendations to the Governor-in-Council for a final decision.

10. There are two forms of remission: statutory and earned. Earned remission is achieved through good behavior and may equal up to one-third of a sentence. Statutory remission is bestowed at admission and may equal one-quarter of the sentence (Bottomley 1990, 336).

11. Psychiatric and psychological testing are required as a supplement to the risk assessment for offenders sentenced to two years or more for a crime of violence. Such assessments are also required for offenders with a previous conviction for violence for which a sentence of two years or more was imposed, as well as in cases where an offender was sentenced for a disorder that probably contributed to the instant offense.

12. A victim, or a representative of the victim, is allowed to provide input to the board through the regional director. Though the victim is not automatically informed about when the offender is due to be released, he/she may receive such information upon request, including the type of release, the terms and conditions of supervision, and the offender's destination. A victim may also request to be notified if the parolee is returned to custody before his/her sentence expires.
13. The postrelease (supervision) policies have since been revised and implemented, providing comprehensive standards to govern parolee classification and case management.

Chapter 8

The Question of
Parole in the 1990s

Parole is experiencing a period of transition. Two states that had at one point abolished discretionary release have recently restored the parole board (Colorado and Connecticut). Other states have chosen to retain the function of parole release but now call it something else (e.g., Florida). Although the movement to abolish paroling authorities appears to have peaked in the mid-1980s, the parole board in Delaware was recently eliminated as a result of actions taken by the Sentencing Accountability Commission (1989).

While parole boards remain controversial and subject to challenge, they are nonetheless found in the vast majority of states. Moreover, even though the proportion of inmates granted mandatory release relative to discretionary release has jumped sharply, the latter is still the modal form of release from confinement. Regardless of the method of release, for the past several years the fastest growing component of corrections, which includes prison, jails, and probation, has been parole supervision.

These developments carry significant implications for the future of parole. They reflect the continuing trend toward determinate sentencing reform or structured sentencing and the incessant pressures caused by prison crowding.

Although the adoption of determinate sentencing does not lead invariably to the demise of the parole board (e.g., New Jersey, Pennsylvania), in states where sentencing commissions have been formed and are considered success stories, the authority of the parole board has been abolished (e.g., Minnesota and Washington). Where the problem of prison crowding has been left solely to the parole board to manage (e.g., Texas), the integrity of parole release decision making has been compromised, if not debased.

Paroling authorities occupy both a pivotal and a vulnerable position relative to these developments. While there are steps they can take in response, these measures will prove insufficient, if not counterproductive, if pursued in isolation from the other components of the criminal justice system.

The most important component is the department of corrections (or its equivalent), both institutional corrections and postrelease supervision. The initiatives taken here must be responsive primarily to the increased demands for community protection. Unless these measures are coordinated, however, with sentencing policies at the front end of the system, the goals most often associated with sentencing reform, such as fairness, equity, and proportionality, will be achieved at an enormous cost and without contributing significantly to public safety (e.g., as in California).

What follows is an argument for revitalizing parole within the context of future sentencing reform. It is based on the recognition that while the traditional goals of determinate sentencing and parole (that is, just deserts and crime control) cannot be integrated at a philosophical level or in a logical fashion, they can and must be balanced as a matter of sensible public policy. It also assumes that parole boards are uniquely positioned to play a pivotal role in helping to achieve this balance.

Nonetheless, for this to occur, parole boards must address the need for structured decision making, the effective management of correctional resources, and growing community concerns for safety and accountability. To the extent paroling authorities are able to resolve these issues in a credible fashion, they will play a key role within the criminal justice system in the 1990s and beyond.

Paroling Authorities, Policy Making, and the Structuring of Discretion

Until the early 1970s, parole boards, like other administrative agencies, were reluctant to place limits on the exercise of their discretion. Board members made individual, case-by-case decisions in an ad hoc fashion. In the absence of explicit agency policy governing their decisions, they were able to emphasize whatever correctional goals (e.g., rehabilitation, incapacitation) they felt applied to particular cases. Ultimately, they were empowered to grant or deny parole within a context of enormous discretion and without concern for accountability.

One of the more salient developments with respect to paroling authorities nationwide and in Canada has been the movement toward structured parole decision making. The initial impetus for this movement may be traced to the development of parole guidelines by the U.S. Parole Commission in 1972 (Gottfredson et al. 1978). Currently, according to the ACA Parole Task Force survey, twenty-three jurisdictions are using formal, structured guidelines. As was discussed in Chapter 3, however, no one definition of what constitutes such guidelines prevails. Nine of the states use what might best be characterized as grid guidelines, while ten jurisdictions use guiding principles. The other four states assign offenders scores and are thus closer to the former, but it is not clear how these scores shape the decision to grant or deny parole.

Various studies of different states' experiences with parole guidelines have concluded that structuring the release decision through guidelines provides for a measure of equity (by reducing both sentencing and parole disparities), greater consistency and fairness, and more accountability relative to parole release standards (Tonry 1987).

Nonetheless, structured parole decision making is not synonymous with the development of parole guidelines. As defined by McGarry, a structured decision-making approach

> refers to the making of individual case decisions in accordance with explicit goals and policies determined by the larger, policy-making body—in this case, a parole board or parole advisory body (1988, 37).

By virtue of the decisions they make, parole boards are policy-making bodies. Whether as a matter of explicit policy or informal practice, parole boards are expected to balance, if not achieve, an array of contradictory sentencing goals, including deterrence, incapacitation, retribution, and rehabilitation. In the absence of a structured framework for decision making, the cumulative impact of individual decisions by board members becomes de facto policy (albeit inconsistent and unreviewable) for the agency.

Structured parole decision making links explicitly the three major components of the parole process: release, supervision, and revocation. It requires that parole boards review their current decision-making practices and (subject to the achievement of a policy consensus among the members) state their goals, explain their decision-making tools (e.g., grid guidelines, risk assessment instruments), and describe the procedures for making decisions and overriding policy (Burke et al. 1987).

In so doing, the parole board conveys clearly to the department of corrections what it expects with respect to institutional behavior and program participation. In terms of field services, such an approach effectively communicates its goals and expectations concerning the enforcement of the conditions of supervision. As a matter of policy, this is especially important in terms of defining the types of responses to parolee violations that are considered appropriate.

Incorporating a structured approach to decision making states the paroling authority's mission, goals, and procedures in a clear and credible fashion. Perhaps of more importance, it provides a coherent policy framework for addressing the management of correctional resources, a responsibility that paroling authorities share with departments of corrections.

Managing Correctional Resources: The Limits of Responsible Participation

Release Policy

For nearly a decade, the attention of policy makers, legislators, and correctional administrators has been riveted on the problem of prison crowding. Both in absolute numbers and in terms of rates, each new report on the subject shows further record-breaking growth. Although crowding is a deceptively elusive, if not fluid, concept and provides prison administrators as well as prison reformers with "a useful vehicle for pursuing their individual agendas" (Bleich 1989, 1,127), it is also the case that in many jurisdictions chapel space, recreation areas, and schoolrooms have been converted to accommodate growing inmate populations.

Despite a dramatic expansion in prison beds through the construction of new facilities and the renovation of others, most jurisdictions continue to operate above their rated capacity. Current projections suggest that prison populations will continue to exhibit comparable growth at least through the middle of the 1990s (Austin and

McVey 1989; Blumstein 1989). While corrections officials must manage the inmate population in a manner that ensures order, avoids escapes, and minimizes violent or disruptive inmate behavior, paroling authorities are increasingly expected to serve as the formal managers of prison population levels.

Parole boards have long served as the "safety valve" of the American prison system (Rothman 1983; Garry 1984). As indicated earlier, escalating prison populations in the 1980s placed unprecedented pressures on parole boards to release inmates. Some paroling authorities have received legislative authority and direction to control the prison population (e.g., Georgia). Other states have enacted emergency powers acts to reduce crowding whenever the prison population level exceeds a specified capacity as defined by legislation or judicial decree (e.g., South Carolina).

Once triggered, emergency powers acts require that the parole board consider certain inmates for release earlier than they normally would have. In still other jurisdictions, quota systems have been established so that the number of parole releases must equal the number of admissions (e.g., Texas).

Regardless of the strategy that is adopted, once the role of a paroling authority is reduced or narrowed to an exclusive preoccupation with managing prison population levels, the concept of parole release as "earned" is lost, as is determining suitability for release. Under such circumstances, the demands of prison crowding often compromise adherence to any overriding principles of policy (Bottomley 1990).

Nonetheless, where prison crowding is severe, the parole board must form a responsible partnership with the department of corrections in assisting in the management of finite correctional resources. In states with still-effective emergency powers acts, the two agencies should together determine how often and under what circumstances to trigger emergency release. Although EPAs are not a panacea to solve prison crowding, if they are not used often, those released do not appear to present a threat to public safety (Austin 1987).

Given that EPAs are by their very nature politically controversial, parole boards should work in concert with the department of corrections to ensure that mutual agreement programs and parole contracts are available for suitable inmates (Cullen and Gilbert 1982). In addition, criteria and procedures might be developed to reduce the statutory period of parole eligibility for exceptional inmate progress during confinement. Finally, where program participation is emphasized by the parole board, parole eligibility should be timed to coincide with the successful completion of the program.

Revocation Policy

Though other options might be considered, it may not be possible for paroling authorities to go much further with respect to release policy. Nevertheless, parole boards may also participate in the management of finite correctional resources through the development of intermediate sanctions for responding to parolee violations short of formal revocation.

There are two major avenues of admission to a state correctional facility: new court commitments (inclusive of probation revocation) and parolees returned for violations of the rules. Between 1977 and 1987, the latter increased at a rate nearly three times that of the former: 284 percent compared with 97 percent. During 1987, a total of 80,524 parole violators were returned to prison for failing to abide by the conditions of their supervision. Another 225,267 represented new court admissions (Austin 1989, 3).

In California alone in 1987, there were 62,729 prison admissions. Of these, 31,581 (50.3 percent) represented parole violators. Eighty percent, or more than 25,000 of the parole violators, were returned to custody without a new prison sentence or for technical parole violations (Austin 1989).

There are two basic categories under which parole violations fall: technical violations and new criminal violations. The label "parole violation" covers a wide variety of behaviors, which may range from serious criminal activity to violations as seemingly innocuous as failing to report a change of address to the parole officer. Although it may happen, perhaps often, that parolees are revoked for technical violations and recommitted in lieu of prosecution, parolees returned to custody can exert a significant impact on a jurisdiction's rate of prison population growth.

Until recently, discussions of revocation invariably centered either on compliance with the requirements of procedural due process as defined in *Morrissey v. Brewer* or how long offenders should serve if their parole was, in fact, revoked. Although several parole boards addressed the issue through the creation of revocation guidelines, most focused on developing schedules for setting future eligibility terms. The revocation of parole was relied upon as the singular response to parolee violations of the rules.

This approach to revocation makes it difficult for parole officers to respond in an effective fashion short of commencing formal revocation proceedings whenever parolees fail to comply with the terms of supervision. It also narrows the range of options that the parole board may consider when reviewing revocation cases. What is needed is a continuum of intermediate sanctions that allow the field services agency and the paroling authority to respond in a sensible fashion to such violations.

Generally, the concept of intermediate sanctions has been applied to the front end of the criminal justice system, that is, to that part of the system between prison and probation (McCarthy 1987; Morris and Tonry 1990). Among some parole boards there is a growing recognition that the concept may be usefully extended to cover the back end of the system: that part of the system that falls between parole and reincarceration.

As noted in Chapter 6, several states (e.g., South Carolina, Tennessee) have developed a range of intermediate sanctions for dealing with parole violators. Such sanctions encompass an array of responses, including changing the level of supervision, requiring more contacts or office visits, increasing the frequency of urine testing, imposing community service, mandatory placement in a treatment program, or placement in a day or residential center (e.g., a halfway-back program).

Paroling authorities should develop intermediate sanctions or alternatives for responding to violation behavior in cooperation with parole field services. Doing so will afford each agency an opportunity to shape the options that it considers most viable, and once adopted, offer sufficient flexibility when confronted with parolee violations. Within this context, revoking parole represents only one option among many.

Regardless of which sanctions are selected, they should be developed within an explicit policy framework that links release decision making, the setting of conditions, supervision practices, and revocation policies. By clarifying the goals and purposes behind the use of such sanctions, the paroling authority will be able to respond to the community's concern for offender risk management, and at the same time, offer parolees appropriate forms of intervention to assist in the reintegration process.

If parole boards must assume a significant role in managing limited correctional resources, they must also define the limits of responsible participation. Parole boards alone cannot solve the problem of prison crowding. Moreover, as will be discussed later, any policies that are developed in this area must be crafted within the framework of future sentencing reforms.

Managing the Transition to the Community: Shared Accountability

Prison Programs and Parole Release

The unrelenting pressures associated with prison crowding often overwhelm classification systems, create widespread inmate idleness, and reduce the availability of educational and other programs. While the range of treatment programs in institutions continues to display considerable diversity, from traditional concerns emphasizing educational and vocational training to computer programming and "est" seminars (Hawkins and Alpert 1989, 209), most of the programs that are offered are of limited appeal to inmates (Johnson 1987, 171), do not aim at appropriate behavioral targets (e.g., mature coping skills), or are not provided at a point during confinement when they might be maximally effective (Zamble and Porporino 1990, 67).

Such programs are retained, in part, because they provide activities for the inmate population and are thus functional to prison management. Given their primary mandate—the maintenance of security and control and the provision of essential support services—departments of corrections must of necessity focus inward. Prison managers must attend to the daily concerns of administering a self-sufficient community in a manner that ensures order, avoids escapes, and minimizes violent or disruptive inmate behavior. They must of necessity concentrate on the present.

With respect to parole, prison administrators are not inclined to consider how decisions made at any given moment may affect the eventual transition to the community. When paroling authorities weigh various factors in deciding whether to grant parole, their focus is on the future, on an inmate's readiness and preparation for release. Release decision making is compromised when inmates are ill-prepared due to the absence of meaningful program participation or the failure to provide adequate prerelease training. The task of supervision is likewise made far more difficult under these circumstances.

Although parole boards are not responsible for developing or running treatment programs, they must cooperate with corrections officials to ensure that effective programs are in place, especially those emphasizing mature coping skills and prerelease training (Johnson 1987; Zamble and Porporino 1988, 1990). As inmates near parole eligibility, their participation must be coordinated or timed to their release.

Parole boards themselves must be explicit about the types of program participation they consider important to the release decision and how such involvement factors in to the granting or denial of parole. They cannot afford to keep corrections administrators guessing about the weight they give to such participation relative to other release decision-making criteria.

Parole Boards and Parole Field Services

The transition from confinement to the community is a critical and difficult passage for many offenders, especially during the first twelve months (Irwin 1970; Clear and Cole 1990). Paroling authorities are uniquely situated within the correctional continuum not only to look backward at what is done during confinement, but forward to how the transition to the community will be managed during supervision. Doing so, however, requires a fully integrated relationship between the parole board and parole field services.

The long-term trend has been to separate parole supervision from paroling authorities. Since 1966, the number of boards with administrative responsibility for parole supervision has declined dramatically. Most parole field service agencies are currently located within the department of corrections and thus are separate and autonomous from the parole board.

By its very nature, the decision by the parole board to release an offender reflects a "judgment about the appropriateness of continuing a prisoner's sentence outside of an institution...[supervision] in the community is the carrying out of the decision goals of the board" (McGarry 1988, 55). Parole field services, however, are large operations and are often organized into geographical units. Even where the paroling authority is explicit about its decision-making policies and goals, the organizational separation of field services undermines the ability of the former to effectively manage or oversee the parolee's transition from confinement.

More important, the separate responsibilities and organizational locations undermine a sense of shared accountability for parolee success or failure. If parole field staff often feel that the conditions of supervision are unrealistic and unenforceable or that the offender was not a suitable candidate for release, parole board members frequently express concern that monitoring of parolee behavior in the community is haphazard and inconsistent.

The ACA Parole Task Force survey revealed strong support for merging field services under the paroling authority. Parole board chairs were asked to respond to the following statement: "[the] merging of release, supervision, and revocation into a separate and autonomous parole agency would contribute to a more effective parole system." Thirty-nine chairs (or 77 percent) agreed or strongly agreed with this statement. Eight chairs expressed disagreement, while four were uncertain.

The need for coherent policy with respect to release, supervision, and revocation will not be achieved by organizational reform alone. In those jurisdictions where the parole board has clear-cut policies, maintains close contact with the field service agency, and conveys its expectations with respect to monitoring parolee behavior and responding to violations of the rules, an organizational merger may not be feasible or desirable.

Where these conditions are absent, however, consideration should be given to such a step. Incorporating parole supervision under the parole board would help ensure the consistent enforcement of the decision goals and policies of the latter, increase the level and frequency of communication between functionally interdependent agencies, and provide a sense of shared accountability for each case as it moves from release to supervision to discharge or revocation.

Public Opinion, Community Safety, and Parole

Until recently, parole boards were largely immune from public scrutiny. They were able to grant or deny parole without regard to public opinion. In most jurisdictions the primary constituency of the paroling authority was the governor's office. Neither media reporting nor the concerns of victims shaped parole board policy or practice.

The situation has changed dramatically. The legislative challenges to paroling authority and judicial discretion that ushered in the sentencing reforms of the 1970s and 1980s continue to be accompanied by critical media commentary every time a parolee, or a mandatory releasee labeled a parolee, is charged with a new crime. Perhaps more important, in sensitive parole cases, citizens' rights groups are mobilizing to block parole release and failing that, to determine where the parolee is placed while under supervision.

In 1987, residents in several California communities began a successful media and legal campaign to block the placement of Lawrence Singleton, who was nearing release (Barkdull 1988). Eventually, after he moved several times from areas throughout the state due to strident local opposition, parole officials were forced to house him on the grounds of San Quentin prison (Barkdull 1988).

More generally, citizens' and victims' rights groups are engaging in letter-writing campaigns, securing supportive editorials, appearing on talk shows, and protesting on the steps of state capitols, usually in opposition to parole release in a particular case. It is likely that protests of this kind will increase in the future. To the extent that community protest serves only to politicize parole, the impartiality of parole board decision making is undermined.

The effect such protests actually have on specific cases is difficult to assess. In terms of parole board chairs, the ACA Parole Task Force survey showed that it may very well be a significant concern for some. One of the questions asked the chairs to respond to the following statement: "[the] biggest fear parole board members have are releasees who commit new crimes and get a lot of media attention." Fifty-six percent agreed or strongly agreed with this statement, while 36 percent disagreed. Another 8 percent were uncertain.

The visible presence of organized opposition to parole is matched by a countervailing trend that shows support for the function of parole in both the United States and Canada. In 1984, 1,004 adults were surveyed through a telephone poll for their understanding and views on the parole system—both release and supervision. The survey results indicated "a high level of understanding among the general public about the parole system, particularly about the criteria used to determine parole eligibility" (Figgie International 1985, ix).

Of even greater significance, the research found that only 8 percent of the sample believed that parole should be abolished. Another 24 percent felt that the system of parole should be retained as it was. The majority of respondents (61 percent), while supportive of parole, agreed that it was in need of reorganization (Figgie International 1985).

Across the border, a total of 2,006 in-person interviews were conducted in December 1988 to assess Canadian public opinion on parole. The survey showed that while the respondents believed that the parole system is flawed, they were not supportive of its outright abolition.

When presented with an explanation of parole and asked whether it should be abolished, be made more strict, be left as it is, or be expanded, only 7 percent of those interviewed said it should be abolished. The majority of Canadians (69 percent) favored making the system more strict, while 11 percent said that the status quo should be maintained. Another 9 percent supported its expansion (Goldberg 1989).

Growing evidence suggests that the public is not as punitive or harsh as is often depicted in the media or perceived by legislators (Gottfredson and Taylor 1984; Cullen and Gendreau 1989). The research that is accumulating indicates that while the public wants offenders punished for their crimes, they are far more concerned with assurances of personal safety.

This research also shows that the public believes in and is supportive of rehabilitative programs if such programs do not compromise public safety. A recent study in Alabama showed particular support for work and reparative programs (e.g., community service; Doble and Klein 1989), while research in Ohio revealed citizen support for inmates earning early release for good behavior and for participation in education and work programs during confinement (Skovron et al. 1988).

As this illustrates, there are various cross-currents of public opinion affecting parole. Within this context, paroling authorities must be able to defend the reasonableness and consistency of their decisions. They must be able to articulate a credible role in relation to correctional resource management and effective offender supervision.

Ultimately, they must be able to show how their decision making balances fairness and offender rehabilitation with a firm commitment to community protection. If such efforts are to achieve legitimacy, they must be done within the framework of sentencing reform more generally.

Sentencing Reform and the Continuing Challenge to the Legitimacy of Parole

In 1972, federal judge Marvin E. Frankel first introduced the concept of a sentencing commission to provide explicit standards to structure the discretion available to judges at the time of sentencing (von Hirsch et al. 1987). Three key features were incorporated within the framework he proposed: the formation of a permanent sentencing commission to create and revise presumptive sentencing guidelines, the development of such guidelines specifying for judges whom to imprison and for how long, and the creation of a formal mechanism permitting appellate sentence review whenever the sentencing judge departed from the guidelines.

In 1978, Minnesota became the first state to form a sentencing commission and subsequently adopt presumptive sentencing guidelines. Other jurisdictions have since followed suit, including the District of Columbia, Pennsylvania, and Washington. In 1983, Florida moved from voluntary to presumptive sentencing guidelines. At the federal level, the U.S. Sentencing Commission implemented a system of presumptive sentencing guidelines in 1987.

In contrast to the demise of voluntary sentencing guidelines projects and a declining interest in statutory determinate sentencing, two to three states each year establish sentencing commissions or their equivalent (Morris and Tonry 1990, 39). Such bodies are currently found in Kansas, Louisiana, New Mexico, Oregon, and Tennessee. Whether they will be successful, however, remains an open issue. Sentencing commissions were created in Connecticut, Maine, New York, and South Carolina, but they were unable to achieve a consensus on sentencing policy, or the guidelines they recommended for adoption failed to win legislative approval (Tonry 1987, 45-75).

As was discussed in Chapter 1, the movement toward sentencing reform has exerted a significant impact on sentencing practices across the country. Before 1975, most states' sentencing codes (as well as that of the federal system) could be characterized as indeterminate. In the relatively short span of ten years, most replaced or revised their sentencing schemes in the direction of greater determinacy (Shane-DuBow et al. 1985; Tonry 1987).

The first wave of sentencing reforms occurred within a political and legislative arena that also stiffened penalties for criminal convictions and increased the average time served in prison through mandatory sentencing laws, sentencing enhancements, and reductions in discretionary parole release. In many jurisdictions, these reforms have contributed to, and occurred simultaneously with, the rapid growth of prison populations (and ironically, to the early release of many inmates). Mainly in response to the enormous costs to accommodate this growth, a second phase of sentencing reform has developed, one that may be characterized as "making the punishment fit the crime . . . and the prison budget" (Strasser 1989).

Across the country, fiscal constraints are beginning to emerge as a primary determinant of sentencing policy. During the 1980s, correctional budgets increased at a rate far in excess of other sectors of states' budgets (National Association of State Budget Officers 1989). Moreover, even in states that have begun ambitious prison construction programs, the recognition has developed that it is not possible to build bedspace sufficient to keep pace with the ever-escalating demand (e.g., California Blue Ribbon Commission on Inmate Population Management 1990).

In response, a number of states are considering changes in their sentencing policies that would, in effect, link offender sentencing to correctional resources. Several of the sentencing commissions mentioned previously (e.g., Louisiana) have been asked to draft comprehensive sentencing changes that as a matter of policy treat prison beds as a scarce resource, a resource that must be rationally allocated to only the most serious or violent offenders.

If the impact of the first wave of sentencing reforms on parole was dramatic, the second wave presents paroling authorities with an opportunity to help restore coherence and balance to a state's sentencing structure. Whatever reforms are enacted in the years ahead, they will in all likelihood continue to emphasize fairness, proportionality, and certainty in sentencing (Morris and Tonry 1990). They will also be influenced, however, by fiscal constraints and increased demands on the part of the public for a criminal justice system that manages offender risk and thus provides some measure of community protection.

Paroling authorities are uniquely situated to balance the goals associated with greater determinacy in sentencing and utilitarian concerns focusing on offender risk management at release and during supervision. They also occupy a critical position relative to establishing just and effective intermediate sanctions for responding to parole violations.

How paroling authorities achieve these objectives may only be crafted in relation to a given jurisdiction's framework for sentencing reform. To the extent that they do so successfully, paroling authorities will contribute to greater public safety and provide real assistance to parolees. The net effect will be a more rational approach to offender release and community supervision.

Appendix

Missouri Salient Factor Score

1. Conviction and Confinement Measures

A. No prior convictions = 2
One prior conviction = 1
Two or more prior convictions = 0
B. No prior incarcerations = 2
One prior incarceration = 1
Two or more prior incarcerations = 0
C. Total prior incarceration time does not exceed five years = 1
Prior incarceration time exceeds five years = 0

2. Stability Measures

A. Age at first commitment
18 or older = 1
17 or younger = 0
B. No history of alcohol or drug abuse = 1
Alcohol or drug abuse history = 1
C. Five years conviction-free prior to present offense = 1
Conviction within previous five years = 0

3. Performance and Behavior Measures

A. Has never had parole, probation, or conditional
release revoked = 1
Has had parole, probation, or conditional release
revoked = 0
B. Has never escaped or attempted to escape = 1
Has escaped or attempted to escape = 0
C. Has had no prior conviction for burglary = 1
Has had prior conviction for burglary = 0

Total:

11-9: Excellent   8-6: Good   5-3: Fair   2-0: Poor

State of Minnesota
Assessment of Client Risk

1. **Number of address changes during past twelve months client was in community**

   None = 0
   One = 2
   Two or more = 3

2. **Age at first conviction (or juvenile adjudication)**

   24 or older = 0
   20-23 = 2
   19 or younger = 4

3. **Number of prior probation/parole adjudicated violations (adult or juvenile)**

   None = 0
   One or more = 4

4. **Number of prior felony convictions (or juvenile adjudications)**

   None = 0
   One = 2
   Two or more = 4

5. **Convictions for juvenile adjudications for: (select applicable and add to score; do not exceed a total of 5, include current offense)**

   Burglary, theft, auto theft, or robbery = 2
   Worthless checks or forgery = 3
   n/a = 0

6. **Percentage of time employed during past twelve months client was in the community**

   60% = 0
   40%-59% = 1
   under 40% = 2
   n/a = 0

7. **Alcohol usage problems (past twelve months in community)**

   No interference with functioning = 0
   Some interference with functioning = 2
   Serious interference with functioning = 4

8. **Other drug usage problems (past twelve months in the community)**

   No interference with functioning = 0

   Some interference with functioning = 1

   Serious interference with functioning = 2

9. **Attitude**

   Motivated to change; receptive to assistance = 0

   Dependent or unwilling to accept responsibility = 3

   Negative; rationalizes/justifies behavior or not motivated to change = 5

10. **Number of prior supervised periods of probation/parole (adult or juvenile)**

    None = 0

    One or more = 4

11. **Conviction or juvenile adjudication of any crime against a person (felony, gross misdemeanor, or misdemeanor) within the past five years**

    Yes = 15

    No = 0

Level of Supervision	Risk
Maximum	15 or above
Medium	8 to 14
Minimum	7 and below

Maine Adult Caseload Management System

A. Severity of Instant Offense

A	B	C	D	E
15	12	8	3	1

B. Prior Record

All misdemeanors and felonies for the past ten years are counted and two points are assigned for each conviction, for a maximum of twenty points. Juvenile convictions are not counted unless the juvenile was convicted for a criminal offense in an adult court.

C. Education

1. 8th grade or less = 10
2. 9th to 11th grade = 5
3. High school graduate, GED, or higher = 0

D. Occupation

1. Regularly employed/occupied = 0
2. Intermittent employment = 4
3. Seldom employed = 8
4. Not employed/occupied = 13

E. Substance Abuse

1. Frequent abuse and/or serious impairment of daily functioning = 15
2. Occasional abuse and/or some impairment of daily functioning = 8
3. No apparent problem = 0

F. Living Arrangements

1. Ongoing constant relationship = 0
2. Somewhat stable relationship = 4
3. Unstable or nonexistent relationship = 8

G. Residence

1. Constant, stable address = 0
2. Occasional changes of address = 2
3. Frequent changes of address = 4

H. Mental Stability

1. Symptoms prohibit adequate functioning = 15
2. Symptoms limit but do not prohibit adequate functioning = 8
3. No apparent symptoms of emotional instability; adequate responses to crises = 0

Low Supervision = 1 - 12
Medium Supervision = 13 - 45
High Supervision = 46 - 100

Michigan Department of Corrections Risk Screening

Risk of New Violent Felony on Parole (Recidivism, Base Rate = 10.5%):

- *Very High Risk*: Instant offense of rape, robbery, or homicide, and serious misconduct or security segregation, and first arrest before fifteenth birthday. (40.0% recidivism rate)
- *High Risk*: Instant offense of rape, robbery, or homicide, and serious misconduct and age of arrest was over fifteen. (20.7% recidivism rate)
- *Middle Risk*: Instant offense either rape, robbery, or homicide, and no serious misconduct; or instant offense not rape, robbery, or homicide, and reported felony while juvenile. (11.83% recidivism rate)
- *Low Risk*: Instant offense not rape, robbery, or homicide (may be other assaultive crime), and no reported felony while juvenile and never been married at time of instant offense. (6.3% recidivism rate)
- *Very Low Risk*: Instant offense not rape, robbery, or homicide, and no reported felony while juvenile and not serving on other assaultive crime and had been married. (2% recidivism rate)

Risk of New Nonviolent Felony While on Parole (Base Rate = 28%):

- *High Risk*: Reported felony while juvenile and major misconduct, or reported felony while juvenile and no major misconduct, and age of first arrest before fifteenth birthday. (39.5% recidivism rate)
- *Middle Risk*: Reported felony while juvenile and no major misconduct, and age of first arrest over fifteen; or no reported felony while juvenile and drug problem at the time of instant offense. (27% recidivism rate)
- *Low Risk*: No reported felony while juvenile and no drug problem at time of instant offense. (15.1% recidivism rate)

Maryland Parole Commission Policies

A. Prior Adult Criminal Record

1. None or very minor = 0 (minor crimes with incarceration of less than six months, probation, fines)
2. Minor = 2 (bad checks, driving while intoxicated, shoplifting, with incarceration longer than six months)
3. Moderate = 4 (assault and battery with sentence less than ten years, auto theft, etc.)
4. Major = 8 (murder, rape, robbery, burglary, handgun, etc.)

B. Pattern Offender

1. No prior convictions for current commitment offense or for similar type of offense = 0
2. One prior conviction for current commitment offense or for similar type of offense = 1
3. Two or more prior convictions for current commitment or for similar type of offense = 2

C. Juvenile Delinquency

1. At time of offense, age twenty-six or over, no information, or not more than one finding of delinquency = 0
2. Two or more findings of delinquency without commitment or one commitment = 1
3. Two or more commitments = 2

D. Adult Supervised Probation and/or Parole Status at the time of the instant offense:

1. None = 0
2. Probation = 1
3. Parole = 2
4. Both Probation and Parole = 3 (except for split sentences)

E. Prior Adult Parole/Probation Revocation

1. None = 0
2. Probation Revocation = 1
3. Parole Revocation = 2
4. Both Parole and Probation Revocation = 3

Classification: I = 0-6
II = 7-12
III = 13-18

Bibliography

Allen, Francis A. 1981. *The decline of the rehabilitative ideal: Penal policy and social purpose.* New Haven, Conn.: Yale University Press.

Allen, Harry E., Chris W. Eskridge, Edward J. Latessa, and Gennaro F. Vito. 1985. *Probation and parole in America.* New York: The Free Press.

American Correctional Association. 1947. *Handbook on classification.* New York: American Correctional Association.

American Correctional Association. 1981. *Standards for adult paroling authorities.* College Park, Md.: American Correctional Association.

American Correctional Association. 1981. *Standards for adult probation and parole field services.* College Park, Md.: American Correctional Association.

American Friends Service Committee. 1971. *Struggle for justice.* New York: Hill and Wang.

Archambault, J. 1938. *Royal commission to investigate the penal system of Canada.* Ottawa: King's Printer.

Arluke, Ned R. 1956. A summary of parole rules. *National Probation and Parole Journal* (January): 6-13.

Arluke, Ned R. 1969. A summary of parole rules: Thirteen years later. *Crime and Delinquency* 15 (April): 267-74.

Austin, James, and William Pannell. 1986. *The growing imprisonment of California.* San Francisco: National Council on Crime and Delinquency.

Austin, James. 1987. The use of early release and sentencing guidelines to ease prison crowding: The shifting sands of reform. In *Prison and Jail Crowding: Workshop Proceedings.* National Research Council; National Institute of Justice.

Austin, James, and Aaron D. McVey. 1988. *The NCCD prison population forecast: The growing imprisonment of America.* San Francisco: National Council on Crime and Delinquency.

Austin, James. 1989. *Parole outcome in California: The consequences of determinate sentencing, punishment, and incapacitation on parole performance.* San Francisco: National Council on Crime and Delinquency.

Austin, James, and Aaron D. McVey. 1989. The impact of the war on drugs. In *Focus.* San Francisco: National Council on Crime and Delinquency.

Bibliography

Baird, S. Christopher, Richard C. Heinz, and Brian Bemus. 1979. *The Wisconsin case classification/staff deployment project: A two-year follow-up report*. Madison, Wis.: Bureau of Community Corrections.

Baird, S. Christopher, and Donna Lerner. 1986. *A survey of the use of guidelines and risk assessments by state parole boards*. Washington, D.C.: Government Printing Office.

Banks, J., A. L. Porter, R. L. Rardin, T. R. Silver, and V. E. Unger. 1977. *Summary phase I evaluation of intensive special probation project*. Washington, D.C.: National Institute of Corrections.

Barkdull, Walter L. 1988. Parole and the public: A look at attitudes in California. *Federal Probation* (September): 15-20.

Barry, John V. 1972. Alexander Maconochie (1787-1860). In *Pioneers in criminology*, 84-106. Hermann Mannheim, ed. Montclair, N.J.: Patterson-Smith.

Berk, Richard A., and Peter Rossi. 1977. *Prison reform and state elites*. Cambridge: Ballinger.

Bleich, Jeff. 1989. The politics of prison crowding. *California Law Review* 77: 1,125-1,180.

Blumstein, Alfred. 1988. Prison populations: A system out of control? In *Crime and justice: A review of research*, 231-66. Michael Tonry and Norval Morris, eds. Chicago: University of Chicago Press.

Blumstein, Alfred. 1989. American prisons in a time of crisis. In *The American prison: Issues in research policy*, 13-22. Lynne Goodstein and Doris L. Mackenzie, eds. New York: Plenum Press.

Boyd, James W., and Jeffrey D. Padden. 1984. *The Michigan prison overcrowding emergency powers act: A political analysis of enactment and implementation*. Paper presented at the Annual Meeting of the Academy of Criminal Justice Sciences.

Bottomley, A. Keith. 1990. Parole in transition: A comparative study of origins, developments, and prospects for the 1990's. In *Crime and justice: A review of research*, 319-74. Michael Tonry and Norval Morris, eds. Chicago: University of Chicago Press.

Breed, Allen F. 1984. Don't throw the parole baby out with the justice bathwater. *Federal Probation* 48 (June): 11-15.

Breed, Allen F. 1990. *Overview and future*. Address given at the Sixth Annual Conference of the Association of Paroling Authorities International, Toronto, Ontario, Canada.

Bruce, A. A., E. W. Burgess, and A. J. Harno. 1928. *The working of the indeterminate sentence law and the parole system in Illinois.* Springfield: Illinois Parole Board.

Bureau of Justice Statistics. 1984. *Returning to prison.* Washington, D.C.: U.S. Department of Justice.

Bureau of Justice Statistics. 1985. *Examining recidivism.* Washington, D.C.: U.S. Department of Justice.

Bureau of Justice Statistics. 1986. *State and federal prisons, 1925-85.* Washington, D.C.: U.S. Department of Justice.

Bureau of Justice Statistics. 1987a. *Probation and parole 1986.* Washington, D.C.: U.S. Department of Justice.

Bureau of Justice Statistics. 1987b. *Recidivism of young parolees.* Washington, D.C.: U.S. Department of Justice.

Bureau of Justice Statistics. 1987c. *Time served in prison and on parole, 1984.* Washington, D.C.: U.S. Department of Justice.

Bureau of Justice Statistics. 1988a. *Probation and parole 1987.* Washington, D.C.: U.S. Department of Justice.

Bureau of Justice Statistics. 1988b. *Sourcebook of criminal justice statistics.* Katherine M. Jamieson and Timothy J. Flanagan, eds. Washington, D.C.: Government Printing Office.

Bureau of Justice Statistics. 1989a. *Probation and parole 1988.* Washington, D.C.: U.S. Department of Justice.

Bureau of Justice Statistics. 1989b. *Recidivism of prisoners released in 1983.* Washington, D.C.: U.S. Department of Justice.

Bureau of Justice Statistics. 1990. *Prisoners in 1989.* Washington, D.C.: U.S. Department of Justice.

Burke, Peggy B., Linda M. Adams, Gerald Kaufman, and Becki Ney. 1987. *Structuring parole decisionmaking: Lessons from technical assistance in nine states.* Washington,D.C.: National Institute of Corrections.

Burke, Peggy B. 1988. *Current issues in parole decisionmaking: Understanding the past; shaping the future.* Washington, D.C.: National Institute of Corrections.

Burke, Peggy B., Linda Adams, and Becki Ney. 1990a. *Policy for parole release and revocation: The National Institute of Corrections 1988-89 technical assistance project.* Washington, D.C.: National Institute of Corrections.

Burke, Peggy B., Chris Hayes, Helen Connelly, Linda Adams, and Becki Ney. 1990b. *Classification and case management for probation and parole:* A *practitioner's guide.* Washington, D.C.: National Institute of Corrections.

Burke, Peggy B., Chris Hayes, Helen Connelly, Linda Adams, and Becki Ney. 1990c. *The National Institute of Corrections model case management and classification project: A case study in diffusion.* Washington, D.C.: National Institute of Corrections.

Byrne, James M., Arthur J. Lurigio, and Christopher Baird. 1989. The effectiveness of the new intensive supervision programs. *Research in Corrections* 2 (2). Washington, D.C.: National Institute of Corrections.

California Blue Ribbon Commission on Inmate Population Management. 1990. *Final report.* Sacramento, Calif.

Canadian Bar Association. 1988. *Preliminary perspectives: Parole and the report of the sentencing commission.* Special Committee on Imprisonment and Release. Submitted to the Standing Committee on Justice and Solicitor General.

Canadian Sentencing Commission. 1987. *Sentencing reform: A Canadian approach.* Minister of Supply and Services.

Carlson, Eric. 1979. *Contemporary United States parole board practices.* San Jose, Calif.: San Jose State University Foundation.

Cavendar, Gray. 1982. *Parole: A critical analysis.* Port Washington, N.Y.: Kennikat Press.

Champion, Dean J. 1990. *Corrections in the United States.* Englewood Cliffs, N.J.: Prentice-Hall.

Citizen's Inquiry on Parole and Criminal Justice. 1975. *Prison without walls: Report on New York parole.* New York: Praeger.

Clear, Todd R., and Vincent O'Leary. 1983. *Controlling the offender in the community.* Lexington, Mass.: Lexington Books.

Clear, Todd R., and Kenneth W. Gallagher. 1985. Probation and parole supervision: A review of current classification practices. *Crime and Delinquency* 31: 423-43.

Clear, Todd R. 1988. Statistical prediction in corrections. *Research in Corrections* 1 (March). Washington, D.C.: National Institute of Corrections.

Clear, Todd R., and George F. Cole. 1990. *American corrections.* 2d ed. Pacific Grove, Calif.: Brooks/Cole.

Clear, Todd R., and Patricia L. Hardyman. 1990. The new intensive supervision movement. *Crime and Delinquency* 36 (January): 42-60.

Clemmer, Donald. 1958. *The prison community.* New York: Holt, Rinehart and Winston.

Criminal Justice Newsletter. 16 January 1990. *Florida plan: More prisons, and restoration of parole.*

Cromwell, Paul F. Jr., George G. Killinger, Hazel B. Kerper, and Charls Walker. 1985. *Probation and parole in the criminal justice system.* 2d ed. St. Paul, Minn.: West.

Cullen, Francis T., and Karen Gilbert. 1982. *Reaffirming rehabilitation.* Cincinnati: Anderson.

Cullen, Francis T., and Paul Gendreau. 1989. The effectiveness of correctional intervention. In *The American prison: Issues in research policy,* 23-44. Lynne Goodstein and Doris L. Mackenzie, eds. New York: Plenum Press.

Cullen, Francis T., Sandra Evans Skovron, Joseph E. Scott, and Velmer S. Burton Jr. 1990. Public support for correctional treatment: The tenacity of rehabilitative ideology. *Criminal Justice and Behavior* 17 (March): 6-18.

Daubney Committee. 1988. *Taking responsibility.* Report of the Standing Committee on Justice and Solicitor General on Its Review of Sentencing, Conditional Release, and Related Aspects of Corrections. Ottawa: Queen's Printer.

del Carmen, Rolando V., and Paul T. Louis. 1988. *Civil liabilities of parole personnel for release, nonrelease, supervision and revocation.* Washington, D.C.: National Institute of Corrections.

DiIulio, John J. Jr., ed. 1990a. *Courts, corrections and the constitution.* New York: Oxford University Press.

DiIulio, John J. Jr. 1990b. Managing a barbed wire bureaucracy: The impossible job of the corrections commissioner. In *Impossible jobs.* Erwin Hargrove, ed. East Lansing, Mich.: Michigan State University Press.

Doble, John, and Josh Klein. 1989. *Prison overcrowding and alternative sentences: The views of the people of Alabama.* New York: Public Agenda Foundation.

Erwin, Billie. 1987. *Evaluation of intensive supervision probation in Georgia: Final report.* Atlanta: Department of Offender Rehabilitation.

Fauteux Report. 1956. *Report of a committee to inquire into the principles and procedures followed in the remission service of the Department of Justice of Canada.* Ottawa: Queen's Printer.

Figgie International. 1985. *Figgie report part V—Parole: A search for justice and safety.* Richmond, Va.: Figgie International.

Bibliography

Finckenauer, James O. 1978. Crime as a national political issue: 1964-1976—From law and order to domestic tranquility. *Crime and Delinquency* 24: 13-27.

Fischer, Daryl R. 1986. *The Rand recidivism report: Summary and critique.* Phoenix: Board of Pardons and Paroles.

Fogel, David. 1975. *We are the living proof: The justice model for corrections.* Cincinnati: Anderson.

Garry, Eileen. 1984. *Options to reduce prison crowding.* Rockville, Md.: National Institute of Justice/NCJRS.

Gendreau, Paul, and Robert R. Ross. 1987. Revivification of rehabilitation: Evidence from the 1980's. *Justice Quarterly* 4: 349-407.

Genevie, Louis, Eva Margolies, and Gregory Muhlin. 1986. How effective is correctional intervention? *Social Policy* (Winter): 52-57.

Glaser, Daniel. 1987. Classification for risk. In *Prediction and classification: Criminal justice decision making*, 249-91. Don Gottfredson and Michael Tonry, eds. Chicago: University of Chicago Press.

Glaser, Daniel. 1964. *The effectiveness of a prison and parole system.* Indianapolis: Bobbs-Merrill.

Glueck, Sheldon, and Eleanor Glueck. 1946. *After-conduct of discharged offenders.* New York: Macmillan.

Goldberg, Linda. 1989. Personal correspondence to the authors summarizing a survey by Environics Research Group Limited.

Goldenberg, H. Carl. 1974. *Parole in Canada.* Standing Senate Committee on Legal and Constitutional Affairs. Ottawa: Information Canada.

Goodstein, Lynne. 1985. *Determinate sentencing and imprisonment: A failure of reform.* Cincinnati: Anderson.

Gottfredson, Don, Leslie T. Wilkins, and Peter B. Hoffman. 1978. *Guidelines for parole and sentencing.* Lexington, Mass.: Lexington Books.

Gottfredson, Don, and Ralph B. Taylor. 1984. Public policy and prison populations: Measuring opinions about reform. *Judicature* 68 (October-November): 190-201.

Gottfredson, Don, and Michael Tonry, eds. 1987. *Prediction and classification: Criminal justice decision making.* Chicago: University of Chicago Press.

Gottfredson, Michael R., and Don M. Gottfredson. 1988. *Decisionmaking in criminal justice: Toward a rational exercise of discretion.* New York: Plenum Press.

Griset, Pamela L. 1987. *The rise and fall of the determinate ideal in New York state.* Dissertation. State University of New York at Albany.

Hawkins, Richard, and Geoffrey P. Alpert. 1989. *American prison systems: Punishment and justice.* Englewood Cliffs, N.J.: Prentice-Hall.

Herrick, Emily. 1988. Intensive probation supervision. *Corrections Compendium* 12 (12): 4-14.

Herrick, Emily. 1989. Survey: Parole revocation. *Corrections Compendium* (March): 8-19.

Hofstadter, Richard. 1955. *The age of reform.* New York: Alfred A. Knopf.

Hugessen, H. J. 1973. *Report: Task force on the release of inmates.* Ottawa: Information Canada.

Hussey, Frederick A., and Stephen P. Lagoy. 1983. The determinate sentence and its impact on parole. *Criminal Law Bulletin* 19 (2): 101-130.

Irwin, John. 1970. *The felon.* Englewood Cliffs, N.J.: Prentice-Hall.

Irwin, John. 1980. *Prisons in turmoil.* Boston: Little, Brown and Company.

Irwin, John, and James Austin. 1987. *It's about time.* San Francisco: National Council on Crime and Delinquency.

Jackson, Ronald W., Al Hegedorn, Pablo Martinez, and Michael Eisenberg. 1987. *Parole and prison population control: At a crossroads.* Austin, Texas: Board of Pardons and Paroles.

Jackson, Ronald W., Edward E. Rhine, and William R. Smith. 1989. Prison crowding: A policy challenge for parole. *Corrections Today* (August): 118-23.

Jacobs, James. 1983. *New perspectives on prisons and imprisonment.* Ithaca, N.Y.: Cornell University Press.

Johnson, Robert. 1987. *Hard time: Understanding and reforming the prison.* Monterey, Calif.: Brooks/Cole.

Klein, Stephen P., and Michael N. Caggiano. 1986. *The prevalence, predictability, and policy implications of recidivism.* Santa Monica, Calif.: Rand Corporation.

Knight, Barbara B., and Stephen T. Early Jr. 1986. *Prisoners' rights in America.* Chicago: Nelson-Hall Publishers.

Kramer, John H., and Robin L. Lubitz. 1985. Pennsylvania's sentencing reform: The impact of commission-established guidelines. *Crime and Delinquency* 31: 481-500.

Krauth, Barbara. 1985. *Parole in the United States.* Washington, D.C.: National Institute of Corrections.

Lauen, Roger J. 1990. *Community-managed corrections.* 2nd ed. Laurel, Md.: American Correctional Association.

Bibliography

Lindsey, Edward. 1925. Historical sketch of the indeterminate sentence and parole system. *Journal of the American Institute of Criminal Law and Criminology* 16: 9-126.

Lipton, Douglas, Robert Martinson, and Judith Wilks. 1975. *The effectiveness of correctional treatment: A survey of treatment evaluation studies.* New York: Praeger.

Lunden, Richard. 1986. *Risk and recidivism among Massachusetts parolees: An exploratory study.* Boston: Massachusetts Parole Board.

Lunden, Richard. 1987a. *Prison behavior and parole outcome in Massachusetts.* Paper presented at the annual meeting of the American Society of Criminology, Montreal, Canada.

Lunden, Richard. 1987b. *Risk and recidivism among Massachusetts parolees: An update.* Boston: Massachusetts Parole Board.

Lunden, Richard. 1988. *The parolee's perception of the parole experience in Massachusetts: Follow-up interviews with two groups of parolees.* Paper presented at the annual meeting of the American Society of Criminology, Chicago.

Lurigio, Arthur J. 1990. Intensive probation supervision: An alternative to prison in the 1990's. *Crime and Delinquency* 36 (1).

Maltz, Michael D. 1984. *Recidivism.* New York: Academic Press.

Mannheim, Hermann, ed. 1972. *Pioneers in criminology.* Montclair, N.J.: Patterson-Smith.

Marcelli, Ralph J., ed. 1977. *Reorganization of state corrections agencies: A decade of experience.* Lexington, Ky.: Council of State Governments.

Markley, Greg. 1989. The marriage of mission, management, marketing, and measurement. In *The effectiveness of the new intensive supervision programs,* by James M. Byrne, Arthur J. Lurigio, and Christopher Baird. *Research in corrections* series, vol. 2, no. 2 (September). Washington, D.C.: National Institute of Corrections.

Marshall, Ineke H. 1981. Correctional treatment processes: Rehabilitation reconsidered. In *Critical Issues in Corrections: Problems, Trends and Prospects,* 14-46. Roy R. Roberg and Vincent J. Webb, eds. New York: West.

Martinson, Robert. 1974. What works? Questions and answers about prison reform. *Public Interest* 35: 22-54.

Martinson, Robert. 1979. New findings, new views: A note of caution regarding sentencing reform. *Hofstra Law Review* 7: 243-58.

Mathias, Robert, and Diane Steelman. 1982. *Controlling prison populations: An assessment of current mechanisms.* Washington, D.C.: National Institute of Corrections.

Matusow, Allen J. 1984. *The unraveling of America: A history of liberalism in the 1960's.* New York: Harper and Row.

McCarthy, Belinda R., ed. 1987. *Intermediate punishments: Intensive supervision, home confinement, and electronic surveillance.* Monsey, N.Y.: Criminal Justice Press.

McCleary, Richard. 1978. *Dangerous men: The sociology of parole.* Beverly Hills, Calif.: Sage.

McGarry, Peggy. 1988. *Handbook for new parole board members.* 2d ed. Washington, D.C.: National Institute of Corrections.

McKelvey, Blake. 1977. *American prisons: A history of good intentions.* Montclair, N.J.: Patterson-Smith.

Megathalin, Susi. 1973. *Probation/parole caseload review.* Atlanta: Department of Offender Rehabilitation.

Merritt, Frank S. 1980. Parole revocation: A primer. *University of Toledo Law Review* 11: 893-938.

Messinger, Sheldon L., John E. Berecochea, David Rauma, and Richard A. Berk. 1985. The foundations of parole in California. *Law and Society Review* 19: 69-106.

Messinger, Sheldon L., John E. Berecochea, Richard A. Berk, and David Rauma. 1988. *Parolees returned to prison and the California prison population.* BCS Collaborative Report (January): 1-13. California Attorney General's Office and the University of California.

Michigan Department of Corrections. 1985. *Prison crowding in the state of Michigan.* Lansing: Michigan Department of Corrections.

Miller, Frank P. 1976. Parole. In *Crime and its treatment in Canada.* W. T. McGrath, ed. Toronto: Macmillan.

Modley, Phyllis. 1985. *Emergency powers acts: Talking notes.* Washington, D.C.: National Institute of Corrections.

Monahan, John. 1981. *The clinical prediction of violent behavior.* Rockville, Md.: U.S. Department of Health and Human Services.

Moore, Silas. 1989. Early releases just latest in long series. *Georgia Parole Review* 1 (Winter).

Morris, Norval. 1974. *The future of imprisonment.* Chicago: University of Chicago Press.

Morris, Norval, and Marc Miller. 1985. Predictions of dangerousness. In *Crime and justice: An annual review of research.* Michael Tonry and Norval Morris, eds. Chicago: University of Chicago Press.

Morris, Norval, and Michael Tonry. 1990. *Between prison and probation: Intermediate punishments in a rational sentencing system.* New York: Oxford University Press.

Morse, Wayne, ed. 1939. *Attorney General's survey of release procedures.* Washington, D.C.: U.S. Department of Justice.

National Advisory Commission on Criminal Justice Standards and Goals. 1973. *Corrections.* Washington, D.C.: Government Printing Office.

National Association of State Budget Officers. 1989. *State expenditure report 1989.* Washington, D.C.: National Association of State Budget Officers.

National Commission on Law Observance and Enforcement (Wickersham Report). 1931. *Report on penal institutions, probation, and parole.* Washington, D.C.: Government Printing Office.

National Conference of State Legislatures. 1989. *State legislatures and corrections policies: An overview.* Denver: National Conference of State Legislatures.

National Criminal Justice Association. 1990. Drugs and prison issues top criminal justice concerns in governors' 1990 state of the state addresses. *Justice Bulletin* 10 (2).

National Governors' Association. 1988. *Guide to executive clemency among the American states.* Center for Policy Research. Washington, D.C.: National Institute of Corrections.

National Parole Board. 1988. *National parole board prerelease decision policies.* Ottawa: Ministry of Supply and Services.

National Parole Institutes. 1963. *A survey of the organization of parole systems.* New York: National Council on Crime and Delinquency.

National Prison Project. 1988. *Status report: The courts and the prisons.* Washington, D.C.: American Civil Liberties Union.

National Prison Project. 1989. *Status report: The courts and the prisons.* Washington, D.C.: American Civil Liberties Union.

National Probation and Parole Association. 1957. *Parole in principle and practice.* New York: National Probation and Parole Association.

Newman, Charles L. 1971. *Personnel practices in adult parole systems.* Springfield, Ill.: Charles C Thomas.

New York Division of Parole, Office of Policy Analysis and Information. 1985. *Guideline application manual.* Albany, N.Y.: New York Division of Parole.

New York State Special Commission on Attica. 1972. *Attica: The official report of the New York State special commission on Attica.* New York: Bantam Books.

Ohlin, Lloyd, and O. D. Duncan. 1949. The efficiency of prediction in criminology. *The American Journal of Sociology* 54: 441-52.

Ohlin, Lloyd. 1951. *Selection for parole.* New York: Russell Sage Foundation.

O'Leary, Vincent, and Joan Nuffield. 1972. *The organization of parole systems in the United States.* Hackensack, N.J.: National Council on Crime and Delinquency.

O'Leary, Vincent, Michael Gottfredson, and Arthur Gelman. 1975. Contemporary sentencing proposals. *Criminal Law Bulletin* (September/October): 555-86.

O'Leary, Vincent, and Kathleen J. Hanrahan. 1976. *Parole systems in the United States.* Hackensack, N.J.: National Council on Crime and Delinquency.

O'Leary, Vincent, and Todd R. Clear. 1984. *Directions for community corrections in the 1990's.* Washington, D.C.: National Institute of Corrections.

Ouimet Report. 1969. *Toward unity: Criminal justice and corrections.* Report of the Canadian Committee on Corrections. Ottawa: Queen's Printer.

Outerbridge, William R. 1990. *Some reflections of a former parole board chairman, then and now: A modest apologia.* Address given at the Sixth Annual Conference of the Association of Paroling Authorities International, Toronto, Ontario, Canada.

Palmer, Joseph R. 1984. *Parole selection, abolishment, and determinate sentencing creation: Role and influence in the change process.* Washington, D.C.: National Institute of Corrections.

Parent, Dale. 1990. *Recovering correctional costs through offender fees.* Washington, D.C.: National Institute of Justice.

Parker, William. 1975. *Parole: Origins, development, current practices and statutes.* College Park, Md.: American Correctional Association.

Pearson, Frank. 1987. *Research on New Jersey's intensive supervision program: Final report to the National Institute of Justice.* Washington, D.C.: National Institute of Justice.

Petersilia, Joan, Susan Turner, James Kahan, and Joyce Peterson. 1985. *Granting felons probation: Public risks and alternatives.* Santa Monica, Calif.: Rand Corporation.

Petersilia, Joan. 1987. *Expanding options for criminal sentencing.* Santa Monica, Calif.: Rand Corporation.

Petersilia, Joan, and Susan Turner. 1987. Guideline-based justice: Prediction and racial minorities. In *Prediction and classification,* 151-81. D. Gottfredson and M. Tonry, eds. Chicago: University of Chicago Press.

Pisciotta, Alexander W. 1983. Scientific reform: The 'new penology' at Elmira, 1876-1900. *Crime and Delinquency* (October): 613-30.

Pray, Roger T. 1987. *An updated analysis of adherence to Utah sentence and release guidelines by the Board of Pardons.* Salt Lake City: Utah Department of Corrections.

President's Commission on Law Enforcement and Administration of Justice. 1967. *The challenge of crime in a free society.* Washington, D.C.: Government Printing Office.

President's Commission on Law Enforcement and Administration of Justice. 1967. *Task force report: Corrections.* Washington, D.C.: Government Printing Office.

Rhine, Edward E. 1986. Prison overcrowding emergency powers acts: A policy quandary for corrections. *Proceedings of the 116th Congress of Correction.* College Park, Md.: American Correctional Association.

Rhine, Edward E., and Ronald W. Jackson, eds. 1987. *Observations on parole: A collection of readings from Western Europe, Canada, and the United States.* Washington, D.C.: National Institute of Corrections.

Rhine, Edward E., William R. Smith, Ronald W. Jackson, and Lloyd G. Rupp. 1989. Parole: Issues and prospects for the 1990's. *Corrections Today* (December): 78-83.

Rothman, David J. 1980. *Conscience and convenience: The asylum and its alternatives in progressive America.* Boston: Little, Brown and Company.

Rothman, David J. 1983. Sentencing reform in historical perspective. *Crime and Delinquency* (October): 631-47.

Rubin, Sol. 1949. *Adult parole systems of the United States.* New York: National Council on Crime and Delinquency.

Schmidt, Janet. 1977. *Demystifying parole.* Lexington, Mass.: Lexington Books.

Sechrest, Lee B., Susan O. White, and Elizabeth Brown, eds. 1979. *The rehabilitation of offenders: Problems and prospects.* Washington, D.C.: National Academy of Sciences.

Sentencing Accountability Commission. 1989. *Delaware sentencing accountability commission: The first year.* Wilmington, Del.: Sentencing Accountability Commission.

Shane-DuBow, Sandra, Alice P. Brown, and Erik Olsen. 1985. *Sentencing reform in the United States: History, content, and effect.* Washington, D.C.: National Institute of Justice

Skovron, Sandra E., Joseph E. Scott, and Francis T. Cullen. 1988. Prison crowding: Public attitudes toward strategies of population control. *Journal of Research in Crime and Delinquency* 25: 150-169.

Stanley, David T. 1976. *Prisoners among us.* Washington, D.C.: Brookings Institution.

Star, Deborah, and John E. Berecochea. 1984. Rationalizing the conditions of parole. In *Probation, parole and community corrections,* 286-305. Robert M. Carter, Daniel Glaser, and Leslie T. Wilkins, eds. 3d ed. New York: John Wiley and Sons.

Strasser, Fred. 1989. Making the punishment fit the crime and the prison budget. *Governing* (January): 36-41.

Studt, Elliot. 1978. *Surveillance and service in parole: A report of the parole action study.* Washington, D.C.: National Institute of Corrections.

Texas Attorney General. 1987. *Crime Prevention Newsletter* 69 (11 February 1987): 732.

Texas Board of Pardons and Paroles. 1985. *Thirty-seventh annual statistical report.* Austin, Texas: Board of Pardons and Paroles.

Thomas, Jim. 1988. *Prison litigation: The paradox of the jail house lawyer.* Totowa, N.J.: Roman and Littlefield.

Tonry, Michael. 1987. *Sentencing reform impacts.* Washington, D.C.: National Institute of Justice, U.S. Department of Justice.

Tonry, Michael. 1988. Structuring sentencing. In *Crime and justice: A review of research,* 267-337. Michael Tonry and Norval Morris, eds. Chicago: University of Chicago Press.

Travis, Lawrence F. III, and Vincent O'Leary. 1979. *Changes in sentencing and parole decisionmaking: 1976-1978.* Washington, D.C.: National Institute of Corrections, U.S. Department of Justice.

Travis, Lawrence F. III, and Edward J. Latessa. 1984. A summary of parole rules thirteen years later: Revisited thirteen years later. *Journal of Criminal Justice* 12 (6): 591-600.

Twentieth Century Fund Task Force on Criminal Sentencing. 1976. *Fair and certain punishment.* New York: McGraw-Hill.

USA Today. 9 September 1990. *Prison population at record level.*

Useem, Bert, and Peter Kimball. 1989. *States of siege: U.S. prison riots 1971-1986.* New York: Oxford University Press.

Vassar, B. Norris. 1987. *Parole today: A jurisdiction by jurisdiction analysis.* Richmond, Va.: Association of Paroling Authorities.

von Hirsch, Andrew. 1976. *Doing justice: The choice of punishments.* New York: Hill and Wang.

von Hirsch, Andrew, and Kathleen J. Hanrahan. 1979. *The question of parole: Retention, reform or abolition?* Cambridge: Ballinger.

von Hirsch, Andrew, Kay A. Knapp, and Michael Tonry. 1987. *The sentencing commission and its guidelines.* Boston: Northeastern University Press.

Wenninger, Robert A. 1985. Unjustified sentence disparity: A case study of the levelling effect of parole. *Syracuse Law Review* 36: 715-57.

White, Stephen. 1976. Alexander Maconochie and the development of parole. *Journal of Criminal Law and Criminology* 67 (March): 72-88.

Wiebe, Robert H. 1967. *The search for order: 1877-1920.* New York: Hill and Wang.

Wooton, Barbara. 1959. *Social science and social pathology.* London: George Allen and Unwin.

Wright, Erik O. 1973. *The politics of punishment: A critical analysis of prisons in America.* New York: Harper and Row.

Zalman, Marvin. 1987. Sentencing in a free society: The failure of the President's Crime Commission to influence sentencing policy. *Justice Quarterly* 4 (December): 545-69.

Zamble, Edward, and Frank J. Porporino. 1988. *Coping, behavior, and adaptation in prison inmates.* Secaucus, N.J.: Springer-Verlag.

Zamble, Edward, and Frank J. Porporino. 1990. Coping, imprisonment, and rehabilitation: Some data and their implications. *Criminal Justice and Behavior* 17 (March): 53-70.

Court Cases

Blackwell v. Commonwealth of Pennsylvania, 516 A.2d 856 (Pa. Cmwlth. 1986)

Gagnon v. Scarpelli, 411 U.S. 778 (1973)

Greenholtz v. Inmates of the Nebraska Penal and Correctional Complex, 442 U.S. 1 (1979)

Mathis Carl Williams v. State (see *Crime Prevention Newsletter*, no. 69, 732, 11 February 1987, Texas Attorney General, July 1987)

Mistretta v. U.S., 109 S.Ct. 102 L. ed. 2d 714 (1989)

Montana Board of Pardons v. Allen, 41 CrL 32581 (1987)

Moody v. Dagett, 429 U.S. 789 (1976)

Morrissey v. Brewer, 408 U.S. 471 (1972)

Nelson v. Balazic, 802 F.2d 1077 (8th Cir. 1986)

Ruiz v. Estelle, 503 F. Supp. 1265 (S.D. Tex 1980), aff'd, 679 F.2d 1115 (5th Cir. 1982), cert. denied, 460 U.S. 1042 (1983)

U.S. v. Lustig, 555 F.2d 751 (1977)

Index

judges, 10, 11, 22, 75, 76, 77, 78, 160, 176
just deserts, 22, 26, 29, 57, 60, 61, 160, 166

Kansas, 52, 57, 64, 80, 83, 120, 176
Kentucky, 37, 52, 64, 66, 83, 98

life imprisonment, 35
Louisiana, 52, 65, 83, 120, 176, 177

Maconochie, Alexander, 5-7, 29
Maddox, Lester, 89
Maine, 25, 30, 52, 64, 66, 80, 83, 101, 119, 176
mandatory proportions, 62, 79
marks (earned by prisoners), 6, 9
Martinson, Robert, 22
Maryland, 15, 37, 52, 65, 66, 67, 72, 83, 120
Massachusetts, 13, 37, 52, 57, 64, 83, 116, 133, 135, 136
Mathis Carl Williams v. State (of Texas), 127
Michigan, 37, 50, 51, 52, 64, 67, 83, 84, 85, 86-88, 91, 93, 96, 97, 120, 135
Minnesota, 25, 37, 50, 51, 52, 64, 66, 80, 83, 120, 160, 166, 176
Mississippi, 11, 18, 51, 53, 57, 65, 83, 84, 120
Missouri, 15, 53, 65, 66, 67, 73, 83, 120
Mistretta v. U.S., 30
Montana, 36, 53, 64, 83, 84, 98, 137
Montana Board of Pardons v. Allen, 137
Moody v. Dagett, 126
Morrissey v. Brewer, 125-128, 129, 138, 170

National Conference on Parole, Second, 18

National Congress on Penitentiary and Reformatory Discipline, 8
National Parole Conference, 16
National Council on Crime and Delinquency, 20, 123
National Institute of Corrections, 31, 57, 105, 107, 133, 137
National Probation and Parole Association, 18
Nebraska, 33, 53, 57, 65, 66, 83, 101, 120, 124
needs assessments, 108, 109, 116
Nelson v. Balazic, 138
Nevada, 53, 65, 67, 72, 83
New Hampshire, 50, 53, 64, 83, 104,
New Jersey, 25, 53, 64, 83, 84, 85, 101, 117, 120, 138, 166
New Mexico, 23, 53, 64, 83, 120, 176
New York, 13, 17, 23, 30, 37, 53, 54, 57, 59, 65, 66, 67, 72, 83, 101, 133, 176
New York City, 15
New York Prison Association, 9
Norfolk Island, 5, 6, 29
North Carolina, 25, 51, 53, 65, 83, 84, 98, 120
North Dakota, 50, 53, 64, 83, 101, 120

Ohio, 8, 13, 36, 37, 50, 51, 53, 57, 64, 67, 83, 84
Oklahoma, 33, 50, 53, 65, 66, 83, 84, 120
Ontario, 156-157
Oregon, 53, 65, 67, 72, 83, 120, 176

pardons, 9, 12, 15, 35
parole
    abolition of, 24
    criticism of, 20

About the Authors

Ronald W. Jackson

Ron Jackson is the director of the Field Operations Division, Georgia State Board of Pardons and Paroles. He served as Parole Commissioner for the Texas Board of Pardons and Paroles from 1984 to 1990. He has served as manager of Membership Services for the American Correctional Association, executive director of the Texas Corrections Association, and worked in several capacities in the Texas Department of Corrections.

Jackson has served in several offices of the Association of Paroling Authorities International, including President from 1986 through 1988. He was the cochair of the ACA Task Force on Parole.

Jackson holds a B.S. in Criminal Justice from Sam Houston State University.

Edward E. Rhine

Edward E. Rhine is an assistant chief in the Probation Services Division, Administrative Office of the Courts, Trenton, New Jersey. He has worked as an executive assistant to the chairman of the state parole board and as an accreditation manager for the New Jersey Department of Corrections. He served as cochair of the ACA Task Force on Parole and has written and presented numerous papers on parole. He is coeditor of *Observations on Parole: A Collection of Readings from Western Europe, Canada and the United States* (1987) and *Correctional Theory and Practice* (in press).

He received his B.A. in sociology from Ohio University and his M.A. and Ph.D., also in sociology, from Rutgers University.

William R. Smith

William R. Smith is an assistant professor of sociology at Rutgers University. He also served as a research associate and assistant research professor at the Institute for Criminological Research there. Smith is currently a coprincipal investigator of a research grant funded by the National Institute of Justice on the effects of sentencing on subsequent criminality.

He received his Ph.D. in 1984 and his M.A. in 1977 (both in sociology) from Rutgers University and his B.A. in 1973 (in sociology) from St. Norbert College, DePere, Wisconsin.

Peggy B. Burke

Peggy B. Burke is a senior associate with the Center for Effective Public Policy, a nonprofit organization in Washington, D.C., that provides technical assistance and research on policy matters to state and local criminal justice agencies. She has directed three national technical assistance projects for parole agencies and has worked with more than twenty different paroling authorities as they have refined their decision-making policy for release and revocation. She is a frequent guest faculty member at the National Academy of Corrections and the author of two practitioner-oriented handbooks on classification. She is presently working with courts interested in the more appropriate use of intermediate sanctions and is conducting a study of residential community corrections facilities around the country.

Burke received her B.A. in English Literature from Manhattanville College, Purchase, New York, and her M.P.A. from George Washington University in Washington, D.C.

Roger Labelle

Roger Labelle was executive director and vice-chairman of the National Parole Board of Canada. He also served as director of the Quebec Jail System for eight years. Labelle has worked in Canadian federal and provincial corrections since 1961 and has taught corrections administration at the University of Ottawa. He received his B.A. in Business Administration and Labour Relations from Montreal University.

Community-Managed Corrections and Other Solutions to America's Prison Crisis – *Revised*
Roger J. Lauen, Ph.D.

An examination of the social and political factors affecting crime and sentencing, offering some new ideas and effective remedies. This edition has been updated statistically and a new chapter has been added that reviews the status of crowding and other issues. Gain valuable information on the subject of community corrections from an author with 15 years of community corrections experience.

Probation and Parole Directory

Includes listings of parole, pardon, and release boards; names, addresses, and telephone numbers of key personnel; data on probation and parole programs and services; statistics on budgets, beginning salaries, personnel, and client caseloads.

Getting High and Doing Time: What's the Connection?
A Recovery Guide for Alcoholics and Drug Addicts in Trouble with the Law

A workbook-style guide aimed at giving the reader a better understanding of his/her own problem. It explores the definition and causes of addiction through true-life accounts from other recovering alcoholics and addicts.

Counseling the Involuntary and Resistant Client
George A. Harris, Ph.D., David Watkins, Ph.D.

Practical help for counselors, officers, medical teams, and others working with clients who don't want to be helped. Reviews the causes and the types of resistant behavior and offers useful techniques for working with these clients.

Correctional Issues: Probation and Parole

Contains readings on parole decision making, the responsibility of parole boards and the media to inform the public about parole issues, how crowding effects the parole decision, and a look at parole in the 1990s.

Correctional Issues: Intermediate Punishment/Community-based Sanctions

Examines critical topics on community corrections and how to enhance the public's acceptance of it. Also included is an article on a new pre-release strategy, day reporting centers. Special attention is given to electronic monitoring and house arrest.

Available from the American Correctional Association

Call 1-800-825-BOOK to order a complete catalog!

Supplement your career...

The Female Offender: What Does the Future Hold?

Summarizes three recent nationwide surveys conducted by the ACA Task Force on the Female Offender. It highlights information about the dramatic increase in the number of female offenders, facility design and location, demographics, security issues, and much more. It also includes recommendations from the Task Force for dealing with the problems associated with the growing female offender population.

The Mentally Retarded Offender and Corrections

Miles B. Santamour

Mentally retarded offenders are frequently the victims of more sophisticated inmates. They also serve longer sentences – often because their slow adjustment to prison routine limits parole opportunities. Santamour's updated handbook will help you identify these offenders, improve assessments of their needs, provide appropriate programs, and reduce recidivism.

Standards for Adult Parole Authorities

129 standards covering 13 program areas associated with parole decision making.

Standards for Adult Probation and Parole Field Services

208 standards concerning 11 important areas for sound and progressive noninstitutional services.

Guidelines for the Development of Policies and Procedures: Adult Parole Authorities/Adult Probation and Parole Field Services

Model policies and procedures relating to both probation and parole field services and parole authorities.

99 Days and A Get Up

Ned Rollo

A highly practical pre-release manual for inmates. Both realistic and optimistic, Rollo examines the steps involved in "getting short" and "hitting the bricks." His premise is that release from prison is only the midpoint of a total experience.

Legal Issues for Probation and Parole Officers – *Correspondence Course*

Provides a basic understanding of legal issues to help corrections practitioners comply with the law and reduce the likelihood of being held liable in a lawsuit. Covers types of lawsuits, use of force, inmates rights, supervisor's liability, current legal cases, court rulings, and more.

Available from the American Correctional Association

Call 1-800-825-BOOK to order a complete catalog!